Cover artwork and design by Allie Daigle

Printed in the United States of America.

25 24 23 22 21   5 4 3 2 1

Library of Congress Cataloging-in-Publication Data

Names: Harmening, William M., author.
Title: The deadly force script : How the Police in America defend the use of excessive
    force / William Harmening.
Description: Chicago, Illinois : ABA Publishing, American Bar Association, [2021] |
    Includes index. | Summary: "The job of the expert witness is to offer opinions
    about a case based on a subjective understanding and analysis of the evidence. It is
    the nature of litigation that the opposing side will always dispute those opinions
    and offer their own counter-opinions. The opinions offered in this book about the
    cases discussed have all previously been disclosed in publicly available expert
    witness reports and court documents. They are just that, opinions. Only a judge or
    jury can rule on the ultimate issue of guilt or innocence"— Provided by publisher.
Identifiers: LCCN 2021023236 (print) | LCCN 2021023237 (ebook) |
    ISBN 9781639050048 (hardcover) | ISBN 9781639050055 (ebook)
Subjects: LCSH: Police—United States—Digests. | Police shootings— United States—
    Digests.
Classification: LCC KF5399.A53 H37 2021 (print) | LCC KF5399.A53 (ebook) |
    DDC 344.7305/232—dc23
LC record available at https://lccn.loc.gov/2021023236
LC ebook record available at https://lccn.loc.gov/2021023237

Discounts are available for books ordered in bulk. Special consideration is given to state bars, CLE programs, and other bar-related organizations. Inquire at Book Publishing, ABA Publishing, American Bar Association, 321 N. Clark Street, Chicago, Illinois 60654-7598.
www.shopABA.org

THE DEADLY FORCE SCRIPT

How the Police in America Defend the Use of Excessive Force

WILLIAM HARMENING

CONTENTS

Foreword by Carl E. Douglas.. viii

Chapter 1   **A State of Mind**... 1

Chapter 2   **The Case of Kajieme Powell: St. Louis, Missouri**
An Accidental Expert: Leveling the Playing Field........... 13

Chapter 3   **The Case of Cedrick Chatman: Chicago, Illinois**
How the Police Justify Shooting an Unarmed
Suspect in the Back 25

Chapter 4   **The Deadly Force Theater**
Those Who Make the Wheels Turn and Those Who
Attempt to Apply the Brakes 37

Chapter 5   **The Case of Dontre Hamilton: Milwaukee, Wisconsin**
The Thousand-Yard Stare: How the Police Use a
Misunderstood Phenomenon to Create an Illusion
of Danger... 53

Chapter 6   **The Case of Michael Brown: Ferguson, Missouri**
The Myth of the Superhuman Black Man: How the
Police Weaponize Negative Stereotypes........................ 67

Chapter 7   **The Case of John Deming Jr.: Pleasanton, California**
The De-escalation Paradox: Who Responds When
It Is the Police Who Need to Be De-escalated?.............. 87

Chapter 8   **The Case of Anthony Soderberg: Los Angeles, California**
Perceptual Distortion: How the Police Strategically
See Things That Are Not There and Fail to See
Things That Are... 99

Chapter 9   **The Case of Michael Dial: White County, Tennessee**
The Vehicle Pursuit: Pavlov's Bell for a
Deadly Ending 115

Chapter 10   **The Case of Nicholas Dyksma: Columbus, Georgia**
Compressional Asphyxia: How the Police
Conceal and Defend a Deadly Tactic........................... 131

Chapter 11   **The Case of Isaiah Murrietta: Fresno, California**
The Waistband Defense: When the Police
Reach for an Excuse.. 145

Chapter 12   **The Case of Drew Edwards: Maquoketa, Iowa**
Excited Delirium: A Popular Excuse with Deadly
Consequences... 159

Chapter 13   **The Case of Jorge Ramirez: Bakersfield, California**
Contagious Fire: When One Shoots,
They All Shoot... 173

Chapter 14   **The Case of Tommy Le: Seattle, Washington**
How the Police Can Turn Anything (Even an Ink Pen)
into a Deadly Weapon.. 189

Chapter 15   **The Case of Bryan Carreño: Santa Barbara, California**
Suicide by Cop: The Perfect Justification for a
Perfectly Unjustified Shooting...................................... 203

Chapter 16   **The Case of John Cruz Jr.: Edgewater, Colorado**
The Cost of Being Expendable...................................... 219

Chapter 17   **The Case of George Floyd: Minneapolis, Minnesota**
Lessons Learned and the Path Forward....................... 235

Index.. 254

The job of the expert witness is to offer opinions about a case based on a subjective understanding and analysis of the evidence. It is the nature of litigation that the opposing side will always dispute those opinions and offer their own counter-opinions. The opinions offered in this book about the cases discussed have all previously been disclosed in publicly available expert witness reports and court documents. They are just that, opinions. Only a judge or jury can rule on the ultimate issue of guilt or innocence.

William Harmening

Foreward

For almost 40 years, I have heard police officers in the United States use the same excuses when trying to justify virtually any and every type of police shooting. Anyone who has followed a highly-publcized police shooting has heard the routine. The suspect was reaching for his waistband; the officer thought the cell phone was a gun; the suspect had a thousand-yard stare. All are designed to support a particular state of mind that is difficult to disprove. It is a routine that has been perfected over the years, making it difficult for the victims of police violence, or their surviving families, to enjoy a just outcome and the closure they so desperately need.

For the first twelve years of my legal career, I was lucky to work for my friend and mentor, Johnnie L. Cochran Jr. In those days, the Law Offices of Johnnie L. Cochran Jr. were ground zero in the fight for civil rights justice. It was a time when public sentiment favored the police, and when the civil and criminal justice systems placed substantial roadblocks like qualified immunity all along the winding and seemingly endless road to justice.

Civil rights litigation has only recently moved to the forefront of America's collective conscience. The brutal death of George Floyd, the shooting of Breonna Taylor, and many other similar disturbing acts of police violence have broadened our exposure to questionable and dangerous police tactics. The truth is, police violence has not increased dramatically over the past few years as it may seem rather, police misconduct has been more widely revealed through the increased availability of video recordings. Every citizen on the street now has a camera in their pocket ready to shine a much-needed light on police–citizen interactions. It is in this new environment of accountability that experts such as William Harmening are particularly important. Juries have always been more willing to accept the official police version of a shooting incident than a plaintiff's alternative account. It takes bold experts like William Harmening, himself a retired lawman, to level the playingfield. I first met William several years ago when my law partner, Jamon Hicks, was working on a particularly tough police shooting case in Indiana. Jamon was excited because he had finally met a knowledgeable police practices expert who was willing to review the case, and even prepare a draft report, without first demanding a hefty up-front retainer. Soon, I learned just how special and unique William was. His calm and deliberate manner, coupled with his unique combination of law enforcement experience and his tenure as a professor of forensic psychology at one of America's elite universities, adds tremendous power to every word he speaks. I learn from him whenever we discuss the problem of police violence, and I am certain the reader will too as he walks through some of his most important cases over the past several years. His breadth of knowledge and common-sense approach to a decades-long problem should be welcomed and embraced by all who truly have an interest in police reform and the ideal of an equitable system of justice for all.

Attorney Carl E. Douglas
Beverly Hills, California

CHAPTER 1

A State of Mind

When I had my shoot, it was no big deal really. Some dirt head with a pocketknife. Pulling the trigger was easy. I can't say that I felt much at all . . . at least not until the union guy showed up and advised me what to say. Suddenly it became the most frightening moment of my life, and somehow, I had misperceived the pocketknife to be a friggin' samurai sword!

—Anonymous Chicago police officer

It began with a cynical chuckle. Another nameless Black kid shot in the back as he ran from a stolen vehicle. The reporter appeared to accept without question the chief of police's narrative that the kid had reached for his waistband just prior to being shot. It did not surprise me that no gun was found. I chuckled because I knew the fix was in. The lie had begun. Standard practice when a cop shoots an unarmed Black kid in the back. The press always swallows it hook, line, and sinker. They maintain a symbiotic relationship with the police. The police knowingly provide disinformation. In return, the press provides cover by not aggressively seeking out the truth. One gets a story, the other avoids a public relations nightmare and hopefully a multimillion-dollar lawsuit. Like so many similar cases before this one, I knew the press would quickly lose interest after a few obligatory follow-ups, if they did any at all. It was all quite predictable. Another Black kid lying dead in someone's backyard; another cop who would eventually be cleared of any wrongdoing by a district attorney who counts on the support of the police union each election cycle; and another fractured family forever haunted by questions that would likely never be answered. Life goes on. And all I could do was shake my head and chuckle.

Every police officer in the United States knows that in the event of a questionable shooting, or any questionable use of force, the most important defense they have against potential criminal and civil liability is their state of mind. They know that even the best attorneys are seldom able to defeat it. It is an intangible, an abstract get-out-of-jail-free card that can be twisted and shaped to meet almost any set of circumstances. Consequently, very few police officers have ever been criminally prosecuted for using deadly force without justification. Even in videotaped cases that appear obvious, once the officer's state of mind is included in the equation, suddenly the excessiveness of the officer's actions becomes less obvious to the casual observer, and even more confusing to a juror who must weigh those actions against a perplexing set of jury instructions. Making it even more difficult, any criminal or civil litigation will likely include a pro-police expert witness who will support the officer's actions with an array of research conducted by pro-police researchers, much of it with conclusions that have been reverse-engineered to get to a desired result—a result that will always support an officer's actions no matter how excessive.

In times past, an officer's state of mind, as well as the research used to support it, was seldom challenged, or even an issue at all. In fact, such cases rarely saw the inside of a courtroom. More often than not, the officer's actions were weighed against the character of the person against whom the force was used rather than any relevant legal standards. One of the unspoken realities of the criminal justice system in America is that it has always placed an intrinsic value on the lives of those who pass through its doors; both those who break the law and those who enforce it. In decades past, the value assigned to a criminal offender's life was very low, and to that of a Black offender even lower. Neither compared to the value assigned to a police officer's life and livelihood. This intrinsic value was apparent in the laws and policies that guided the use of deadly force in times past. There were even written standards for when a police officer could justifiably shoot a suspect in the back just for trying to evade arrest. The level of risk to the officer or others if the suspect were allowed to escape was not a factor to be considered. It was simply implicit in the policy that the life of an individual suspected of committing certain types of crimes had no intrinsic value. Thus, the state of mind of the officer was not even a relevant topic, at least not in the case of a fleeing felon.

As a new Illinois police cadet in 1982, I do not recall our useof-force instruction being very long or complicated. It was actually rather formulaic and dispassionate. It was true then, as it is now, that a police officer could use deadly force against someone attempting to cause death or serious bodily harm to the officer or others. But there was another circumstance discussed in our training that surprised me. I was introduced to the name Mark V. Bart, a name that after ten weeks of academy training became chiseled in my mind like the words on a granite memorial. M.A.R.K.V.B.A.R.T. was actually an acronym for a series of crimes—murder, arson, robbery, kidnapping, vehicular theft, burglary, aggravated battery, rape, and treason—for which a police officer could justifiably shoot a fleeing suspect in the back. Certain of these crimes, especially rape and murder, made perfect sense to me. But others, vehicular theft, for example, were a bit confusing. In my mind, it seemed that the value of human life had been relegated to a place somewhere below motor vehicles and personal property. Some of the more tactless cadets even found comedic value in the whole thing. Mark V. Bart quickly became a pejorative for every Black kid who appeared in our training films. One overly aggressive cadet joked that he intended to introduce Mark V. Bart to some of the gang members back in his hometown on the outskirts of Chicago. None of us recognized that we were already conditioning ourselves—either actively by engaging in such humor or indirectly by laughing at it—to devalue the lives of criminal offenders, especially young Black men.

Perhaps the reason that the rules of deadly force, such as they were, were not a real intensive block of instruction during my academy training—how to kill took up a great deal more of our curriculum

than when to kill—was because in those days the police simply were not scrutinized, neither by the courts nor by the public at large. Growing up in a small Illinois farm town, I could recall only a single incident when a police officer used deadly force. A part-time officer in my town pursued two kids one evening on a stolen motorcycle they had purchased for $50. When the kids wrecked and attempted to get away by running into a cornfield, the officer shot both of them in the back with a shotgun. The state's attorney was outraged and convened a grand jury, but in the end the officer was cleared of any wrongdoing. The two kids, both of whom survived, admitted to knowing that the motorcycle was stolen. They had caused themselves to become the "V" (vehicular theft) in the deadly force acronym, and both paid a near fatal price for their indiscretion.

A few years after I finished my academy training and hit the streets as a full-time deputy sheriff in a rural Illinois county, the U.S. Supreme Court weighed in on the issue of deadly force, specifically the practice of shooting suspected criminal offenders who were not shooting back but attempting only to escape arrest. Their ruling in the case of Tennessee v. Garner remains one of the Court's most important decisions affecting how police officers do their jobs. The Court had finally recognized the terrible reality that when deadly force by an officer was justified to prevent a suspected felon from escaping, it was always up to the officer's discretion whether to fire upon the suspect. It was three times more likely that deadly force would be used if the suspect were Black rather than Caucasian, regardless of the crime they were suspected of committing. It took nearly a decade for the case to make its way to the U.S. Supreme Court, but when the Court finally rendered its decision in 1985 on a 6–3 vote, with Justices O'Connor, Burger, and Rehnquist dissenting, it became necessary to retrain every police officer in the United

States, myself included, on the issue of deadly force. The rules of engagement had changed in a major way.

The Case of Eddie Garner

On an October night in 1974, two Memphis police officers, Leslie Wright and Elton Hymon, responded to a residential burglary in process. As Officer Hymon walked to the rear of the house, he spotted 15-year-old Eddie Garner, a Black kid, running across the backyard toward a six-foot-high chain link fence. Hymon properly announced his presence and ordered Garner to stop, but Garner refused, and when he began to climb the fence, Hymon fired one shot to the back of his head and killed him instantly. It turned out that Garner had taken a mere ten dollars and a purse from the house. Hymon later stated that he could clearly see that Garner was unarmed and that he had fired his weapon only to prevent him from escaping. Garner had become the "B" (burglary) in our deadly force acronym.

Officer Hymon was cleared of any wrongdoing because his actions were consistent with both Tennessee law and the policiesof the Memphis Police Department. Garner's father filed a lawsuit against the Memphis Police Department and Officer Hymon, arguing that the fleeing felon law was unconstitutional. A decade-long legal battle ensued. The District Court disagreed with Garner and dismissed the lawsuit. Garner appealed the decision to the Sixth U.S. Court of Appeals, which reversed the District Court and concluded that the law was "severe and excessive" and gave police officers too much discretion in the use of deadly force. But then the state of Tennessee appealed, and finally, in 1985, three years after I went on patrol as a deputy sheriff, the U.S. Supreme Court affirmed the decision. The old way was done, and Mark V. Bart would quickly fade from the collective memory of America's law enforcement community.

The effect of the Garner decision was that a police officer could no longer shoot a fleeing felon in the back simply because they were suspected of committing a particular crime. Now there had to be an imminent threat of death or serious harm to someone if the suspect were allowed to escape. The police were always able to use deadly force to protect themselves or others in the immediate. That did not change. The decision had a systemic impact, and in addition to officers all over the country being retrained, departmental policies were rewritten and state statutes governing the use of force were either changed or amended. I recall attending a one-week law update to learn about the new standards. Of course, I also recall that a subtle theme throughout the training was ways to work around the new law and avoid being forced to make significant changes to how we did our jobs. The deadly force script was about to be born.

The law enforcement community quickly figured out that police officers could still shoot people in the back. Now they just needed to offer a particular state of mind defense to go with their use of force. Statements such as "I thought he had a gun in his hand" or "he was reaching for his coat pocket" became commonplace in police reports. The police had essentially found a workaround to justify an indefensible shooting. Their own state of mind became the most important piece of evidence, and one that was difficult, if not impossible to disprove. What some might call lying, the police called an unwritten, unspoken, and acceptable tactic in their mission to rid the streets of the ne'er-do-wells who made it their aim to victimize the law-abiding public.

Graham v. Connor

In 1989, the U.S. Supreme Court again addressed the issue of deadly force, this time to tackle the problem of how to reconcile an officer's state of mind with the available evidence or lack of. The case involved a man who, while in the throes of a diabetic emergency, had received significant injuries at the hands of an officer who had detained him because of suspicious behavior. In its decision, the Court imposed a new standard. It essentially said that an officer's state of mind would no longer be the primary measure of the reasonableness of their use of force, but rather, the state of mind of a reasonable officer would be paramount in making that determination. In other words, the Court instructed that the following question be asked: "Would a reasonable officer in this same situation and faced with these same set of circumstances have acted in a similar manner?" To answer that question, the totality of the evidence would now be weighed to determine how an officer who did not even exist would have acted in the same situation. So, while Garner made it unlawful for a police officer to shoot a fleeing suspect in the back unless the officer had reason to believe the suspect posed a significant threat to someone, with the Graham decision, the Court imposed a standard for determining whether the officer's belief was reasonable. Furthermore, while Garner dealt only with the fleeing felon problem, the Graham decision impacted every incident in which an officer uses force, regardless of its level of intensity.

For the second time in less than five years the rules of force had changed, and law enforcement agencies once again had to retrain their officers and update their policies. And once again police officers found ways to adapt. Now it was not enough to say they shot a suspect because they feared for their safety. Now they had to convince a judge or jury that a reasonable officer in that same situation would have feared for their life as well. The vast majority of police shootings were then, as they are today, unquestionably justified. But in those cases where the shooting was questionable, it now required a more sophisticated approach by the police to make it appear justified. Not only had a deadly force script been born out of Garner, but now with the Graham standard an entire deadly force industry was about to spring into existence, its various legal, academic, and pseudoscientific components ready and willing to defend the police in almost every case, no matter how blatantly unreasonable their use of force happened to be.

Rodney King and the PCP Defense

Perhaps no single event in modern times has had a more dramatic impact on law enforcement than the 1991 videotaped beating of Rodney King by four LAPD officers and the riot that followed, the deadliest in U.S. history. Police brutality and discriminatory enforcement for the first time since the days of Bull Connor and the civil rights movement were laid bare at the nation's feet in all their ugliness. When the incident occurred, I had by then risen to the position of chief deputy sheriff. I was now the person responsible for ensuring that the department's personnel were properly trained and that they understood the restrictions and limitations placed on their use of force by the Graham decision. But until that day, it never seemed to be the focus of much discussion. There were the usual "if you shoot someone, make sure you say this . . ." type of comments around the station, but none of us expected any problems anytime soon. The fact was, most complaints of excessive force were quickly dismissed, and if a citizen, after being roughed up by the police, went to a local attorney seeking to file a lawsuit, chances were good the attorney would tell them they had little chance of winning and to forget about it. That all changed on the morning of March 3, 1991, when America awakened to the Rodney King video being broadcast by every news outlet in the nation. I remember watching it with two of my deputies, one of whom sighed and said, "Well, fellas, the game just changed."

Four LAPD officers—Stacey Koon, Ted Bresino, Laurence Powell, and Timothy Wind—were criminally charged in the beating of King. It would become one of the most watched trials in U.S. history. The case represented a number of firsts. It was the first time a police action of that nature had been videotaped and nationally televised. It was the first time the public at large, especially the White segment of American society, began to question the tactics of the police. The social blindness White America suffered during the civil rights movement was no longer there. The videotape was a sharp contrast to how the LAPD had been depicted heretofore in shows like Adam-12, S.W.A.T., and T.J. Hooker, the last-named involving the fictional LCPD. But the case represented another important first. It would be the first major public test of Graham, just two years on the books when the beating occurred. At trial, both sides would attempt to define the reasonable officer. Making that task more difficult, the defense would have to overcome a videotape that depicted nothing even remotely appearing to be reasonable.

During direct examination, it was Sergeant Stacey Koon, the senior officer at the scene of the beating, and who twice deployed his

Taser against King, who testified to the following when asked to describe King's actions following the second Taser deployment:

> He repeated this groan, similar to like a wounded animal and then I could see the vibrations on him but he seemed to be overcoming it. At this time, I thought the suspect was under the influence of PCP. PCP is a dangerous drug, it's kinda like a policeman's nightmare that the individual that's under this is super strong, they have more or less a one track mind, they exhibit super strength, they equate it with a monster is what they equate it with.

Koon's description of the effects of PCP (phencyclidine) was a rehearsed and calculated tactic, though at the time that was not apparent to the larger law enforcement community. It had the effect of adding to the narrative a threat that clearly was not visible on the videotape. Now, instead of appearing to beat King mercilessly, the officers' actions were portrayed as a futile attempt to hold back a drug-crazed man with superhuman strength. The tactic very effectively defined the reasonable officer's state of mind. After all, any experienced officer would have recognized the symptoms of PCP usage—toxicology tests revealed that King had no PCP in his system— and thus would have recognized the extreme danger of a noncompliant suspect with superhuman strength. The nearly all-White jury swallowed the argument hook, line, and sinker, and the four officers were acquitted of their crimes. And while two of the officers—Koon and Powell—were later convicted of federal civil rights violations, it came too late to prevent the worst riot in U.S. history, one that left sixty-three people dead, nearly 2,400 wounded, and over $1 billion in property damage.

Within law enforcement circles, there was a great deal of support for the four officers. Police officers all over the country followed the case. In my own department it was the subject of many discussions. One thing I vividly recall was that the subject of PCP and its effects almost immediately began to appear in police training modules. Notwithstanding the fact that today I cannot recall a single case of having to arrest someone on PCP with superhuman strength, back then we were on the lookout for it each and every time we dealt with someone suspected of being under the influence of drugs. Thanks to Stacey Koon, it seemed to have taken on a life of its own. If someone appeared to display some of the symptoms, which by the way were not unlike the symptoms of most other types of drug intoxication, we prepared for battle. Our heightened vigilance only increased our willingness to use more force than was necessary.

Following the King case, there was a proliferation in the use of video cameras to tape officers using excessive force. Not surprisingly, there was an increase in the number of officers who were criminally charged for such behavior. America was not about to risk sparking another LA riot. During that time, there was also an increase in the use of the PCP defense by police officers who found themselves answering to a judge or jury for their actions. Although it was true that the law enforcement community suffered from a bit of PCP hysteria— the same thing happened a few years later when law enforcement became convinced that satanic groups around the country were sacrificing human babies—officers realized early on that it was a powerful defense, even if not a completely truthful one. I recall officers actually joking about using the PCP defense almost as a get-out-of-jail-free card. It was a sign that the law enforcement community was not about to roll over without a fight. Quite the contrary, it was adapting to Graham and becoming better at playing the game.

Business as Usual

By the time the new millennium rolled around, Rodney King, then a millionaire as a result of a civil settlement with the city of Los Angeles, was barely mentioned any longer in police circles. Police officers had become more adept at keeping a sharp eye for video cameras, and the deadly force industry had blossomed into a formidable force inside the courtroom. When a police officer used deadly force, a lawyer from the police union—the Fraternal Order of Police being the largest and best organized—typically arrived at the scene before the officer's own commander, their only job being to protect the officer from self-incrimination. And if the officers did eventually find themselves in either a criminal or civil courtroom, there were now pro-police expert witnesses, most of them recommended by the police unions, ready to testify with a compelling argument about why the officer's use of force was reasonable under Graham, no matter how unreasonable in reality it was. And to make their argument even more convincing, there were now pro-police academicians and researchers who were willing to provide all the pseudoscientific studies necessary to bolster the expert's testimony, most of them serving up reverse-engineered conclusions designed to benefit the police in every situation.

By the time of the terrorist attacks on September 11, 2001, it seemed that we had returned to a time when the press reported only on the most sensational police shootings and when police officers again were seldom being criminally charged with using excessive force. Thanks in part to the 9/11 attacks, the intrinsic value society assigned to the lives and livelihood of its law enforcement professionals again was very high. The deadly force industry had perfected its protocols and arguments and had successfully stacked the deck in its own favor inside the courtroom. The script had become quite well developed, and police officers became masters at using it when necessary. For example, if an officer shot someone with a knife and the shooting was questionable, then the 21-foot rule became their savior. If they shot someone in the back who was armed but running away from them, then the action v. reaction argument was invoked. And if the person turned out not to be armed at all, then nothing worked better than the waistband defense. Of course, since Graham, the state of mind of the reasonable officer, though inextricably linked to the real officer's mindset at the time of the deadly encounter, continued to be paramount. To present to a jury a more compelling picture of a reasonable officer who would have feared for their lives in the same situation, pro-police lawyers and experts routinely assigned such characteristics as the thousand-yard stare and superhuman strength to a suspect who was now likely dead and unable to defend themselves. And when all else failed, the catch-all perceptual distortion argument was offered to explain why an officer saw something that was not there or failed to see something that was. Truly, the deadly force script had evolved to the point where its use could provide a police officer an effective defense to essentially any allegation of questionable force.

And there, things remained for over a decade as the law enforcement establishment became a critical link in the war on terror, and society in general grew insensitive to the occasional reported case of a police officer killing someone without justification. With the tragic reality of sixty dead police officers following the 9/11 attacks, communities across the United States embraced their police officers with a new patriotic vigor. Society was willing to give a little to gain a lot, and what it wanted was to be kept safe from a radical form of Islam that wanted to destroy America. But eventually that mission began to wind down, and on August 9, 2014, an incident took place on a street in Ferguson, Missouri, that would change forever the dynamic that existed between the police and the public it serves. The era of policing that began with the Garner decision would end abruptly when an image of Michael Brown's lifeless body lying on the pavement in the hot Missouri sun was broadcast around the world. Just like in the days following the Rodney King incident, for police officers across the nation, suddenly everything was different.

- CHAPTER 2 -

The Case of Kajieme Powell

St. Louis, Missouri

An Accidental Expert: Leveling the Playing Field

By the time the streets of Ferguson, Missouri, erupted in violence in August 2014, I had long before, over twenty years before in fact, left my position with the Sheriff's Department for a state-level law enforcement job investigating cases of securities fraud. Such investigations are lengthy and very detail oriented. It was not uncommon for me to investigate a case involving millions of dollars in fraud and to take as long as three years to complete the investigation. I had become especially good at these investigations and was routinely called upon to provide training to new securities investigators around the country. In late 2001, shortly after the attacks of 9/11, I was promoted to the position of chief special agent. I would eventually come to recognize the benefits of having done such tedious and detail-oriented investigations when I began to offer my services as an expert in police shooting cases where the difference between justified and excessive often depends on what happens in the seconds, or even microseconds, just before the trigger is pulled.

Along the way I had also started teaching part-time at various colleges. With a graduate psychology degree and my police experience, I had no problem finding adjunct professor jobs teaching criminology or criminal justice. I had over a number of years worked my way up the professor food chain, teaching first at a local community college, then at a small Catholic university, and finally, in 2006, at Roosevelt University in downtown Chicago. It was during my time at Roosevelt that I jumped headfirst into the discipline of forensic psychology. The use of psychological principles and techniques in the pursuit and apprehension of criminal offenders had long fascinated me. Over the years I had become certified in forensic hypnosis and was eventually licensed as a polygraph examiner. I had also studied offender profiling, and for my graduate thesis I constructed a psychological test that could be used to test potential police recruits for various types of internal bias that could potentially impact their job performance. Eventually, I developed a new theory of criminality—criminal triad theory—and published four textbooks, including a popular forensic psychology text that went on to be used at a number of U.S. and Canadian colleges and universities. I was even given the opportunity to present my ideas on how the criminal personality develops to the British Criminological Society at the University of Wales and to academic institutions throughout the United States. The role psychology plays in essentially every aspect of the criminal justice system in the nation had become the focus of my reading, writing, and teaching. I would soon come to understand just how critical an understanding of psychology is to being able to unravel the complex dynamics of a deadly force encounter. I would also come to learn just how scarce such knowledge is among the purported experts who testify in court and offer opinions on such matters. It is a systemwide deficit of knowledge that I eventually learned to use to my advantage.

In January 2012, I was offered a dream teaching position at Washington University in St. Louis, one of the nation's top research institutions. Not only did it provide me the opportunity to teach some of the top students in the world, but more importantly, I was offered the challenging task of designing and implementing a new undergraduate certificate in forensic psychology program. I had rather accidentally become a marketable commodity—a career law enforcement professional with a graduate psychology degree and the ability to write textbooks. The program very quickly became among the most popular of the University's certificate programs.

I developed a curriculum of new courses, at least three of which dealt extensively with the issue of deadly force. Little did I know that I was fast developing the knowledge and credentials to act as an expert witness on the subjects of deadly force and police practices, something I had never even considered up to that point, likely because my loyalties were still firmly entrenched on the side of law enforcement. That all began to change with the shooting death of 25-year-old Kajieme Powell by two St. Louis police officers shortly after noon on August 19, 2014.

The city of St. Louis, especially the police department, was already on edge the day Kajieme Powell was shot. Less than 4 miles away, Michael Brown had been shot and killed just nine days earlier, and the city of Ferguson, a contiguous suburb of St. Louis, was dealing with nightly violence and rioting. The Missouri National Guard had been called in the day before. It was not a good time for another questionable shooting. The difference with this one was that it was recorded by a citizen's cell phone and was now being broadcast around the nation and in other parts of the world.

Leading up to that day, I had taken a special interest in the happenings in Ferguson. Washington University is only 5 miles from ground zero where the rioting was taking place, and because I was teaching courses like crisis intervention and policing—the only professor at Washington University teaching such courses—any media calls to the university seeking an academic expert to comment on the happenings in and around Ferguson were referred to me. I was doing radio and print media almost daily, and while I was careful not to comment on the Brown shooting itself, I did discuss the tactics of the area police departments that came together in an effort to quell the chaos. I tried my hardest to support the police. Most of them were decent and hard-working professionals who found themselves in a difficult situation with little command and control at the top. On that issue, I was very critical. I was also critical of the politicians who decided to involve themselves, especially Missouri Governor Jay Nixon, who, on an apparent mission to protect free speech and make himself appear as a man of the people, only empowered the malefactors in the crowd who were using the riots as a cover to loot and burn the city.

Following the Powell shooting, Sam Dotson, chief of the St. Louis Metropolitan Police Department, wasted no time in driving out to the scene to hold a short press conference. This was before the video became public later in the day and before the police even knew it existed. Dotson's biggest concern was to prevent the rioting that was occurring in Ferguson from spreading into the city, something that eventually happened in spite of his best efforts. This was the type of incident that could easily cause a new front in the civil unrest to explode wide open. The scene of the Powell shooting, as well as the Brown shooting and resulting riots, were situated along the I270 corridor about 5 miles north of downtown St. Louis. If another riot were to erupt near the Powell shooting and then consolidate with the Ferguson riot a few miles to the west, the result would be devastating.

Dotson took to the microphone when the press arrived and quickly attempted to portray the Powell shooting as a justified use of force by his two officers. He began by describing the initial 911 call from an employee of Six Stars Market who reported a shoplifting incident. The caller advised the 911 dispatcher that the suspect, later identified as Powell, had taken two energy drinks and a donut and was refusing to give them back. A few seconds after the initial 911 call, a second caller, this time the proprietor of a barber shop next door to the market, reported that Powell was in front of her shop acting very upset and carrying a knife in his hand. Dotson described how the caller had locked her doors to prevent Powell from entering her building. Dotson was painting a picture of an individual who appeared dangerous and threatening to those near him. And then he described how Powell had walked toward the two officers when they arrived and exited their vehicle, and how he had raised the knife above his head as he prepared to attack. To portray the officers as having no other choice but to shoot, Dotson described how Powell had gotten to within 2–3 feet of their position when the shots rang out.

While at the time I was quite engaged in the happenings in Ferguson, after hearing Dotson's description of the Powell shooting, I saw little reason to spend much time thinking about it. After all, Powell had a knife and was preparing to attack. My first thought was that the officers had waited too long to shoot and that their reluctance was no doubt influenced by what was happening a few miles to the west. But then the video was made public and very quickly found its way onto YouTube.com for the world to see. When I saw it, almost immediately I realized that practically everything Dotson had said about Powell and his actions were untrue. The first thing I noticed was that before the police arrived, Powell was threatening no one, including the man filming him just a few feet away. Further, Powell had placed the two energy drinks and the donut on the sidewalk, and there was no knife visible in his hand. He hardly had the appearance of a menacing felon ready to attack anyone who confronted him.

Within a minute of the initial 911 call, the two-man police SUV pulled up to the scene. Both officers exited the vehicle and immediately drew their weapons and began yelling at Powell to drop the knife. Before even reaching the deadly conclusion of the incident in the videotape, I had two thoughts. First was the possibility that Powell was attempting to commit suicide by cop, something I had seen many times before, including my own case as a uniformed police officer. Officers are trained to recognize this type of situation—typically involving someone in the throes of a mental health crisis—and how to avoid a violent outcome. My second thought was that by yelling at Powell at the top of their lungs with their guns raised, the two officers were going to have the opposite effect and emotionally escalate Powell. That is exactly what happened.

In the video I could not see a knife in Powell's hand, and he certainly had nothing raised above his head. I learned later that the knife, which at that time was likely in his hoodie pocket, was a 4-inch steak knife, hardly the type of knife that will cause an experienced police officer to fear for their life at just the sight of it. It is a knife that will snap into pieces against the ballistic plate of an officer's bullet-proof vest. The officer's commands became even louder as Powell walked toward them yelling "SHOOT ME, KILL ME NOW!" He stopped his advance approximately 20 feet from where the officers stood with their weapons aimed. There was still no visible knife. He then turned to his left, stepped over a small retaining wall into a parking lot, and again began walking forward as if his intent was to pass by where the officers were standing. Only later did I learn that he was walking in the direction of where he was then living with his grandmother. Powell took eight steps forward in the general direction of the officers, but not directly at them, and on his last step, turned slightly toward one of the officers. Suddenly the shots rang out, twelve in all, and Powell fell to the ground dead.

It seemed that either Dotson had lied to the press or the two officers had lied to Dotson. At no time in the video did Powell ever raise the knife above his head—the knife is never actually seen in the video—nor did he do anything that appeared threatening. Also, Dotson's statement that Powell had approached to within 2–3 feet of the officers before being shot was pure fiction. In fact, Powell was nearly 15 feet away when he was hit by the first shot and immediately began his fall. While he did end up 2–3 feet from the officers, he had rolled down an incline in the pavement for 10 of those feet, likely already dead. I also noticed something else, something that was especially clear when I slowed the video down to half speed; as many as nine of the twelve shots had hit Powell when he was on the ground, some of them in his back as he rolled toward the officers. Truly, it had the look of an execution.

The Kajieme Powell video was my eye-opener, perhaps because it was the first time I had ever paid such close attention to a police shooting video. Or maybe it was the fact that I was beginning to look at such things from an academic perspective rather than through the biased eyes of a police officer. I found myself admitting, maybe for the first time, that perhaps the officers were wrong and that the shooting lacked justification. I wondered why they had not deployed their Tasers or their OC (oleoresin capsicum) pepper spray. That question had not even entered my mind when I thought Powell was only 2–3 feet away and attacking the officers, but now that I could see for myself what had happened, either option seemed an obvious choice for the officers before elevating their level of force and firing their handguns.

The shooting of Kajieme Powell opened my eyes to one other reality—the speed and efficiency with which the deadly force industry responds to a questionable police shooting. I really had never noticed it before, but now I saw a well-oiled machine shifting into gear. First came the police union's spokesman doing interviews with every major news outlet in the St. Louis area. Police union personnel, especially if the union happens to be the Fraternal Order of Police (FOP), typically arrive at the scene of a police shooting even before the detectives who are tasked with investigating it. Their sole purpose for being there is to protect the officers involved, regardless of whether the shooting was justified. Unlike a lot of unions, the FOP represents only law enforcement personnel. Most of their field reps are former or retired police officers, so they know well how the game is played. In many cases, it is a union lawyer who responds to the scene to advise the officers involved. The union lawyer tells them what to say and what not to say—not just to reporters but to their own commanders and detectives—and how to present themselves when the media cameras are rolling. The police unions seem to have little or no interest in the truth, or even in justice being served. Their only goal is to protect their dues-paying members, and to facilitate that goal, they will immediately begin a public relations campaign designed to cast the most negative light possible on the individual shot by their officers. If the person has a criminal history, even if their crimes were committed as a juvenile—juvenile records are sealed and protected—the police unions will find a way to leak that information to the media.

Shortly after the Powell shooting, I began to see a local university professor doing interviews and talking about how people should be careful not to judge the officers' actions based solely on the video. St. Louis has two other major universities besides Washington University. One is well known for its criminal justice program. Most of the professors are former or retired police officers. It is also a cog in the deadly force industry's wheel. I did not realize it at the time, but when I eventually became involved in providing expert witness testimony, I often came across opposing experts who used research generated by this particular university program. It was the professor I saw commenting in the local media who first stated the relevance of the 21-foot rule, one of the major elements of the deadly force script and one that has likely contributed to the deaths of hundreds, if not thousands, of individuals over the years, many of them battling mental illness. It was also this same professor who wasted no time in attacking me when I finally gave a local interview in which

I was critical of the officers involved in the Powell shooting and the 21-foot rule. It was my first taste of just how organized the deadly force industry is and how hard they will fight to protect a police officer from public scrutiny. Every police officer knows that a person with a knife can attack an officer before the officer can unholster their weapon and fire if the suspect is within 21 feet of their location. It is part of every deadly force training module at every police academy in America. More importantly, it has been accepted almost as axiomatic by the courts in America. But where did such a notion come from, and is it even couched in science? To find its origins, we must go back to 1983 and to the Salt Lake City Police Department's (SLCPD's) weapons range. There, SLCPD Sergeant Dennis Tueller decided to carry out a simple experiment. At one end of a predefined space was an actor-suspect with a raised knife. At the other end was a police officer with a holstered firearm. At the sound of a signal, the knife-wielding suspect was directed to charge the officer with the knife. At the same time, the officer was directed to unholster their weapon, aim at the suspect, and pull the trigger. Using different distances, Tueller wanted to determine the distance at which the suspect could reach the officer with the knife before the officer could fire. That distance turned out to be 21 feet.

Since 1983 and since Tueller published the results of his experiment in a popular police publication, the 21-foot rule has evolved from a piece of pseudoscientific research with limited relevance to the real world, to what is now considered an objective criterion for shooting a suspect with a knife. But a few things seem to have been lost along the way, things that suddenly seemed especially relevant to the Powell case. Most important was the fact that in the Tueller experiment the officers began the race with their guns holstered. This was not the case with Powell. The two officers had their guns out and on target long before they pulled the trigger. Also, in the Tueller experiment, both participants knew what the other was going to do beforehand. There was no doubt that the knife-wielding actor was going to attack. But in Powell's case, as was obvious in the video, that level of certainty was absent. In fact, from the video it was not at all clear if Powell intended to even walk toward the officers, much less run.

As I considered the improper use of the 21-foot rule in this case, I was struck by how quickly the St. Louis media accepted it as a plausible justification for shooting Powell. Even the Circuit Attorney's Office eventually invoked the rule in their analysis of the incident, as well as their reasoning behind the decision to clear the officers of any wrongdoing. And then the FBI followed suit in their announcement that no civil rights case against the officers would be pursued. As I watched it all unfold, even when my police officer friends privately shook their heads in disbelief after watching the video, I realized that Kajieme Powell, a young mentally ill man who was guilty only of taking from the market two energy drinks and a donut, had become a victim not just of two St. Louis police officers, but also of a highly organized deadly force industry that viewed his death as nothing more than an inconvenient obstacle to getting the officers cleared and back out on the street. It was also my first critical look at one of the main principles embedded in the deadly force script—that is, if an officer shoots a suspect who was armed with a knife but not attacking at the time they were shot, and the incident either was caught on video or witnesses were present, the officer should invoke the 21-foot rule and make sure to say they were scared for their life, no matter how small or insignificant the knife.

In the days following the Powell shooting, and as the turmoil in Ferguson continued to worsen, I found myself a bit haunted by the image of the two officers repeatedly shooting Powell as he rolled toward them on the pavement. I knew the rules of deadly force. After all, I was a career law enforcement officer. But the more I watched the video, the more troubled I became. I decided to discuss the case with one of my classes and to complete a more detailed analysis. At the same time, I began looking at other questionable police shootings around the country, specifically whether the families of the victims of those shootings had access to knowledgeable expert witnesses who understood the police culture, and who could effectively battle against the tactics of the deadly force industry. What I found was a deck of cards that over the years had become overwhelmingly stacked in favor of the police.

It is no secret that very few police officers are ever actually convicted—or even charged for that matter—of killing someone without justification. The ugly truth is, the same communities that elect their prosecutors also support the police for the most part, and rightly so. The consequence of that is that bad officers, those who have no business being police officers, slip through the prosecutorial crack when they become entangled in a questionable shooting. For a prosecutor, the deadly force script allows them an easy way out. In the Powell case, it was the 21-foot rule that allowed Circuit Attorney Jennifer Joyce to publicly pronounce that the shooting was justified. She did not need to understand the science, or lack of, behind the concept, only that the detectives investigating the case, as well as a local esteemed criminology professor, found it to be the deciding factor. She had a quick way out of the case, and in the event the science was questioned, she could point her finger at the detectives and plead ignorance. As I would soon come to learn, the use of this strategy by a prosecuting attorney in a police shooting case was the rule rather than the exception.

The case of Kajieme Powell not only opened my eyes to the reality of the deadly force industry and the script it employs to defend the indefensible, but it convinced me to at least try to do something about it. The playing field needed to be leveled, and I felt that I could contribute to that by acting as an expert witness. It did not matter who hired me, or so I thought, since experts are required to be independent. Of course, I would discover that independence is seldom part of the equation. While I had no desire to participate in the criminal prosecution of police officers, at least not at that point, I decided to offer my services in civil cases, or those cases where the victim of a police shooting, or the family of a deceased victim, has filed a lawsuit seeking monetary damages against the officer and their employer. I knew that in most cases the officer involved would already have been cleared by the appropriate prosecutor of any criminal wrongdoing and, further, that any monetary damages would ultimately be paid by an insurance company.

I began by discussing the business with a couple of use-of-force experts I found on the internet. Both were retired police officers, and not surprisingly, both assumed I wanted to work on behalf of the officers who were being sued in civil court for excessive force. I never told them otherwise. Cops will quickly open up to other cops, and these gentlemen were no different. Both wanted to tell me how much money could be made providing expert witness services, and both described the process as a game of sorts where the only goal is to find a way to justify the officer's actions. There was nothing said about independence or objectivity. The possibility that an officer's actions may not have been justified never entered the conversation.

One thing both individuals were adamant about was that if I wanted to get involved in the "business," I had to become familiar with the Force Science Institute and with a man by the name of Dr. Bill Lewinski. Lewinski is a Ph.D. who provides much of the research used by pro-police experts. He also provides testimony himself, as well as police training. He is, so it seems, the academic guru for the deadly force industry in the United States. It certainly sounded like a worthwhile task to study up on his research and perhaps even give him a call. I was told by both experts that I could get certified by Lewinski's company as a force science specialist, and that such a certification would give me a great deal of credibility in the courtroom when battling against the "liberal assholes" on the other side.

Almost immediately in my search for information about Lewinski and his company, I came across a number of negative articles. I also found an evaluation conducted by a legitimate academic researcher who called the Force Science Institute's research "pseudoscience." I found that one province in Canada had even issued a warning against using Lewinski and his research in their court cases. For some reason it did not surprise me that the deadly force industry had found a way to get its own body of research into America's courtrooms, most of it, as some have suggested, reverse-engineered to reach a predetermined conclusion that will always support the police no matter how indefensible their actions. At the time, however, I had no idea just how far the Institute's reach and influence extended or how organized their efforts were. I would very quickly see their tactics firsthand.

- CHAPTER 3 -

The Case of
Cedrick Chatman

Chicago, Illinois

How the Police Justify Shooting an Unarmed Suspect in the Back

The case of Cedrick Chatman was the first case where I contacted a lawyer and offered my services. I read about the case in the Chicago Tribune and decided to send an email to the plaintiff's attorney, Brian Coffman, one of Chicago's best civil rights lawyers. Having no real experience as an expert witness, I figured Brian would not even reply to the email. But he did, and after a brief telephone discussion about the case, Brian agreed to hire me to evaluate a report submitted by the opposing expert in the case. Expert reports, or "Rule 26" reports as they are called, are a requirement in federal court where most police use-of-force cases are tried. In fact, an expert cannot testify to anything that is not included in their analysis and report. There are no surprises in these cases, no newly discovered evidence, no secret witnesses bursting through the courtroom door to testify.

Once both sides have their Rule 26 reports submitted, then each side has the opportunity to force the opposing expert to submit to a pretrial deposition to allow the opposing attorney to go through the expert's report and ask questions about their qualifications and methodology. Of course, the real purpose of the deposition is to trip up the expert and get them to say something on the record that can then be used against them during the trial.

Brian asked me to evaluate the report of the opposing expert and pointed out that he was a Harvard-educated lawyer. He was also one of the Force Science Institute's certified force science specialists. It was going to be baptism by fire. Here I was, completely inexperienced as an expert, and going up against an Ivy League lawyer. Not one to be easily intimidated, I saw it more as a challenge. But I also knew that if I screwed things up, my career as an expert would be over before it even began. Word travels fast and far among the relatively small group of lawyers across the United States who do federal civil rights cases. Bad experts do not last long; the good ones get more work than they can handle.

Like most use-of-force cases, by the time I became involved, the state's attorney in Cook County had already cleared the officers involved in the shooting of any criminal wrongdoing. That did not surprise me. Police officers are seldom prosecuted. In most cases the prosecutor looks for reasons not to prosecute the officers. It was the city of Chicago that hired the Harvard guy and paid a handsome fee of $30,000 to get the reason they were looking for. It was all under the guise of an "independent" investigation. I have seen the public and local media many times commend a prosecutor for going outside the local law enforcement community for such an investigation. I have even watched the families of those killed by the police be manipulated into thinking the prosecutor is doing what is best for them. Seldom is that the case. What the prosecutor never discloses is how they found their purported independent expert. Typically, it is the police union that recommends them from their list of pro-police experts. When that is the case, the fix is in from the beginning. The expert finds that the police officers did nothing wrong, and the prosecutor washes their hands like Pontius Pilate. The family will even be given a copy of the professionally written and expert-sounding report but will have little chance of recognizing the pseudoscience and unsupported conclusions it contains.

Before evaluating the Harvard guy's report, I first reviewed the evidence and case facts. Cedrick Chatman was a 17-year-old Black kid who carjacked a vehicle in Chicago's South Shore neighborhood in early 2013. He was quickly confronted at a traffic light by two plainclothes Chicago police officers—Lou Toth and Kevin Fry. The officers exited their unmarked squad and commanded Chatman to exit his vehicle. Chatman jumped from the stolen vehicle and ran with an iPhone box in his hand. Both officers followed, but the teenager was quicker and immediately put distance between them. As he rounded a corner at the intersection of 75th and Jeffery Avenue on the verge of getting away, Officer Fry stopped, raised his weapon, and fired four times at Chatman's back. Two of the bullets hit their mark and caused him to collapse on the street. He died a short time later.

The entire incident was captured by a security camera posted across the street. I first reviewed the video and then read the officers' statements. It was clear that Chatman was running away from the officers and making no movements with his hands that would indicate he was armed with a weapon. Even on the security video it was obvious that the iPhone box was not a firearm. I could not imagine how any supposed expert could possibly justify this shooting. The use of deadly force requires a deadly threat. Fry would have to argue that he believed and perceived the iPhone box to be a gun. I expected him to do that. I had seen that ploy used many times before in police shootings. But he had another problem. Chatman was running away from his location and was rapidly creating distance between them. Fry would somehow have to find a way to argue that Chatman was still a threat with the iPhone box he purportedly mistook for a gun. It seemed impossible to me that he could make such a case with the entire incident caught on video. As it turned out, he did not have to. That was the Harvard guy's job.

In theory, an expert witness on either side of a civil case—plaintiff or defendant—should be independent and impartial. While both sides may hire their own expert, who pays their fee should have no bearing on the expert's conclusions about the matter. In reality, independence and impartiality are of little concern to the purported experts who defend the police in every case, no matter how wrong their actions. In the legal community they are known as "hired guns," and they will offer all sorts of novel theories and supposed scientific principles to make their case. It took only about four paragraphs of the Harvard guy's report to realize how far he was willing to stretch the facts to declare that the shooting was justified. I got the sense that he had used this same report before in other cases—change the names and a few other facts, add a novel theory, and wrap it all together in page after page of boilerplate language.

The Harvard guy focused his analysis and report on Fry's two problems, the iPhone box and the fact that Chatman was running away from their position and not threatening the officers. He first provided a theory regarding the box. He argued that Fry fell victim to the psychological phenomenon of perceptual distortion. He described how the level of stress present in any deadly force encounter can cause a police officer to see something that is not there or not see something that is. As a psychology professor I was quite aware of this phenomenon, including the current research. Given that the Harvard guy's curriculum vitae showed no behavioral science background, I was surprised that he would attempt to apply such a complex psychological concept to this case. As I would come to learn however, the concept of perceptual distortion, like the 21-foot rule, is one of the most often-invoked components of the deadly force script. It allows the officer to simply say they did not see something that was right in front of them, or conversely, they did see something that was not even there. There is no disputing that an officer in any deadly force encounter is under some amount of stress, so to invoke the concept of perceptual distortion is a great strategy. It is impossible to disprove. Even in a case where an officer shoots an unarmed kid in the back, it is impossible to prove that the officer was not impacted by the stress of the moment.

To buttress his argument, the Harvard guy used two academic studies that are used by pro-police experts in every case where perceptual distortion is part of the officer's defense. These studies are presented as the latest and greatest research on the issue. But the fact is, there is no latest and greatest scientific research on the issue of perceptual distortion during a deadly force encounter, and there never has been. A deadly force encounter, and the stress that accompanies it, is a psychological exchange between two or more people that cannot be replicated in the laboratory. There is no independent variable that can be manipulated, and no scientific method that can be applied. We are left with studies that have little ecological validity or with anecdotal surveys of small nonrepresentative samples. The two studies cited by the Harvard guy both fall way short of the standard for legitimate scientific research. Both studies use samples so small that generalizing their results to a larger population is impossible. And both suffer from an obvious and fatal flaw that renders them invalid, a circumstance that should also render them inadmissible in the courtroom. The deadly force industry, however, has been quite successful in presenting the two studies as authoritative and scientific, and at least until the Cedrick Chatman case, appear to have done so with little or no challenge from the opposing side.

Before discussing the two studies in question, it is important to understand an important statistic, and that is the number of deadly force cases that occur each year. While this number has been difficult to come by in years past, the Washington Post now maintains an online and easily accessible database of all police killings in the United States since January 1, 2015. They have reported, with identifying data, 997 deadly police shootings in 2015; 962 in 2016; 986 in 2017; 992 in 2018; and 1,004 in 2019. It is reasonable to assume that these numbers are relatively stable over time. And thus, we can say that since the year the earliest of the two studies was begun (1994), there have been roughly 20–25,000 police shootings in the United States.

I found it interesting, but not surprising, that the first study was completed by the very professor who had attacked my opinions in the Kajieme Powell case. A professor of criminal justice at a university in St. Louis just a few miles from Washington University, this professor is a former LAPD officer. It did not surprise me that he would carry out a study that would almost guarantee a result that was positive for the police, especially those who use the study to defend themselves in a questionable shooting. In his study, he interviewed just 80 police officers who had been in a deadly force encounter. The author of the second study, also a professor, was at the time heavily involved in police training. It was easy to see from her credentials that she had a long history of involvement in various law enforcement activities. In her study, data was collected from just 157 officers over a six-year period.

From a scientific perspective, the results of these studies offer little useful data that can be used to reach a determination of reasonableness (the legal standard) in a police shooting. First of all, the majority of their conclusions only validate the obvious: that in a moment of high stress, activation of the sympathetic nervous system will cause a person's perception of time and distance, as well as their auditory experience, to be changed. This topic is well researched and documented. But there are two problems with these studies. First, both fail to quantify the amount of distortion that occurred. And second, neither study makes an effort to correlate the level of distortion to an officer's training and experience. There is a great deal of research that supports the idea that with more training and experience, the officer will feel more in control of a situation and better able to anticipate the outcome. This in turn leads to less stress, less activation of the sympathetic nervous system, and consequently, less perceptual distortion. Without this correlational data, neither study has much utility.

The bigger problem is when lawyers and pro-police experts attempt to use this data to construct a whole new reality, such as arguing that because of perceptual distortion, the officer saw a gun that in reality was not there, or, in the case of Cedrick Chatman, saw something they thought was a gun that turned out to be an iPhone box. Both researchers mostly avoided this issue in their study and thus offered no conclusions beyond those relating to distortions of speed of motion, auditory experience, and visual acuity. The first study did include a category called "other distortion," which was reported by just ten officers. The second study included a category called "Memory distortion: saw, heard,orexperiencedsomethingthatdidn'treallyhappen."Theresults were not much better. Only thirty-two officers reported experiencing this type of distortion. Neither study offers any quantitative data on the level of distortion, or on the training and experience of those who reported this type of distortion. And neither distinguishes those officers who argued perceptual distortion in defense of their actions in a questionable shooting, as opposed to those who were clearly and unquestionably justified in their use of deadly force.

Aside from the very small samples used in the two studies, as compared to the total number of police shootings during the relevant time period, both studies have a fatal flaw, or a confounding variable that renders them invalid. It is a variable that should be apparent to any attorney, and that is the statute of limitations on murder and federal civil rights violations. Every police officer involved in a deadly force encounter is acutely aware of the possibility of criminal, civil, or administrative action against them. It is a possibility that may take years to diminish. Take, for example, the case of St. Louis Metropolitan Police officer Jason Stockley. Stockley and his partner were involved in a vehicle pursuit of a suspected drug dealer in 2011. At the end of the pursuit, Stockley shot into the suspect's crashed vehicle and killed him. At the time he was cleared of any wrongdoing (the suspect had a gun) by his own prosecuting attorney and the FBI. Five years later, and for reasons that remain a mystery, the prosecuting attorney presented the case to a St. Louis grand jury, and Stockley was indicted for first degree murder. Not surprisingly, he was acquitted in a 2017 trial.

Following a deadly force encounter, police officers have little to risk by reporting that they experienced perceptual distortion. It can help diminish their responsibility for what happened and lessen the impact of any questionable judgment. But saying that their thoughts were clear and unobstructed may place them at risk of prosecution even years later. In the second study, the researcher admitted to interviewing officers only days after their deadly force encounters. In most cases, this would have been before the various state and federal investigations of the incident had been completed or even begun. It is little wonder that some of the officers reported perceptual distortion. The authors of both studies avoid any discussion of this problem, and their methodologies include no strategy for controlling for this confounding variable. Both studies are thus invalid as a means of determining the reasonableness of an officer's actions.

Both studies include yet another problem. In the second study, the researcher admits that the survey she used was not completed until after the officers involved had been informed of the facts of the case during required critical incident debriefings following the incident. She also admits that a full third of the surveys were administered by other people, including other police officers. She does not say if these other police officers were union representatives, internal affairs investigators, commanders, or just helpful friends. This is a major problem in terms of scientific methodology, especially if those administering the survey have any command authority over the officers. In the first study, the one completed by the former LAPD officer, there is an additional problem related to how the participants were selected. The officers taking the survey were either personal acquaintances of the researcher or acquainted with other officers who were. The potential for the officers to answer the survey questions in ways they believed would validate the research was greatly increased because of these close associations.

In the civil and criminal court systems in the United States, there is an avenue for arguing that a purported expert should not be allowed to testify, either because they are not properly qualified in the area they are testifying about or because their methodology and analysis were problematic. I felt certain that I could be of assistance to Brian in getting the Harvard guy disqualified, at least on the issue of perceptual distortion and his assertion that while under stress, a police officer can easily mistake a square iPhone box for a gun. Not only did he lack the necessary behavioral science background, but the research he used to support his case was fatally flawed.

Finding a way to show a jury how the officers could have mistaken the iPhone box for a gun solved only one of their problems. The Harvard guy also had to find a way to mitigate the fact that Chatman was running away rather than toward the officers. For that he had another piece of purported science in his arsenal—the concept of action versus reaction. This piece of research, which unknown to me at the time had already been discredited by the scientific community, was created by the Force Science Institute. It is a handy little piece of research that purportedly proves that a suspect running from the police will always be able to turn and shoot faster than the officer can pull the trigger on their own weapon. I could see the strategy the Harvard guy was following. First, he would find a way to argue that the officers thought the iPhone box was a gun and then, that Chatman could have stopped, turned, and fired quicker than two experienced and highly trained Chicago police officers who already had their guns on target and were ready to shoot.

The first thing I did was search for the study that reached this conclusion. As it turned out, Dr. Lewinski has authored or co-authored a number of studies relating to human reaction time, all of which, as I discovered, have been found by the scientific community to be wrought with methodological errors and erroneous conclusions. One esteemed scholar, Dr. Lisa Fournier, who at the time was a professor of cognitive psychology at Washington State University and editor of the American Journal of Psychology, was contracted in 2012 by the U.S. Department of Justice to review Lewinski's reaction time research.

Professor Fournier called Lewinski's research "pseudoscience," adding that it was "invalid and unreliable." She went on to state:

> In my opinion, this study questions the ability of Mr. Lewinski to apply relevant and reliable data to answer a question or support an argument. That is, if one cannot report relevant and reliable data to answer a question posed in one's own research study, how can one trust that this person can apply relevant and reliable data to support conclusions he has drawn from the current case. The loose connections between data and one's premise can lead to misleading, inaccurate, and unreliable statements/conclusions.

The Justice Department subsequently denounced Lewinski's findings as lacking in both foundation and reliability.

The Harvard guy certainly was not providing the court an objective survey of the current research on perceptual distortion and human reaction time, two of the more complex issues in the field of cognitive psychology. Instead, he was offering research that ranged from methodologically flawed at its best to junk science at its worse. In theory, neither is allowed in a courtroom. I wondered how often he had gotten away with this. Given his lack of behavioral science credentials, I wondered if he even realized the research was invalid. I put my opinions in an affidavit for Brian Coffman to submit to the court with his motion to exclude the Harvard guy's testimony. Given that the trial date was fast approaching, the judge quickly ruled on the motion and agreed with my findings. Almost the entirety of the Harvard guy's report was disallowed, and his testimony was limited to one minor issue that would serve little purpose. With no expert now to testify on their behalf, the attorneys representing the city of Chicago and Officer Fry threw in the towel a few days later and agreed to settle the case for $3 million.

It was a good feeling to be on the winning side. It was an even better feeling to see Cedrick Chatman's family get some justice and much-needed closure. While it was true that Cedrick Chatman was not the best-behaved kid—carjacking is a serious offense, and there was a good chance he would have received jail time if convicted— he was still just a kid, slightly younger than my youngest son at the time. The case caused me to reflect on certain feelings I once held. There was a time when I would not have given such a story the time needed to read about it in a newspaper. Cedrick Chatman, as well as Kajieme Powell, caused me to see the dark side of policing, the side that assigns its own value to human life; the side that places the lowest value on a Black kid who just committed a felony, even if no one was hurt. I always knew it was there, but I had never truly witnessed it up close and personal. It was only magnified by the lawyers, experts, and academic types who came to the defense of Officer Fry and the officers who killed Kajieme Powell. In just two cases I had seen a significant part of the deadly force script employed—perceptual distortion, action versus reaction, the 21-foot rule, and four highly trained police officers allegedly fearing for their lives from an iPhone box and a brittle steak knife. In these two cases I had gotten a full taste of the deadly force industry in America. I came away more committed than ever to do my part to level the playing field.

It would not be the last time I would do battle with the Harvard guy. In fact, in the years to come, we would find ourselves on opposing sides many times, including my very next case. At least for now I quite enjoyed the fact that the city of Chicago had paid $30,000 for a report I was able to defeat with an affidavit I charged Brian Coffman $900 to write. I was never comfortable charging a lot of money for my services. It felt like I was benefiting from the death of someone's child, no matter how old they were. I understood the attorneys charging their normal fees, but I enjoyed the benefit of a police pension and a paycheck from teaching, not to mention the royalties on my textbooks. I figured the less I charged, the more that eventually would go to the families if the case were settled in their favor.

As for Officer Fry, while he was never criminally charged with the death of Cedrick Chatman, or even disciplined for that matter, he was eventually fired from the Chicago Police Department in 2018 for committing perjury in another case in which he and his partner beat a domestic violence suspect. In his fifteen-year career, Fry had amassed thirty-three citizen complaints ranging from excessive force to illegal arrests. Not surprisingly, he had never been disciplined for any of them. As I would come to learn, it is not uncommon for officers involved in questionable shootings to eventually be fired for various reasons. Sadly, Cedrick Chatman had paid the price for the Chicago Police Department's inaction.

- CHAPTER 4 -

The Deadly
Force Theater

Those Who Make the Wheels Turn and Those Who Apply the Brakes

In a perfect world the process would be predictable. In response to a blatantly bad police shooting, one where some degree of malice is obvious, the local prosecutor would file charges against the officer, and the municipality would offer the family a monetary settlement. In cases where the officer's actions can be attributed to accident or inexperience, while the local prosecutor might perhaps pass on criminal charges, there would still be disciplinary action for the officer and a monetary settlement for the family. But this is not a perfect world, and the process a family goes through to seek some amount of justice and closure in these cases is often as ugly as the shooting itself.

The first actor to take the stage in the deadly force theater, typically before the detectives charged with investigating the matter even arrive at the scene, is the police union representative. There is only one major police union in America. The Fraternal Order of Police (FOP) is a nationwide organization that includes a fraternal component, not unlike the multitude of service organizations across the nation, and a labor component that negotiates union contracts and provides legal representation to any of its members who are the subject of a disciplinary action. The FOP is not like other unions. They represent only law enforcement. They are politically powerful, and most candidates for state or local office will seek out their endorsement. Most of the union representatives are former or retired police officers. They will aggressively protect their members.

If you were to listen to a police scanner during a police shooting, you would likely hear one of the officers at the scene very quickly afterwards ask the dispatch center something a bit cryptic like "Has Pete been called?" The dispatcher's response will almost surely be, "He's on his way." Pete of course is the union representative, and they are typically called to the scene even before the investigating detectives. Their one and only purpose is to protect the officers involved. They do this by acting as a filter for the officer's account of what happened. The public may think that after a shooting, the officer involved is immediately taken to police headquarters and questioned about every fine detail of the incident. But that is not the case. Police officers enjoy constitutional rights just like the people they protect and sometimes kill. Furthermore, they may enjoy additional rights and protections under their union contracts. It is the union representative's mission to guarantee that those rights and protections are respected.

Once the detectives and evidence technicians arrive at the scene, the officer involved will be required to do a public safety walk-through with one or the other, or even both. The purpose of this walk-through is for the officer to provide a bare-bones narrative of the incident. They will answer the *what*, *when*, and *where* of what happened but will avoid the *why*. The union representative will be at their side as they are doing this. The goal is to provide enough information for the detectives and evidence technicians to properly investigate the case without the officer incriminating himor herself. The detectives are always tolerant of the union representative's presence because they are typically union members themselves. The public safety walkthrough is the only time the officer will provide a narrative of the incident without a lawyer present. In many cases a union lawyer will respond to the scene along with the union representative. The deck is already being stacked in favor of the officer involved.

After the initial activities at the scene of the shooting, the officer will be asked to sit for two additional interviews during which the *why* will be addressed in great detail. The first will be a voluntary interview conducted by the investigating detectives. Because a potential outcome of this interview is the filing of criminal charges against the officer, the officer is not required to participate. Eventually, but not always, the officer will next be asked to sit for an interview with internal affairs investigators. This interview is a bit tricky in a legal sense for the officer. They will be ordered to sit for this interview, and if they refuse, they can be disciplined, up to and including termination, for refusing a lawful order. Because the U.S. Constitution prohibits forcing public employees to act as witnesses against themselves under threat of disciplinary action, before an internal affairs interview begins, the officer will be read a Garrity warning. This warning advises the officer that they have no choice but to answer the investigators' questions; that the answers may be used against them in an administrative action that could result in discipline or termination; and that the information disclosed by the officer, because they are forced to do so, cannot be used against them in a criminal case. The union lawyer will be present every step of the way and will be cognizant of the fact that even though the compelled statement cannot be used against the officer in a criminal setting, it can possibly be used in a civil lawsuit. Consequently, the officer's narrative will be well rehearsed and will include statements and answers that are part of the deadly force script. The goals of the officer's various statements, or refusals to even provide one, are to avoid criminal charges and/or termination and to provide as little information as possible that can be useful later in a civil lawsuit filed by the victim's family. The union lawyers are masters at achieving these goals.

The next actor to enter the stage is of course the chief or sheriff of the department involved. There are two types of leaders in law enforcement apart from one who lacks any leadership qualities at all. First are those who realize, just as military leaders do, that a true leader must maintain some degree of separation between themselves and the men and women they lead. A certain level of tension is necessary. No great general ever became great by being every soldier's best friend. General George S. Patton's troops never went into battle with an unbreakable will to win because they hoped to gain his friendship. What they hoped for was his respect. They wanted him to be proud of their efforts in the same way a boy wants his father to be proud of him. In law enforcement, this type of leader is seldom seen out front after a questionable shooting defending their officers before the evidence has even been collected and analyzed, nor do they purposely hide or obfuscate the facts of the case. This type of leader meets privately with the family and assures them of transparency in the investigation. They make public what facts they can and offer an explanation and timetable concerning the rest. Once the investigation is complete, regardless of the prosecutor's decision to either charge the officer or close the case, this type of chief or sheriff will pursue disciplinary action against the officer if any policies were violated, up to and including termination of their employment. A true leader does not hide the truth but rather, attempts to uncover it even at their own political peril.

The other type of law enforcement leader, and unfortunately the most common, is the chief or sheriff who believes that a true leader is one who supports their officers to the bitter end. In the area of police violence, this type of leader can perpetuate the problem by sending the message to their officers that they will have their backs regardless of how egregious their actions may be. The necessary tension between leader and soldier is simply not there. Without that tension the controls on organizational behavior begin to break down. You can always tell this type of leader because they tend to show up at the scene of the shooting to start offering a defense of their officers immediately.

From the perspective of one who investigates these cases on behalf of plaintiffs, this second type of chief does serve a purpose. Often in their haste to defend their officers, they will say things that may become important evidence. In the 2014 case of 18-year-old VonDerrit Myers Jr., another St. Louis shooting that occurred during the turmoil in nearby Ferguson, Chief Sam Dotson came to the scene and described how Myers Jr. wanted to kill his officer,

Jason Flannery, so badly that he continued to pull the trigger on a jammed gun. He even demonstrated it for reporters. Initially I had failed to see this statement because it was only reported in the Los Angeles Times. By the time I did, I had made the case through my own investigation that Myers Jr. initially fired his gun in self-defense against Flannery, a rogue off-duty St. Louis police officer. I had developed the theory that Flannery was actually shaking Myers Jr. down for drugs to use himself. When it was over, Myers Jr. had been shot multiple times, including one shot to the head from close range. When I eventually came across Dotson's statement, I realized that he had essentially confessed for Flannery that Flannery had killed a kid he knew was holding a jammed gun.

Not surprisingly, Dotson never repeated that statement after the night of the shooting, and Flannery changed his narrative to leave out the part about seeing that Myers Jr.'s gun was jammed. He was the only officer present and thus the only officer who could have told Dotson about it. I eventually met with Circuit Attorney Jennifer Joyce and her group of four attorneys who were working police shooting cases. I outlined my investigation step by step, which also included the fact that some of Flannery's empty shell casings were missing from the scene, and the fact that Myers Jr.'s empty casings were not where they should have been if Flannery's version of events were true. I also pointed out Dotson's statement about the jammed gun. And finally, I offered my opinion, which was just a gut feeling, that Flannery was looking for drugs when he stopped Myers Jr. and three of his friends on the street. After a few wide-eyed looks from the lawyers, they thanked me for my time and ushered me out the door. Flannery was never charged with any crime.

Like Officer Fry in the Chatman case, Flannery did not last long after killing Myers Jr. A few months later he was involved in a hitand-run accident with his squad car while off duty. His blood test revealed an alcohol level beyond the legal limit, as well as the presence of cocaine. He was subsequently charged with misdemeanor DUI and terminated by the Department. My gut feeling that Flannery was looking for drugs the night he killed Myers Jr. was never confirmed because Circuit Attorney Joyce refused to reopen the investigation. And Sam Dotson had little to say about the matter after

Flannery was arrested.

Another department I would eventually become quite familiar with, and like St. Louis, one of the deadliest in the United States for police violence, is the Fresno, California, Police Department and its former chief, Jerry Dyer. Like Dotson, Dyer came up through the ranks of the department and had many friends within. He also had a past, as reported by local media, that included excessive drinking, public fighting, extramarital affairs, and an alleged sexual tryst with a 16-year-old girl, an allegation he never admitted or denied. He was a "cop's cop"—tough, physically imposing, and outspoken in his support of law enforcement. Such cops are who most other cops want backing them up in dangerous situations, but they do not always make the best chiefs. Dyer never hesitated to hurry to the scene of a police shooting to defend his officers. Having eventually worked a number of cases in Fresno, Dyer's press statements at shooting scenes became an important source of information for me. I paid close attention not only to what he said but also to what he did not say.

It was never his intention to do so, but in his haste to get in front of the microphone to defend his officers without saying something that could later be characterized as a lie, Dyer had a way of signaling the aspects of a police shooting he was concerned about. Such was the case with the 2015 shooting of Casimero Casillas. While most of the cases I worked ended up with the city, county, or state settling the case with the family, the Casillas case was my first where the city chose to go to trial and take their chances. When I began my investigation—by then the officer involved, Trevor Shipman, had been cleared by the local prosecutor's office of any criminal wrongdoing—I first watched video of Chief Dyer at the scene of the shooting. The shooting occurred after officers chased Casillas for nothing more than a seatbelt violation. Casillas led them to his residence, which was a detached apartment in the backyard of a friend's house in Fresno. Casillas ran inside his apartment while multiple officers responded, including a K9 officer. When the dog was released inside one door of the apartment, Casillas ran outside another door with a piece of pipe in his hand, likely for protection against the dog. Refusing officers' commands to stop, Casillas ran into the breezeway between the house and the attached garage, likely intending to run out the front door of the breezeway to escape. Little did he know, Officer Shipman was inside the breezeway covering the entry door into the house. Immediately after Casillas entered the breezeway, Shipman drew his firearm and fired three times, instantly killing Casillas. It was my belief that Casillas never even saw Shipman prior to being shot.

At the scene of the shooting, Dyer got in front of a microphone and stated, "The suspect was armed with about a 2-foot black pipe and had advanced toward the officer." His statement told me something important—that Dyer had information that Casillas had neither attacked nor even raised the pipe toward Shipman. The word advanced also told me that he was likely not even walking in an aggressive manner. Had he been walking toward Shipman in a way that signaled an imminent attack, Dyer surely would have put that fact front and center. Using such a generic term was his way of attempting to portray Casillas in a negative light without being specific in his description. I knew from that statement alone where the defense's weak spot lay and that the success of the plaintiff's case would lie in portraying Casillas's actions inside the breezeway as something other than an attack on Shipman.

By the time the trial began, I had put together a solid case that Casillas had no intention of attacking Shipman with the pipe and that he was merely attempting to escape through the front breezeway door. The family's attorneys, Bill Schmidt from Fresno and Dale Galipo from Los Angeles, two of the very best, successfully made the case to the jury. After a weeklong trial, including my own five hours of contentious testimony, the jury awarded the family $4.75 million.

It is interesting that Sam Dotson and Jerry Dyer, after eventually retiring from their positions, both decided to run for mayor of their cities. Dotson, a White candidate in a majority Black city, barely began his campaign before realizing the futility of his efforts and dropped out of the race. Dyer, on the other hand, also a White candidate, but in a predominantly White and Hispanic city, won his election and became mayor of Fresno in 2020. In a perfect world, law enforcement would be devoid of political influence. In reality, it is quite prejudiced by it.

One popular strategy often employed by chiefs and sheriffs to make a problematic police shooting disappear while avoiding responsibility for its disappearance, is to announce publicly that they are taking the seemingly harsh step of asking the FBI to take over the case. Sadly, it is a strategy that will invariably instill in the victim's family the belief that their loved one's death is being taken seriously and that justice will be served upon the officers involved. Nothing could be further from the truth. The FBI is where problematic police shootings go to die. What the family is never told is that the FBI has no jurisdiction to even investigate a police shooting, nor do they have the experience to even conduct a proper homicide investigation. The FBI investigates civil rights violations, a federal crime, not the use of excessive force by the police. The question the FBI seeks to answer in these cases is whether the officers involved willfully violated the victim's constitutional rights, specifically the right to be free from unreasonable seizures or use of force. In other words, there must be "intent" on the part of the officer to deny the victim of their constitutional rights at the time they pulled the trigger. It is a very tough case to make as a criminal matter because it requires that the prosecutor somehow divine the mind of the officer. Consequently, 99% of the cases that are sent to the FBI eventually lead to a press release by them or the U.S. attorney announcing that they were unable to prove that intent beyond a reasonable doubt and thus had no choice but to close the case.

Every chief or sheriff knows the eventual outcome of asking the FBI to take over the case. It is a convenient way to wash their hands of the matter and still be able to say that they tried. Unlike police or sheriff's departments, the FBI by design has no connection to local communities. They have no obligation to do what is best for a local community or family. Their obligation is to the federal government and to the letter of the federal statutes they are charged with enforcing. They are seldom motivated by the spirit of the law or to do what is just and right for a local community.

Assuming the FBI is not requested to take over an investigation, the next stop on the line is the local prosecutor's desk. Most local prosecutors have two goals when a police shooting occurs in their jurisdiction. First is to publicly proclaim to the family their commitment to conduct a full review and get to the truth of what happened; and second, to privately try their level best to find a way to avoid charging the officers involved. Prosecutors are first and foremost politicians, and they are keenly aware of the public's support for law enforcement. Only in jurisdictions where there is a majority interest in ending police violence—cities like St. Louis and Chicago—and where a prosecutor is elected who is not afraid of the police union's political muscle, is there any chance of an officer being criminally charged for a problem shooting.

Local prosecutors are involved in the criminal prosecution of offenders, including police officers. They are not involved in civil matters where private attorneys representing the families (plaintiffs) bring suit against the officers involved and their employers (defense). Prosecutors, however, will always be careful not to make statements or release evidence that will bolster the plaintiff's case. In those rare cases when a prosecutor does act independently and in the name of justice, especially when they charge an officer after a problematic shooting, there is a good chance the local police, the police union, and any friends they have on the city council or county board will circle the wagons and begin an all-out political assault on the prosecutor. It can get quite ugly as they attempt to portray the prosecutor as anti-police and anti-law-and-order. I have even seen cases where they play a very subtle race card and attempt to portray the prosecutor as siding with the criminally inclined Black community against the law-abiding White community. They never overtly present it that way, but it is clearly implied in their public messaging.

Once the officer is inevitably cleared of any criminal wrongdoing by the local prosecutor, thus ending any possibility of criminal charges being filed against the officer, scene two of the drama begins. It is now time for the civil lawsuit to move forward. Now is when the private attorneys become involved. The attorneys who work these cases are a mixed lot. They tend to work predominantly on one side or the other, representing the families of those shot by the police (plaintiffs), or the officers themselves and their employers (defendants). Those who work as plaintiff's lawyers are truly among the most accomplished and able lawyers I have had the opportunity to work with in the past nearly forty years. Surprisingly, there are only a handful across the nation who work most of the cases—Bill Schmidt and Stuart Chandler in Fresno, John Burris in San Francisco, Dale Galipo in Los Angeles, Craig Jones and Chris Stewart in Atlanta, Jeffrey Campiche and Craig Sims in Seattle, and Brian Coffman in Chicago, to name a few. They are driven by a desire to seek justice and to right the wrongs they witness in their communities. They are mostly experienced lawyers who understand the complexities of civil rights/excessive force litigation and are quite adept at defending against the legal gamesmanship they often encounter in the courtroom.

On the other side of the courtroom table are the lawyers who defend the police and their employers. Most become involved because they have been recommended by the police union. They are a critical and necessary component of the deadly force industry. They represent the individual officers involved, as well as the cities and counties that employ them. Many municipalities have their own corporation lawyers. However, they seldom defend the municipality in a police shooting case, and they never defend the individual officers. This is where the union-recommended private lawyers take the stage. The reason for this, and another example of how the deck is stacked against the victims of police violence, is that the officers and their employer are typically backed by the unlimited wealth of a major insurance company. It is the insurance companies that approve who will defend the officers involved and their employers, and in the process attempt to limit their company's financial exposure.

Unfortunately, everyday citizens have no ability to purchase insurance against police violence. Plaintiff's attorneys must work on contingency, and they must spend thousands of dollars of their own money on expert witnesses, scientific testing, and depositions. In contrast, defense attorneys spend the insurance company's money. If the jury's verdict is in favor of the defense, then the money the plaintiff's attorney was forced to spend is lost. If the verdict is in favor of the plaintiff, the defense attorney loses nothing. Win or lose, they submit their final bill to the insurance company and move on to the next case. It is an inherently unfair process. Many plaintiff's attorneys, especially those who work outside the major population centers and who may not get a steady influx of civil rights cases, often do not have the financial resources to properly work a case that may require experts, costly depositions, and possibly years of motions and other legal filings. The insurance companies and defense attorneys know this. They know how to wear down the opposing side until they no longer have the resources to continue. Many times, knowing full well the resources a complicated case requires, the defense will offer a low-ball settlement in hopes of the plaintiff accepting it to avoid the risk of losing. It is easy to become cynical in this business when you see the defense offer a ridiculously low settlement to the already-impoverished family of a dead Black kid, playing on the shameful belief that even a small amount of money will seem like a lot to them. Often when a family does accept a small settlement, after their own lawyer takes his or her fees, and rightly so, then any liens against the judgment will be satisfied, such as any medical expenses that were incurred trying to save the victim's life. Many times, there is little left for the family.

Many of the defense attorneys who become involved in civil rights cases around the country are ex-cops. It makes sense. They already know the language, the unwritten rules, and the nuances of a profession many attorneys have little understanding of. And they tend to have a close relationship with the police unions. They are among the toughest defense attorneys for an opposing expert because they too know the dirty little secrets of policing. I like to call it the "I know you know what I know" phenomenon. For example, a defense attorney with no police experience may actually think it is appropriate to shoot a teenager in the back when they reach for their waistband during a foot pursuit. They may even believe their client when they describe how scared they were that the kid was going to kill them. But the ex-cop recognizes the absurdity of it. They understand the deadly force script because, like me, they too were once ready to employ it if necessary. Whether in a deposition or a trial, there is no bluffing between an ex-cop defense attorney and an ex-cop expert witness. It is more a battle of wits and creative argument and whether the question itself or the answer given in response will be more influential on the jury's perception.

While the vast majority of defense attorneys are professional men and women who pursue their mission in an ethical manner, unfortunately there are a few exceptions. I personally was always on the lookout for what I termed the wannabe. These attorneys are easy to spot because they are typically involved in police training but have never been a police officer. They may even carry a special or auxiliary officer's badge some chief or sheriff gave them in return for providing free legal training. Most are gun enthusiasts. While there was always some level of respect between me and the ex-cop attorneys I came up against, that was seldom the case with the wannabes. Many of them were actually hostile toward me, as if I were violating some sacred oath by pointing out that it might have been wrong for their client to beat a handcuffed suspect unconscious or to use a Taser on them until the battery ran dry. These defense attorneys are on a mission. Most seem to be motivated not by the ideal of a just outcome, but by a desire to prove their loyalty to a profession they are not even part of—to be seen as a trusted member of the choir. Their tactics are at times questionable and at others, borderline unethical. If there was ever an opportunity during a deposition for one of them to ask an equivalent question to "Do you still beat your wife?," I just expected it. Fortunately, they represent a small fraction of the total, and I very quickly learned to anticipate and preempt such games.

Once both sides have their attorneys in place and are ready for battle, one of the first things they both will do is hire their own expert. Unfortunately, the world of expert witnesses is an unregulated freefor-all. There are essentially no requirements to be an expert. You just call yourself an expert one day and start looking for business. Of course, you must ultimately convince a judge that you are qualified, but even that process is guided by very few controls. In theory, the expert is completely independent, and regardless of who pays them, that should not influence their opinions. In reality, there is nothing further from the truth. I very quickly developed a process where I reviewed the evidence in a case at no charge so that the attorney who contacted me had the option to not hire me if my tentative opinions differed from what they were looking for. That way I maintained the integrity of my practice. Unfortunately, that is not always the case.

Pro-police expert witnesses are an important component of the deadly force industry. The majority of them, in my experience, are nothing more than hired guns who will say anything and stretch the truth as far as possible to defend an officer's actions. They are typically recommended by the police unions and thus act as preferred providers. Few of them are truly qualified, and over the years I was able to assist in getting many of them disqualified by exposing the sometimes-fraudulent nature of their credentials. I have seen pro-police experts use essentially the same report in multiple cases. I have seen them include in their credentials dubious training courses that often amounted to nothing more than an unaccredited online module. And in one case, I even discovered that the organization that provided the professional designation attached to the expert's name was his own organization. They will go to great lengths to fluff up their resumes and appear to have an expertise in an area where they in fact have none. Of course, like all the various professions involved in the deadly force drama, there are good and qualified experts who do predominantly defense work in support of the officers involved in questionable uses of force. In my experience, they are the minority. Pro-police experts are almost always on the wrong side of the evidence, since the vast majority of police actions are obviously justified, and thus they never see the inside of a courtroom. Plaintiff's attorneys tend not to waste their time on cases they know they have no chance of winning. So, the cases that end up being litigated are those that are obviously problematic. The only way to defend the officer's actions once the plaintiff files their lawsuit is for the defense attorney to find an expert who will try to convince a jury with some novel theory or piece of purported science supporting the notion that the officer had no other choice.

And that brings us to the final player in the drama, the judge. In civil rights cases, the judge is the gatekeeper who either allows a case to go to a jury or dismisses it and brings the matter to a quick and abrupt end. Judges are not unique. They are lawyers with political and social beliefs and biases just like everyone else. Most of them had to play the political game for a considerable length of time to even be considered for their jobs. Politics is not an inherently bad thing for someone who eventually becomes a judge, but it is to be expected that a judge's legal decisions might at times be influenced by their personal beliefs. If those beliefs fall on the conservative side of law and order, then chances are their decisions will fall on the side of the police if there is enough legal wiggle room for them to exercise that discretion. If their beliefs fall on the liberal side of reform and restorative justice, then chances are they will be pro-victim in their decisions.

The judge serves as the gatekeeper by ruling on a motion that is filed early on by the defense in almost every civil rights case—a motion for summary judgment based on the legal protection of Qualified Immunity. Only if the plaintiff's attorney can successfully argue against such a motion will the case move forward. Otherwise, it is immediately closed, although either side may appeal the decision to get a second bite at the apple. Qualified immunity is one of the most hotly debated legal issues in the realm of civil rights litigation. It protects all but the plainly incompetent officer or the officer who knowingly violates the law. In its simplest form it says that an officer is immune from litigation unless they knowingly violate the suspect's constitutional rights. The right must be clearly established by law. If it is, then it is expected that a reasonable officer would have known they were violating that right at the time they used force against the suspect. If the right is not clearly established, which seems to be the case most of the time, then a reasonable officer is not expected to have known they were violating that right. In that case, summary judgment is awarded in favor of the officer and the case is dismissed. In reality, the concept of qualified immunity is sufficiently vague that it allows a judge to take whatever position their politics, bias, and legal philosophy compels them to take. While most such decisions are clearly explained in a lengthy written decision that may or may not be couched in sound legal reasoning, I have seen decisions that were barely coherent, and others that were based on a complete misunderstanding of the evidence. Unfortunately, a judge is not required to understand the evidence when they make their decision, and typically, when the defense files such a motion, the evidence is twisted and stretched to support their position.

For an expert, the judge is also the person who decides if the expert's opinions ever see the inside of a courtroom. If the motion for summary judgment is like watching sausage being made, as some like to say, then the inevitable motion to exclude the opposing expert's testimony is like watching the pig being shot. If the case moves forward because the motion for summary judgment was denied, then the next step for the defense is to get the plaintiff's expert disqualified. Such a motion is often less about legitimately questioning the expert's credentials and more about knowingly obfuscating and mischaracterizing those credentials to make the expert appear unqualified. I personally have had defense attorneys omit to disclose my true credentials; knowingly mischaracterize and even flat-out lie about my credentials; and I even had one defense attorney in the Southwestern United States piece together unrelated snippets from a deposition to create a statement purportedly made by me with an entirely different meaning. Unfortunately, there are no consequences to an attorney for playing such games, even when the truth is pointed out by the opposing side. It is viewed as acceptable theater, sometimes with little thought given to the grieving families who are seeking closure through a just outcome.

After one to two years of the plaintiff's attorney fighting to gain access to the case evidence, defending against a motion for summary judgment, and then fighting to keep their expert from being disqualified, eventually, if all goes well, a trial will be held anywhere from two to five years after the incident that led to the lawsuit. There is no constitutional right to a speedy trial like in a criminal proceeding. The speed at which a case gets to trial is at the mercy of the judge's schedule, and judges tend to work at a snail's pace it seems. It is not an enjoyable experience, especially for the families, but also for an expert who at times must testify to case details they have little or no recollection of after so many years of legal wrangling.

The deadly force theater is at times a Greek tragedy, at others a Shakespearean comedy, and at still others, a complete farce. Those who choose to take the stage, especially those with noble intentions, must keep their eyes on what brought them to the stage in the first place—for me, a desire to level the playing field for the victims of police violence; otherwise they will inevitably run the risk of being quickly consumed by their own growing cynicism.

- CHAPTER 5 -

The Case of
Dontre Hamilton

Milwaukee, Wisconsin

The Thousand-Yard Stare: How the Police Use a Misunderstood Phenomenon to Create an Illusion of Danger

For me personally, no other case illustrates the use of the deadly force script better than the case of Dontre Hamilton, a case that led to rioting in the city of Milwaukee. On April 30, 2014, Hamilton was shot 14 times by Milwaukee Police Officer Chris Manney during a physical altercation. His crime? Sleeping in a city park in the middle of the day. Hamilton, a 31-year-old Black man from a close-knit working-class family who battled with homelessness and mental illness, was killed instantly when Manney drew his weapon and fired (the day before his death Hamilton had informed family members that he was tired and hungry, and that someone was going to kill him). When Manney eventually gave his statement, he described Hamilton as having superhuman strength and a thousand-yard stare. He described how Hamilton reached for his waistband as if he were about to pull out a gun and that he was as scared as he had ever been as a police officer that he was about to be killed. Manney invoked just about every component of the deadly force script. He even described how after Hamilton disarmed him of his police baton and struck him in the head, he literally thought his brains were coming out. At the hospital following the incident, Manney was prescribed aspirin after the medical staff was unable to find any wounds.

As is often the case with experts, the attorney representing Hamilton's family came across my name after reading about the Cedrick Chatman case in Chicago and was aware that the Harvard guy had gotten most of his report excluded in that case. The attorney, Ian Wallach from Los Angeles, contacted me after getting my number from Brian Coffman and asked if I would take a look at the Hamilton case. The district attorney in Milwaukee, John Chisholm, had already cleared Manney of any criminal wrongdoing and, much to my surprise, had used the Harvard guy to find a way to justify his actions. I was more than happy to take a look.

I always begin a case by looking at the autopsy report, sometime before I even know from the officers' reports and statements what happened. It tells me how many times the individual was shot, where they were shot, the trajectories of the bullets through the body, possibly their body position at the time they were shot, and in some cases the distance between the gun's muzzle and the victim's body. In many cases I can tell from the autopsy report if the media accounts of what happened are accurate. The media accounts always originate from either the police spokesperson, many times the chief or sheriff, or the prosecuting attorney. In the case of Dontre Hamilton, by the time I became involved, District Attorney Chisholm had already held a press conference announcing that Manney would not be criminally charged, a press conference that was posted online. I also had access to his report of the incident which was posted online.

One thing that became immediately apparent to me was that Chisholm was trying hard to argue that Hamilton was not shot while he was on the ground. In theory, no police officer should ever shoot a suspect on the ground unless the suspect is armed with a gun and threatening to use it. During his press conference, he even used a rubber band to demonstrate how the bullets would have had an upward trajectory through Hamilton's body if Manney had fired from the area of Hamilton's feet while he was on the ground. The trajectories of the bullets, according to the medical examiner, moved mostly sideways through Hamilton's body with either no upward or downward trajectory, or slightly downward. I assumed that the Harvard guy likely explained to him that this meant Hamilton was on his feet and standing sideways when he was shot. They were both wrong.

After reading the autopsy report and Chisholm's summary of the evidence, I knew almost immediately that many of the shots had hit Hamilton while he was in fact on or near the ground. Manney was not at Hamilton's feet but was to his right side shooting perpendicular to Hamilton's body. Shooting from this location, the trajectories would be exactly what the medical examiner reported. I later confirmed my opinion with the physical evidence, especially the locations of Manney's empty shell casings. I also noticed one other important thing about Chisholm's report. The medical examiner reported that Hamilton had seven blunt force injuries to his arms, chin, and the back of his head. Chisholm made no mention of these wounds. I knew there was more to the story.

On the day he died, Dontre Hamilton was bothering no one. He was simply lying on the pavement in Red Arrow Park in the middle of downtown Milwaukee taking a nap. Around 1:50 p.m. an employee of a nearby Starbucks kiosk telephoned the Milwaukee Police Department to report that Hamilton was sleeping in close proximity to the kiosk. The duty sergeant who took the call telephoned Officer Manney, who was the officer typically working that area during the day. Manney was busy on another call a few blocks away and did not answer his phone. Instead, Officers Robert Fitchett and Andrew Fuerte responded to what was described only as a welfare check. When they arrived, they awakened Hamilton and asked if he was okay and if he needed anything. Hamilton was cooperative and polite, and responded that he was fine. The two officers, acting professionally and appropriately, thanked him and departed the area. Hamilton moved from that location but twenty minutes later returned and continued his nap on the pavement. The Starbucks employee again called the police department to report that he had returned. This time Fitchett and Fuerte responded and explained to the employee that Hamilton was doing nothing wrong and that there was nothing they could do. That should have ended the matter, but at approximately 3:30 p.m., it went in a much different and deadly direction when Officer Manney finished his other call and responded to Red Arrow Park.

There is a concept in law enforcement called de-escalation. It originates from the training all officers now receive that is referred to as CIT (Crisis Intervention Team) training. The CIT concept began in the city of Memphis, Tennessee, in the 1980s. It was designed to reduce the high number of mentally ill people who were being shot and killed by the police. The original idea in Memphis was to have a specially trained team of police officers and mental health professionals respond to things like threatened suicides and other cases involving anticipated mental health commitments. Once the Memphis Police Department reported success with the program, the "Memphis Model" spread to other departments across the country. It was eventually realized that all officers could benefit from the training, either in abbreviated form or the full 40-hour standardized training that is now delivered across the United States. Officers are trained either to de-escalate an emotionally escalated individual to avoid the need for some level of force and to avoid escalating them if they are not yet to that point. They learn about the various forms of mental illness, especially schizophrenia and depression, and how their own behavior can negatively impact their efforts to achieve a peaceful outcome.

In reality, the law enforcement community as a whole is still light years away from seeing significant change resulting from widespread CIT training. It seems that every time a chief or sheriff takes to the microphone after the shooting of a mentally ill individual by one of their officers, they cannot wait to tout the fact that their officers are all CIT trained. Therein lies the problem. There was a time when only certain officers received the training and served as crisis intervention specialists within their departments. Those who filled such positions were typically officers who had volunteered and were thus dedicated to the goals of the program. With essentially all officers now being trained—most departments have discontinued specialized units as a result—the CIT concept has become watered-down and the training

routine a necessary inconvenience for most officers. Consequently, there is no longer systemic buy-in. When an officer responds to a CIT case, say a threatened suicide involving a knife, rather than seeing an individual who needs help and who does not have the ability to comply with their commands due to disordered thinking and paranoia, they see someone who is threatening them with a knife and refusing to drop it—no different than the bank robber, rapist, or anyone else attempting to avoid arrest through violence. So many times, I have watched body cam videos of officers responding to such cases and immediately begin yelling at the individual to drop the knife, withholding any attempt at de-escalation until they do, something that in all likelihood will not happen. Those officers who are committed to using their CIT training know to remain calm, modulate their voices, and begin building rapport despite the knife and without focusing on it. Unfortunately, those officers are a minority. Most simply continue to yell commands until the individual inevitably moves in one direction or another and the shooting begins.

When Officer Manney finally approached Hamilton in Red Arrow Park, unaware that Fitchett and Fuerte had already properly handled the situation, he chose a different course of action and one that was lacking any CIT techniques. After commanding Hamilton to his feet, Manney began frisking him. A police officer cannot randomly frisk people. In the case of Terry v. Ohio (1968), the U.S. Supreme Court held that a suspect's constitutional rights are not violated when a police officer stops the suspect on the street and frisks him or her without probable cause to arrest if the police officer has a reasonable suspicion that the person has committed, is committing, or is about to commit a crime and has a reasonable belief that the person may be armed and presently dangerous. Hamilton had committed no crime, nor was there any indication that he was about to.

Manney likely later knew he had a problem and that he had violated Hamilton's constitutional rights by improperly frisking him. He gave three different statements following the incident, and on this issue, he gave three different versions of what happened. He was interviewed first by Detectives Erik Gulbrandson and Charles Mueller inside the ambulance that transported him to the hospital, and then continued immediately after his medical exam. Gulbrandson memorialized Manney's statement in a written report. As recorded by Gulbrandson, Manney provided the following information:

> PO (police officer) Manney states that as the subject stood up and faced away from him, he approached the subject from behind and based on his experience and for officer safety he conducted a Terry pat down. PO Manney states that he informed the subject of what he was about to do and then reached under the subject's arms and lifted them upward as the subject complied.

In a later affidavit in support of a motion for summary judgment, which was ultimately denied by the judge, Manney changed this important part of his narrative. He stated the following:

> After Mr. Hamilton stood up, he was able to stand without assistance. However, without any direction from me, he turned his back to me, and he raised both of his arms so that they were perpendicular to his torso, in an airplane-like position. By turning his back to me, and raising his arms in that fashion, I perceived that Mr. Hamilton had previously been stopped by the police and subjected to pat down searches, and that he was assuming that I wanted to pat him down, and so he was voluntarily consenting to a pat down search.

Knowing that his pat down was improper, Manney changed his narrative to make it appear as though Hamilton had voluntarily consented to the search. It was a weak attempt to justify his actions—quite absurd actually—and in his next statement, his sworn deposition in the civil case, he changed his story once again. Now, he stated the following:

> I never said I conducted a Terry pat-down [referring to Detective Gulbrandson's report]. No, his arms are already back, and I reached my arm up, and I just wanted to build rapport. I was still at the rapport-building stage, and I wanted to get his first name, and I wanted to see if his heart

rate was okay and if it was pounding, and I asked his name.

While Manney obviously believed immediately following the incident that his pat-down search was justified, in his later statements, no doubt with some coaching from his police union representative or lawyer, he attempted to change the entire complexion of the pat down and in fact, attempted to make it appear as something completely different. In his affidavit he attempted to make it appear as a consensual pat down, and then later, in his sworn deposition, he attempted to portray it as merely a check of Hamilton's heart rate, and not a pat down at all. Also, in his affidavit, in which he contradicted his initial statement to detectives that it was in fact an involuntary pat down, he added what I like to call a "just-in-case" rationale. In other words, if the first lie did not work, he offered a back-up lie that hopefully would. He stated the following in his affidavit:

> Based upon all of the information known to me at the time, including 1) my thought that Mr. Hamilton was homeless, by virtue of him sleeping on a blanket on top of cold concrete in the park, with a backpack nearby, in the middle of a weekday afternoon; 2) my observation of bulges in his clothing, which were consistent with the concealment of a bladed-weapon; 3) Mr. Hamilton's twitching; 4) his inability to focus on me; 5) the fact that he had disturbed the Starbucks employees enough for them to call for police service; and 6) my past policing experiences and my training, I decided that I would pat down Mr. Hamilton for my safety, to determine if he was in fact, in possession of weapon.

If Manney could not convince a judge or jury that Hamilton had consented to the pat down or that he was merely checking Hamilton's heart rate, then he had to overcome two obstacles to get past the illegality of his search. First, he had to show that Hamilton had committed, or was about to commit, a crime. And second, he had to provide some basis for why he believed Hamilton was armed with a weapon. In both his affidavit and deposition, Manney testified that he observed "bulges" in Hamilton's pockets. However, when the contents of his pockets were later inventoried by the medical examiner, only cash was found—approximately $160, which included seven twenty-dollar bills, hardly sufficient for creating a bulge consistent with the size of a weapon, whether a gun or a knife.

As for the crime Hamilton had committed? Well, it was District Attorney Chisholm who took care of that problem for Manney. Chisholm concluded that Hamilton was breaking some obscure ordinance that disallowed people from sleeping in city parks. This of course told me that Chisholm knew the pat down was unlawful and was looking for any way possible to justify it. It was an absurd argument on Chisholm's part. The ordinance was intended for overnight campers, not someone lying on the pavement with his eyes closed in the middle of the day. It was impossible to even prove that Hamilton was sleeping. Fitchett and Fuerte stated that he opened his eyes when they approached. Was he asleep? It was simply impossible to prove. And furthermore, I suspected that Chisholm had probably never prosecuted anyone for lying on the pavement in Red Arrow Park.

It is typically the case that when an officer violates a person's constitutional rights things will quickly progress from bad to worse. Manney was an experienced police officer, and he knew from his training that when dealing with the homeless, particularly those suffering from mental illness, one sure way to escalate the situation is to put your hands on them or their meager belongings. When Manney began his pat down, Hamilton predictably resisted his efforts. According to Manney's statement to detectives, while he was reaching around Hamilton from behind to pat down his front pockets, Hamilton lowered his arms and trapped Manney's arms against his body. He further stated that with his arms trapped, he continued to feel Hamilton's pockets and felt some type of object. Here is where he added yet another component of the deadly force script. Manney stated to the detectives that he believed Hamilton's actions were consistent with someone who was armed with a gun. That of course proved to be untrue.

At this point in the incident, according to Manney, he drew his police baton, a long wooden one, and as he did, Hamilton grabbed it from his hand and began striking him with it. Because he feared for his life, Manney drew his firearm while backing up and ordering Hamilton to drop the baton. Hamilton continued his attack, and Manney fired his weapon fourteen times from close range, killing Hamilton instantly. Almost immediately, I knew Manney's account of what happened could not be accurate. Anyone with any police experience would see the absurdity in this account. When conducting a pat down of an individual in this manner, if the individual at any time drops his arms, as Manney described, it is an immediate signal to escalate the situation and to handcuff the suspect. Furthermore, it is physically impossible to trap a person's arms in such a manner without grabbing their hands, something Manney never suggested Hamilton did. A police officer in this situation would immediately slide their arms free or use them as leverage to take the suspect to the ground and initiate an arrest. But Manney provided a strange account of continuing to pat down Hamilton while his arms were trapped. It was obvious that Manney was attempting to leave open the possibility of Hamilton having a gun in order to create a particular state-of-mind narrative that would support and bolster his use of force. This is a common police tactic in cases involving the use of deadly force against an unarmed suspect.

Manney's statement that he had attempted to use his police baton also confirmed, though not intending to, one other thing. Three of the blunt force contusions found on Hamilton's body by the medical examiner were elongated abrasions to the back of his head. I knew Manney had likely struck Hamilton multiple times with the baton before Hamilton, in self-defense, disarmed him of it. Police officers are trained to never strike someone in the head or neck with a baton unless deadly force is justified. Now it made sense why Manney was attempting to create a narrative about the possible presence of a gun. He knew he had crossed the line with the baton, likely even before he was told that his pat down was illegal. His tactic was to deny striking Hamilton with the baton except for a single time in the rib cage, and to leave an out in case he got put into a corner on the issue. Of course, he would also argue that in the heat of the moment, his perception and memory were impacted, and he simply could not recall striking Hamilton multiple times. Another common tactic— offer an explanation that is impossible to disprove.

There were four eyewitness accounts that supported the fact that the blunt force injuries found on Hamilton were caused by baton strikes. None of the witness accounts were consistent with Manney's. One eyewitness stated to detectives that he observed Manney strike Hamilton with the baton at least twice in the back and shoulder area. Two others stated that Manney struck Hamilton at least twice. And a fourth recalled at least four strikes to the hip and the side of the body. It is often the case that eyewitness testimony is highly unreliable. It demands that an investigator use caution when weighing such testimony. However, when all the eyewitnesses in a case are consistent on certain major points of fact, even when inconsistent on specific details, there is a high probability that they are accurately describing those points of fact. They had all observed Manney strike Hamilton multiple times with his police baton, something Manney denied. Their statements confirmed the picture I was beginning to form in my mind of what had actually happened in Red Arrow Park.

One of the most important pieces of physical evidence at a shooting scene is the empty shell casings. Shell casings can tell an investigator much about what happened. And while there is a great deal of variability in how casings are ejected from semiautomatic handguns, we know generally that when a police officer fires their gun in the manner they are trained, the empty casings will eject to the right and rear at an approximately 45-degree angle. The locations of the empty casings can tell us generally about the movement of the shooter, as well as their location at the point when each shot was taken. It is true that ejected shell casings can bounce if they land on a hard surface, but given their weight, any bounce is minimal. And those that land in the grass likely do not bounce at all.

Because the detectives plotted out the locations of Manney's ejected casings, I was able to look at them in relation to Hamilton's body. The casings provided me Manney's path of travel once the shooting sequence began, and his general location when the final shot was taken. I determined that Manney did not shoot all fourteen shots in rapid succession, but there were periods where he paused momentarily as he backed up. The first three to four shots appeared to have been single shots, each followed by a brief hesitation. There were ten empty casings found in the area beyond the point where

Hamilton collapsed, and given the tighter grouping of those casings, it was apparent that Manney had stopped backing up and had begun to shoot more rapidly and without pausing between shots. I concluded that the final seven shots were taken after Hamilton had stopped his forward movement and was either standing still, falling, or already on the ground. The locations of the casings also confirmed that Chisholm had misunderstood the evidence or was given inaccurate information about where Manney was in relation to Hamilton when he fired. Chisholm had inappropriately pronounced in his report that the evidence did not support that Hamilton was shot while he was on the ground.

Based on the available evidence, the eyewitness accounts, and Manney's own statements and sworn testimony, I was able to determine the sequence of events. The incident began when Manney approached Hamilton and ordered him to stand. Manney stated that almost immediately he recognized that Hamilton was possibly suffering from some type of mental illness. His immediate goal should have been to determine if Hamilton needed medical or mental health services, being careful to interact with Hamilton in a way that would avoid escalating the situation. Instead, Manney chose to conduct a pat-down search without lawful justification, and byplacing his hands on Hamilton to conduct the search—always potentially dangerous when dealing with the mentally ill—he quickly escalated Hamilton's demeanor. As Manney conducted the pat down, Hamilton dropped his arms and spun away. He then began to walk away. At that point, Manney drew his police baton and struck Hamilton multiple times, including strikes to his neck and the back of his head.

Acting in self-defense after being struck multiple times with the baton, Hamilton was able to wrestle it away from Manney's grip. He then moved toward Manney, who began to back pedal. At the same time, Manney drew his gun, and, according to one eyewitness, shouted, "So now you want to play?" We will never know why Hamilton continued to move toward Manney with the baton now in his hands and Manney's gun trained on him. One eyewitness described Hamilton holding it like a sword and swinging it in front of him. It is reasonable to conclude that Hamilton's actions were still defensive in nature, especially with Manney now pointing a gun at him. In his mind, he was causing Manney to move backward in order to prevent him from moving forward to continue his attack on him. Perhaps it was an irrational move on his part, but irrational decisions are why people diagnosed with schizophrenia so often get shot by police officers who fail to consider the impact of mental illness on a person's judgment and their ability to comply with commands.

Manney could have ended the incident quickly by simply deploying his OC pepper spray, but instead, he began firing his weapon as Hamilton continued to move forward. Within seconds, and after being struck multiple times, Hamilton stopped his forward motion and fell to the ground. Manney continued to fire his weapon until his slide locked back on an empty magazine. Hamilton died almost immediately.

Once I was able to determine exactly what happened, I drafted my report and submitted it to Ian Wallach in Los Angeles. The next order of business would be to deal with the Harvard guy. He had been paid for his work on behalf of the city of Milwaukee for Chisholm to use to make a decision about criminally charging Manney, but it remained to be seen if they intended to use him as an expert in the civil case, especially after he had recently had most of his report excluded in the Chatman case just 90 miles down the road in Chicago. His report in the Hamilton case was full of the same pseudoscience and improper assumptions I had seen in his Chatman report. In fact, it was almost the same report with the names and a few facts changed. I told Ian Wallach that I was quite certain we could get this report excluded as well, and I began drafting an affidavit for a Daubert motion. A Daubert motion is filed to question the opposing expert's qualifications and to get the court to disqualify them from testifying.

In the end, the affidavit was not necessary. The city decided not to use the report, likely because they knew a Daubert motion would be filed. Instead, they used another expert who was associated with the Force Science Institute. His report was no more accurate or based on sound scientific methodology than the Harvard guy's. I drafted the affidavit to support the Daubert motion. However, before Ian could get it filed, the city of Milwaukee threw in the towel and agreed to settle the case for $2.3 million.

The Hamilton case clearly illustrates the deadly force industry at work, and they nearly succeeded. The police union immediately moved to protect Manney and likely helped him craft a new narrative to get past the problem of the unlawful pat down. The detectives assigned to the case conducted an investigation that in my mind was intended to provide support for Manney's decision to use deadly force. The city hired the Harvard guy to give the appearance that a nationally recognized expert had determined that Manney's actions were justified (he had graduated from Harvard after all. How could he be wrong?). And then District Attorney Chisholm issued a report that misrepresented the evidence and completely avoided the fact that the medical examiner had found multiple blunt force injuries on Hamilton's head and torso.

Manney was ultimately fired from the Milwaukee Police Department, not for improperly shooting Hamilton, but for conducting an unlawful pat-down search. It is common for police departments to terminate officers who have been involved in blatantly unjustified uses of deadly force, even after the district attorney has cleared them of wrongdoing. But they seldom make the reason for the termination the use of force itself. If they did, it would almost guarantee a win by the plaintiff in the civil case to follow. It is a way for a chief or sheriff to publicly wash their hands of the officer while continuingto protect their department. It is a cynical view because it is a cynical process.

I used to tell young police officers that every crime scene will tell the story of what happened. The trick is learning how to listen. In this case the location of the empty casings; the blunt force injuries found on Hamilton, particularly to the back of his head; the trajectories of the bullets through Hamilton's body; the subtle and not so subtle changes to Manney's account of what happened; and the general consistencies found in the eyewitness statements, all combined to allow me to draft a report with an evidence-based chronology of events that in the end was impossible for them to dispute.

The next time I saw any of Dontre Hamilton's family was when his mother, Maria, along with eight other mothers of victims of police violence, appeared on stage at the 2016 Democratic Convention. It was nice to see that she was turning her personal tragedy into something positive and making a difference. Not long after, a documentary about the Hamilton case titled The Blood Is at the Doorstep was released. The truth of what actually happened that day in Red Arrow Park was laid bare for all to see. So too was the deadly force industry and the script they so masterfully employed. I was happy to see that my efforts to level the playing field were perhaps having an impact, however small that impact might have been at the time.

- CHAPTER 6 -

The Case of Michael Brown

Fergusen, Missouri

The Myth of the Superhuman Black Man: How the Police Weaponize Negative Stereotypes

It was the one case I had no intentions of working. Not only was it the most highly publicized police shooting in U.S. history, but it was a little too close to home. In 2017, almost three years after Michael Brown was shot and killed by Officer Darren Wilson, tensions still ran high in and around St. Louis as the civil trial drew near. I had testified in a number of cases around the country by then, but because I was still a professor at Washington University, just 5 miles from where the Ferguson riots took place, I felt that it was best to limit my involvement to discussing the daily trial reports with my students. The fact was, I had not been contacted by the attorney representing the Brown family, St. Louis attorney Anthony Gray, to review the case, nor had I contacted him to offer my services.

I had by this time decided to write a book about the case and the civil unrest that followed. The district attorney in St. Louis County, Bob McCulloch, had posted online the transcripts of the grand jury proceedings in late 2014 after the grand jury decided not to indict Darren Wilson. Embedded in the transcripts were most of the reports, pictures, and diagrams from the investigation that was conducted by the St. Louis County Police Department. It was a treasure trove of information, and I was reviewing every page prior to outlining my manuscript. Like practically everyone else in the United States, I was well aware of the circumstances surrounding the shooting. I had watched the nightly news coverage of the riots and the chaotic police response. I watched live coverage of Attorney General Eric Holder arriving in Ferguson to attempt to calm the tensions. I looked on with disgust as local politicians, particularly Missouri Governor Jay Nixon, made things worse by involving themselves in the police department's tactical planning and decision making. Almost daily there were supposed experts offering opinions in newspapers and on cable news channels, most of them with little factual basis. And I made sure to tune in when District Attorney McCulloch held his press conference on November 24, 2014, to announce the grand jury's decision. McCulloch's words were still fresh in my mind nearly three years later when I pored through the grand jury transcripts one Sunday afternoon in my home office.

After about six hours of reading testimony, I had reached a point where two things were becoming increasingly obvious. Officer Wilson was not telling the truth, and like Chisholm in the Hamilton case, McCulloch gave a very skewed analysis of the evidence in his press conference. McCulloch also focused heavily on the inconsistencies in the eyewitness statements rather than focusing on the physical evidence. Every investigator knows that eyewitness testimony is more unreliable than reliable. In this case there were personal agendas at play on all sides. There was little reason for McCulloch to have focused so heavily on the eyewitness accounts. What little discussion he had provided of the evidence was either done with little or no analysis in the context of all the other evidence, or it was simply misreported. For example, he reported that Wilson had fired two shots from inside his squad car and that one of the bullets—it was apparent that he meant the empty casing—was never recovered. In fact, it was recovered, and its location was very problematic for Wilson's account of what happened. He also glossed over the fact that Wilson's last ten shots had been captured on audio by a gentleman who was on a video chat nearby in the apartment complex. As it turned out, that audio, when viewed in relation to the blood evidence, was one of the most critical pieces of evidence and one that refuted Wilson's account of Brown charging at him before he fired.

While I had no intention of offering my services, I felt compelled to email Anthony Gray and share with him my opinion that Wilson was not telling the truth and why. It did not take long to find Anthony's email address online. I began by telling him that I was not looking to be involved in the case. In fact, being so close to the trial, and nearly three years after the incident, I figured Anthony had already engaged an expert and they were well into their trial preparation. Also, while Anthony was the local attorney hired by the Brown family, attorney Ben Crump, a high-profile attorney who had represented the family of Trayvon Martin, was also involved. It is not unusual for a local attorney to bring a nationally known civil rights lawyer into the case to bolster their efforts. I continued the email by pointing out a number of inconsistencies in Wilson's grand jury testimony, as well as a number of important things about the physical evidence that McCulloch had either ignored, glossed over, or misrepresented during his press conference.

I was surprised when no more than five minutes after sending the email I received a reply from Anthony asking if I would meet him the next day at the spot where Brown was killed. Since I had some business to tend to on campus anyway, I agreed. The story he told when we met was a bit comical. He said that the day before he had been on the telephone with the expert they had hired for the case, and that after many months, and now so close to trial, he still was not seeing the holes in Wilson's account of what happened, nor was he fully grasping the inconsistencies between Wilson's statement and the physical evidence. Anthony said that he was so mad after he hung up the telephone, he literally threw the expert's report across the room and before it even hit the floor my email hit his inbox. He chuckled when he said it was a sign that God had sent me. With a chuckle of my own, I agreed to work the case. How could I refuse? But I had to work fast, and I had to get a report done quickly with the trial approaching. Fortunately, I had already been through almost all the evidence and was ready to immediately begin writing.

According to Wilson, it had been an uneventful morning on the day of the shooting, August 9, 2014. It was close to 11:30 a.m. when he got his first call, a sick child at the Northwinds apartment complex. The call was an Emergency Medical Service (EMS) call, but the police routinely respond to medical emergencies, either to assist the paramedics, to provide traffic control for emergency vehicles, or in some cases to deal with hysterical family members while the paramedics do their job. In this case, a baby had reportedly quit breathing, which fortunately turned out not to be the case. Wilson stood by while the paramedics prepared to transport the baby and its mother to the hospital.

At around the same time Wilson was responding to the EMS call, Michael Brown and his friend Dorian Johnson were walking to the Ferguson Market, a convenience and liquor store located at West Florissant and Ferguson Avenues a few blocks from the Northwinds complex. Johnson would later tell investigators that he came across Brown in the parking lot of the apartment complex while he was walking to purchase "cigarillos" from an acquaintance. The small cigars are used to smoke marijuana by first emptying out the tobacco and then replacing it with the cannabis leaves. By the time they met up, Brown had already been smoking marijuana. The two talked for a short time about sports, music, and Brown's plans to attend technical school, and then they decided to walk to the Ferguson Market to buy cigarillos there.

There were two employees, a man and a woman, inside the Ferguson Market when Brown and Johnson entered. Brown walked past the only other customer in the store at that time to a glass counter that held two boxes of "Swisher Sweets," the preferred cigarillos for smoking marijuana. As if he were oblivious to the two employees, Brown reached over the top of the glass counter and grabbed an unopened box of the Swisher Sweets and handed it to Johnson. He then reached again and grabbed a handful of singles from an opened box. This time the male clerk attempted to push Brown's hand back, but Brown easily defeated his attempt. By now, Johnson surmised that Brown had no money and was planning to steal the cigarillos. He had been in the Ferguson Market many times and was aware of the video cameras scattered throughout. Brown seemed oblivious to those as well and began walking toward the door. Johnson sat the unopened box on the countertop and followed. The last thing he wanted was a robbery charge leveled against him.

By the time Brown reached the front door, the male clerk, who was barely half his size, placed himself between Brown and the door and demanded that he give back the cigarillos. By now a woman and her small son had entered the market. Brown grabbed the clerk by the neck and easily swung him away from the door and into a rack of potato chips. The clerk yelled that he was going to call the police. When he did, Brown turned and approached him once again in an aggressive manner but refrained from touching him. He and Johnson then departed, with Brown still clutching the Swisher Sweets. The encounter was captured by the security cameras. I later learned that Brown had possibly sold marijuana to someone associated with the Ferguson Market the day before and had not been paid as promised. I was unable to confirm that rumor, but it did provide a plausible explanation for why he would take the Swisher Sweets without paying.

Wilson testified to the grand jury that just before leaving the EMS call, he heard a "stealing in progress" call over his radio. The location of the incident was the Ferguson Market. Two other Ferguson units with the call signs "Frank-22" and "Frank-25" responded to the area and began looking for the suspects. The description provided by the employees at the Market—red Cardinals hat, white t-shirt, yellow socks, khaki shorts—was dispatched to the responding officers. There was no sign of anyone walking on the street that matched the description. As he was leaving the Northfield complex, Wilson radioed the two officers and asked if they needed him. Frank-25 responded no and that the two suspects had "disappeared into the woodwork." Frank-22 discontinued the search and proceeded to another call, this one a complaint about illegally parked vehicles. Frank-25 responded to the Ferguson Market to meet with the employees and complete the incident report.

Wilson testified that he departed the Northfield complex and headed west on Canfield Drive toward West Florissant Avenue. Within seconds he noticed two men walking toward him in the middle of the street. He did not know it at the time, but it was Michael Brown and Dorian Johnson returning to Johnson's apartment from the Ferguson Market. The two men seemed to purposely be disrupting the flow of traffic, forcing two oncoming vehicles to stop in the middle of the street to allow an eastbound vehicle to go around them. The two seemed unconcerned about Wilson's squad car approaching and remained in the middle of the street. Wilson testified that he pulled up beside the two, heading in the opposite direction, and without getting out of his squad, lowered his window and asked them to please walk on the sidewalk. Johnson responded that they were almost to their destination and continued walking, with Brown following close behind. Wilson testified that Brown responded to his request with "Fuck what you have to say!" and continued walking. Here is where Wilson's account and the evidence begin to diverge.

Like the point when Officer Manney made the deadly decision to pat down Dontre Hamilton, I knew that whatever happened between Wilson and Brown in the seconds that followed likely sparked the sequence of events that ended in Brown's death. Wilson testified that he chose to drive away since walking in traffic was only a minor offense, and that when he did, he looked in his rear-view mirror and noticed the Swisher Sweets in Brown's hand. He stated that he immediately knew that Brown and Johnson were the suspects in the stealing case, and that he drove in reverse past the two and blocked their path of travel. Wilson attempted to exit his squad, but Brown purportedly slammed the door and began striking him with closed fists through the open window.

Almost immediately after reading Wilson's testimony I had doubts about his story. I was able to view his medical records and pictures of his head and face area following the incident. Like Officer Manney, he had no noticeable injuries. I recalled that much was said three years earlier about Wilson's injuries, but in reality, there were none. He did appear to have some slight redness on his right cheek, something the detectives took a number of pictures of, but when I compared the pictures to how he looked months later in an interview with ABC's George Stephanopoulos, I noticed the redness was still there. It was a naturally occurring skin blemish. Following the shooting, his diagnosis at the hospital was "unspecified injury to face and neck." In other words, there were no specific injuries noted. His X-rays were all "unremarkable." There was a scratch noted on his neck; however no scratch was visible in the pictures, only a small area of very faint redness.

It was hard to believe, as Wilson testified, that Brown had attacked him in a violent manner with his closed fists and struck him multiple times in his face. Brown weighed nearly 300 pounds. A man of that size would have caused considerable physical damage with closedfist blows. Wilson had no hand or knuckle marks, no bleeding, no scratching, and no dark bruising in the days following the incident. Every police officer knows what a person's face looks like after being severely beaten. It is not a pretty sight. I had many police officer friends and associates I discussed the case with before I ever agreed to serve as an expert witness. Although most of them supported Darren Wilson regardless of the evidence, the one thing that seemed to universally cause them to roll their eyes was the complete lack of injury to Wilson's face.

I also questioned whether Wilson ever knew that Brown and Johnson were the suspects in the Ferguson Market case. In his first account of the incident, given to detectives the day after the shooting, Wilson stated the following:

> Um, they had been walking in the middle. I remember seeing two cars I believe go around them and they hadn't moved. I pulled up to them, stopped with them about at my hood as they kept walking towards me. I told them, "hey guys, why don't you walk on the sidewalk." The first one said, "we're almost to our destination," and pointed in this direction. So, I guess that's northeast. . . . I said "Okay, but what's wrong with the sidewalk?" And then, that was as they were passing my window, the second subject said, "fuck what you have to say!" And then after that I put the vehicle in reverse, backed up about ten feet to them, and attempted to open my door. Prior to backing up I did call out on the radio. I said, "Frank 21 out with two, send me another car."

I found it interesting that in his first account of what happened, Wilson said nothing about backing up because he recognized Brown and Johnson as suspects in the Ferguson Market case. This was further corroborated by the statement of Sergeant William Mudd, the first person to talk to Wilson at the scene. When Mudd gave his statement to detectives ten days after the shooting, he stated that Wilson never told him exactly why he backed up his vehicle. In fact, later in the interview he stated that he had no idea if or when Wilson learned about the purported theft from the Ferguson Market, confirming that Wilson had not provided Sergeant Mudd that allegation as his reason for backing up. In his grand jury testimony, Mudd provided a slightly different account. He testified that Wilson stated to him, "They told me to fuck off. I slowed my car down and told him, hey, all you got to do is get out of the street and get on the sidewalk." According to Mudd, Wilson stated that Brown approached his window at that point and started hitting him.

One thing that is almost universally true about excessive force cases, at least those where the excessive force is obvious, is that the officer's account of what happened will change over time as they attempt to "perfect" their story and bring it in line with constitutional standards and department policy. Officer Manney did this when he changed his story to portray the pat down as some bizarre attempt to check Hamilton's heart rate. Needing a suspected crime to make the pat down lawful, in spite of Manney's attempt to perfect his statement, District Attorney Chisholm added the obscure ordinance violation (sleeping in a public park) to the narrative. The similarities between the two cases were striking. Wilson knew that backing up his vehicle out of anger because a teenager had told him to "fuck off" was not a legitimate reason to engage Brown in a physical encounter. He needed a better reason, and by the time he testified before the grand jury, he had added the narrative about seeing Brown in his rear-view mirror holding the Swisher Sweets. And of course, McCulloch did his part by sharing only the later version of events in his press conference and summary report. He said nothing about Wilson's earlier account, nor about the testimony of Sergeant Mudd, a highly respected officer in the community.

The evidence was beginning to tell a story, and the more I listened, the more I realized it was a different version of events than what the news media had broadcast around the world in the weeks following the shooting. It was clear to me that Wilson had backed up his squad car out of anger and not because he recognized Brown and Johnson as the suspects in the Ferguson Market case. He had made a rookie mistake by allowing his anger to get the better of him. It was likely the case that when Wilson opened his door to exit the vehicle, Brown did in fact prevent him from getting it open. Given Wilson's complete lack of visible injury, as well as the reports of at least some of the eyewitnesses, it is reasonable to conclude that Wilson then grabbed Brown through his open window and pulled him toward him. Brown struggled to free himself. There is a line that once crossed by a police officer, there is no retreating. That line is usually when some level of physical contact occurs between the officer and suspect. With Brown struggling to free himself from Wilson's grasp, Wilson made the deadly decision to draw his gun. Brown's DNA was later discovered on top of the gun, indicating that rather than trying to disarm Wilson of the weapon, he instead pushed it downward into Wilson's leg to avoid having it aimed at him. Even Wilson admitted to detectives that Brown pushed the gun into his hip, although he also testified that Brown was attempting to gain control of the weapon when he did. In the matter of just a few seconds things had gone from bad to much worse.

Wilson testified to the grand jury that he fired his weapon twice from inside the squad car. This account was echoed by District Attorney McCulloch, who also stated that only one of the bullets had been recovered. While I suspected that McCulloch actually meant the empty casing, the fact was that both empty casings, as well as both bullets, had been recovered by St. Louis County detectives. I knew even before my email to Anthony Gray that Wilson's account of the two shots inside the vehicle was impossible.

Wilson was clear in describing the shots. He described how, with Brown attempting to gain control of the weapon and with his hand on the barrel, he pulled the trigger only to hear a click. A second pull of the trigger immediately after the first produced the same result. A third attempt and the gun fired. Wilson described how Brown, having been hit in the hand by the shot, appeared to check his body for injuries, and then again began attacking him through the window of the vehicle. Wilson attempted a second shot, but once again heard only a click. We know that Brown's hand was not on the gun at this time because Wilson described how he next "racked the slide," something that would not have been possible had Brown been holding onto the gun. Racking the slide involves manually pulling the slide to the rear and allowing it to spring forward. This action ejects any bad or jammed rounds and loads a new round into the chamber. Wilson stated that he could not figure out why his gun was not firing, and thus made the decision to clear the chamber to allow a new round to be loaded. After completing this maneuver, he again pulled the trigger and the gun fired. He was not sure if this shot hit Brown, although he assumed he missed since he saw dust in an area behind Brown, purportedly from the bullet hitting the ground. He clarified for the grand jury that the sequence of trigger pulls was "click, click, fire, click, fire."

Like all semiautomatic weapons, Wilson's Sig Sauer P229 (.40 cal.) ejects its rounds to the right and rear at an approximately 45-degree angle. The second empty casing was actually found on the opposite side of Canfield Drive from the vehicle, approximately 15 feet away. It was impossible for Wilson to have shot from inside the vehicle while leaning toward the passenger side door to avoid Brown's continued attack, and to have the casing end up outside the vehicle and across the street. Even more impossible was Wilson's account that when the second shot was fired, Brown had returned to the window to reinitiate his attack. Given Brown's size, it would have been impossible for a spent casing to fly through to the outside and with enough force to end up on the opposite side of the street. Furthermore, at near point-blank range, it would have been equally impossible for Wilson to miss Brown, as he obviously did with the second shot.

The bullet from the second shot was found embedded in one of the apartment buildings at 2960 Canfield Drive. Given its location and that of the empty casing, it was relatively easy to determine exactly where Wilson was standing when he fired the second shot. A couple days after agreeing to work the case, I returned to the shooting scene. Using the information included in the investigative reports, I marked the location and orientation of Wilson's squad car on Canfield Drive using orange cones. My suspicions were confirmed when I determined that there was no clear trajectory from inside the vehicle to the location where the bullet was recovered from the apartment building. Wilson could not have fired the second shot from inside his squad car. I determined that he had exited the vehicle and fired the second shot as Brown ran away with his hand now severely injured and bleeding. There was no other conclusion to be reached but that Wilson had attempted to shoot Brown in the back. There was one other piece of evidence that allowed me to determine exactly where Brown was when the second shot was fired. In direct line with the bullet found embedded in the apartment building and approximately 25 feet from the squad car, the detectives had located and photographed one of Brown's sandals. It was clear to me that when the second shot was fired, Brown abruptly changed directions and literally ran out of one of his sandals. Even if Brown had been attacking Wilson through the window of the squad car, and even if the first shot had been justified, the second shot was not. A police officer cannot shoot an unarmed individual in the back as they run away. Wilson's mistakes were now multiplying.

I suppose it was predictable that Wilson would invoke the deadly force script during his testimony. Officer Manney had testified that Dontre Hamilton had superhuman strength and a "thousand-yard stare" in his eyes. Wilson testified that Brown was so strong when he attacked him through the open window that he felt like he was "a five-year-old holding on to Hulk Hogan." And of course, he added in the thousand-yard stare, though in slightly different terms. He testified, "I've never seen a look like that before. He seemed to look right through me." The latter element of the deadly force script is used often. A simple Google search around the time of my report revealed the following:

- Jamar Clark (killed by two Minneapolis police officers on November 15, 2015). "Clark allegedly had what Dustin Schwarze called a thousand-yard stare."
- Terrence Crutcher (killed by a Tulsa, Oklahoma, police officer on September 16, 2016). "He had a very hollow look in his face, kind of a thousand-yard stare, so to speak, and would not communicate."

- Laquon McDonald (killed by a Chicago police officer on October 20, 2014). Apparently confused, "the officer stated that McDonald has a hundred-yard stare."
- Che Taylor (killed by a Seattle police officer on February 21, 2016). "I recall him standing and giving us the, quote, unquote, thousand-yard stare as we move. . . ."
- Michael Santiago (killed by a Brattleboro, Vermont, police officer on April 4, 2014). "Described as having a thousand-yard stare in his eyes and his face was completely emotionless. . . ."
- Antonio Lopez (killed by San Jose State University police on February 21, 2014). "They said Lopez appeared catatonic, his face frozen in a thousand-yard stare."

It was likely that none of the judges, juries or family members in these cases had any awareness of the deadly force script or the extent to which such testimony, seemingly novel at the time, finds its way into civil rights cases across the United States. The sad fact is, if you ask ten police officers to define what the thousand-yard stare is, you may get different answers. It has actually been redefined by the law enforcement community to mean the exact opposite of its original usage. The term was coined during World War II to describe the condition known as shell shock. Physiologically speaking, it occurs when an individual is so overwhelmed by stress and fear that the parasympathetic nervous system is unable to return the body to a state of equilibrium. It is the final stage in the fight, flight, or freeze mechanism, when the person's ability to function normally simply shuts down, resulting in a catatonic-like state. The law enforcement community, especially those charged with training new officers, has redefined the term to mean a manifestation of a heightened state of agitation and fearlessness, almost an animal-like ferocity. It is used to bolster an officer's state of mind defense and is particularly effective since it cannot be disproven.

With Brown running away on Canfield Drive, severely injured and bleeding from his hand, Wilson would have been wise at this point to discontinue his pursuit. He had now fired his weapon twice, once at Brown's back, and without a legitimate reason for having initiated the confrontation in the first place. Instead, he pursued Brown with his gun in his hand. Wilson described for the grand jury the moment when Brown purportedly turned back toward him and charged:

> He turns, and when he looks at me, he made like a grunting, like aggravated sound and he starts, he turns and he's coming back towards me. His first step is coming towards me, he kind of does like a stutter step to start running. When he does that, his left hand goes in a fist and goes to his side, his right one goes under his shirt in his waistband and he starts running at me.

It really is not known to what extent Brown moved forward in an aggressive manner, if at all. By this time, he was severely wounded, likely out of breath and significantly weakened, and was facing a police officer with his gun pointed directly at him. Furthermore, Brown was wearing very loose shorts, a circumstance that would have made charging difficult at best. Like Officer Manney in Milwaukee, Wilson offered his own "just-in-case" defense, the infamous waistband reach. But, given his account, this means that Brown struggled violently, not once, but twice, through the vehicle's open window with a gun in his waistband. I could clearly see in the video from the Ferguson Market, as well as the images of Brown's body in the street, that it was entirely impossible to have had a gun secured in his waistband when his pants were being worn so loosely. Furthermore, by this time, Brown's right hand was severely injured by the first gunshot and bleeding. Consider Wilson's words to Sergeant Mudd when he arrived on the scene. According to his own testimony, Wilson advised Mudd that he had to shoot Brown because Brown had grabbed his gun. He said nothing about shooting Brown because he feared Brown was armed. That concern was never even mentioned. Furthermore, when Wilson was asked in the grand jury what his justification was for using deadly force, he responded that it was the fact that Brown had grabbed his gun. Again, nothing was said about a fear or suspicion that Brown was armed. And finally, when Wilson testified to what he did after he shot Brown, not surprisingly, he says nothing about searching Brown for a gun, nor does he direct the other two responding officers to search Brown for a weapon. In fact, he says nothing about even approaching Brown. Retrieving and securing a weapon would have been his first priority had he truly believed Brown was armed.

Wilson had a problem reconciling his account of Brown's purported "charge" to the known time duration and distance of the final ten shots. I knew from the captured audio that Wilson fired six times, followed first by a three-second pause and then by the final four shots. From beginning to end, the ten-shot sequence, including the pause, took 6.57 seconds. But here Wilson had a problem. He testified as follows:

> As he is coming toward me, I tell, keep telling him to get on the ground, he doesn't. I shoot a series of shots. I don't know how many I shot, I just know I shot it.
>
> At this point I start backpedaling and again, I tell him to get on the ground, get on the ground, he doesn't. I shoot another round of shots. Again, I don't recall how many it was or if I hit him every time. I know at least once because he flinched again. At this point it looked like he was almost bulking up to run through the shots, like it was making him mad that I'm shooting at him.
>
> Well, he keeps coming at me after that again. During the pause I tell him to get on the ground, get on the ground, he still keeps coming at me, gets about 8 to 10 feet away. At this point I'm backing up pretty rapidly, I'm backpedaling pretty good because I know if he reaches me, he'll kill me.
>
> And when he gets about that 8 to 10 feet away, I look down, I remember looking at my sights and firing, all I see is his head and that's what I shot.

The first obvious problem with Wilson's account is that he described three separate clusters of shots with pauses between each. We know from the audio that there were only two clusters of shots, which is further confirmed by two distinct groupings of empty shell casings. It is also important to note that Wilson described Brown as charging in one continuous action without stopping or slowing down. Wilson never deviates from this account. When he was interviewed by detectives from the St. Louis County Police Department, the following was recorded in their report of the interview:

> As P.O. [police officer] Wilson was running, Brown stopped and turned around. According to P.O. Darren Wilson, Brown had an "intense" and "psychotic" look on his face. Brown immediately placed his right hand into the waistband of his pants. P.O. Darren Wilson stopped, leaving a gap of approximately 30 feet. P.O. Darren Wilson gave Brown a command to get on the ground. Due to the recent assault on P.O. Darren Wilson and Brown's action of placing his hand near his waistband, P.O. Darren Wilson still had his firearm in his hand and had it pointed at Brown. Brown then screamed something inaudible and began to "charge" P.O. Darren Wilson. P.O. Darren Wilson stated he began to back pedal with attempts to create or keep the distance between himself and Brown. P.O. Darren Wilson explained that he knew if Brown reached him, he would "be done" as Brown had already overpowered him once during the assault inside of the patrol vehicle.
>
> P.O. Darren Wilson continued to give Brown commands to stop; however, Brown ignored them. Once Brown got within approximately 15 feet of him, P.O. Darren Wilson indicated he discharged five rounds to stop the threat. According to P.O. Darren Wilson, this did not slow Brown down and he continued to advance. P.O. Darren Wilson discharged two additional rounds; however, Brown continued to advance. P.O. Darren Wilson stated that Brown then leaned forward and appeared as if he (Brown) was attempting to "tackle" him. P.O. Darren Wilson then discharged one additional round to stop the threat. Brown then fell to the ground, ending the threat.

The idea that Brown "charged" before the first shots and stopped only when he collapsed after the final shot simply does not reconcile with what we know about those final ten shots. Brown's body was found approximately 29 feet from the light pole that essentially every witness, including Wilson himself, identified as the point where Brown stopped and turned back toward him. Research tells us that an adult male runs at an average speed of 12–15 mph for short distances, and jogs at an average speed of 8.3 mph. Using a conservative estimate that Brown moved forward at 10 mph, in 6.57 seconds he would have covered approximately 96 feet in a continuous charge, as Wilson described. We know with certainty that he covered only 29 feet, using the light pole as a starting point. So, I found it impossible to reconcile Brown's location after he collapsed with Wilson's account.

A further problem with Wilson's account was his assertion that he stopped approximately 30 feet short of Brown and that he shot the final four shots when Brown was 8 to 10 feet away. When I looked at the location of the empty shell casing closest to the light pole, Wilson's first shot of the final ten was found approximately 24 feet 5 inches from the light pole. Given what we know about the ejection patterns of semiautomatic handguns—they essentially all eject to the right and back at an approximately 45-degree angle and a mean distance of 7 feet—I was able to approximate Wilson's distance from Brown to be between 12 and 17 feet when the first shot was fired, and before Brown even began his advance.

Regarding the nature of Brown's advance, there were two additional pieces of evidence that refute the idea of a "charge" by Brown. There were two clusters of Brown's blood located and photographed on the pavement. The first was approximately 14 feet 2 inches from the light pole. This cluster showed a grouping of blood spatter in one location, indicating that Brown was stationary at this point. A few feet later there was a second cluster of blood evidence. This cluster indicated movement forward, but given the closeness of the blood droplets, it did not support the idea that Brown was charging toward Wilson at any significant rate of speed. I was able to say with certainty that when Brown turned at the light pole, Wilson began shooting almost immediately. Brown moved forward slowly, likely a reaction to being shot multiple times, as Wilson moved backward slowly. Brown then stopped in the area of the first cluster of blood evidence, thus the three-second pause in the audio, and then continued to react to the shots. Wilson then fired the final four shots. I was able to conclude that likely what eyewitnesses observed as Brown charging was in fact Brown falling forward. From the location of the first cluster of blood droplets (only five steps from the light pole) to the point where Brown collapsed was slightly less than 15 feet. Given that Brown was already well into his fall when the final shot was taken, I concluded that after stopping his forward movement following the first six shots, Brown took only a few steps more before beginning his fall to the ground.

In the end, Officer Wilson provided an account of the incident that included six major statements I was able to refute with the physical evidence and his own statement to detectives. They were:

1. Wilson did not back up his police vehicle because it "clicked" that Brown and Johnson were the suspects in the incident at the Ferguson Market.
2. Wilson was not violently attacked by Brown in his vehicle and hit repeatedly with Brown's closed fists.
3. Wilson did not shoot a second shot from inside his vehicle. While a perception is difficult to disprove, there is no evidence to support Wilson's purported fear that Brown was armed. In fact, the evidence supports the belief that this part of Wilson's narrative was a later addition.
4. Wilson did not stop 30 feet from where Brown turned back at the light pole, nor did he wait until Brown had charged to within 15 feet before shooting.
5. Brown did not charge in a single continuous charge until he collapsed after the final shot.

The death of Michael Brown was unnecessary and avoidable. It defies logic that a young man with no known criminal convictions or active warrants would risk his life by attacking an armed police officer through the window of his police vehicle; not just once, but twice according to Wilson, and then even a third time after already being shot multiple times. This incident began when Wilson made the decision to put his vehicle in reverse and grab Brown through the open window, apparently only because of a comment that either Brown or Johnson made as they walked past Wilson on Canfield Drive. Both of these behaviors—backing up his police vehicle in a provocative manner and grabbing Brown—only escalated the situation unnecessarily. He then inappropriately drew his weapon and fired it at Brown, wounding Brown in the hand as he attempted to push the gun's muzzle away from his direction. This decision by Wilson escalated the situation further and caused it to quickly spiral out of control. Wilson then fired a second time at Brown's back as he ran. The evidence is clear that Wilson fired six times almost immediately as Brown turned back at the light pole and stumbled toward him. Brown then stopped, as evidenced by the first grouping of blood droplets and the three-second pause in the shooting, and then stumbled forward again toward Wilson, having by then been shot multiple times. I concluded that given the short distance of Brown's final movement forward, what ome of the witnesses perceived as Brown charging was in fact Brown being carried forward by the momentum of falling. Rather than subdue Brown at that point in a manner police officers are trained to do, Wilson instead decided to fire his weapon four more times, including a final and immediately fatal shot to the top of the head as Brown was already well on his way to the ground.

After completing the draft of my report, I forwarded it to Anthony Gray to get his comments. I typically do this in a case, although as an independent expert I am not bound to change the report if I do not agree with the recommended changes. We had to work quickly given that the trial was approaching. Once the report is accepted by the client, then it is submitted to the court and the opposing side. The opposing side has the option to then require a deposition prior to trial. The night before the report was to be submitted, Anthony, Ben Crump, and I had a conference call to discuss. Ben believed there was a racial component to the case and believed that I should address that issue in the report. In other words, he wanted me to play the race card and find a tactful way to allege in my report that Darren Wilson was a racist. Never before nor since had I played the race card in one of my reports. One certain way for an expert to get their report disqualified by a judge is to attempt to discern the mind of one of the participants, either the officer or the suspect. An expert simply cannot testify to what someone is thinking. They can only provide an objective analysis based on the evidence.

Ben was not happy when I refused to address the issue. I explained to him that he did not need to go there and that he had a solid case based on the evidence. I was confident that I had put Wilson in a corner he would not be able to get out of. The more Wilson provided his account of the incident to detectives, the media, and the grand jury, the deeper the hole he dug for himself. I offered my opinion that if the case went to trial, Wilson would have to testify and that it would be a disaster for him when cross examined. We ended the call with Ben agreeing to submit the report the following day with no changes. Shortly after hanging up the phone, Anthony called me back. He wanted me to know that he agreed with my decision in spite of Ben's dissatisfaction. Anthony, an African American attorney, is also an ex-cop, and he understood the evidence in the same way I did. He recognized the corner Wilson had put himself in.

Just a few days after my report was submitted, apparently the city of Ferguson also recognized Wilson's problems. No deposition was requested. They agreed to settle the case for $1.5 million without a trial. Finally, the most heavily publicized police shooting in U.S. history had quietly reached its conclusion long after the riots and media interest had ceased. Like Dontre Hamilton's mother, Michael Brown's parents became activists, even testifying before the United Nations in Geneva, Switzerland. The U.S. Department of Justice forced a set of reforms to be implemented in the city of Ferguson. And Darren Wilson, who never worked another shift for the Ferguson Police Department, quietly left the area and has never since been the focus of the media's attention.

I knew there would be consequences, whether good or bad, for having worked the Brown case. Almost immediately I began getting calls from attorneys all over the country asking me to review their cases. At the same time, I noticed that a few of my police officer acquaintances were acting a bit cold toward me. I understood. I had hoped they would understand that my goal was to make the law enforcement profession better, not to expose its deepest secrets merely for financial gain. It was a tough sell, but most of the truly dedicated and professional officers I had spent the better part of my adult life working with recognized that my intentions were pure. A few even provided a friendly warning to watch my back, especially in places like Chicago and Los Angeles. I frankly did not feel a need to do so. Time would tell.

- CHAPTER 7 -

The Case of
John Deming, Jr.

Pleasanton, California

The De-escalation Paradox: Who Responds When
It Is the Police Who Need to Be De-escalated?

You will never hear a police officer involved in a shooting say they shot to kill the suspect only to "stop the threat." That leads to the obvious question of why they often shoot so many times. The answer, especially if the incident was not captured on video, will almost always be something like "the bullets seemed to have no effect on him." They like to couple that with a pro-police expert who will provide some anecdote about a suspect who continued to attack an officer even after being shot directly in the heart. They will also typically throw in the thousand-yard stare for good measure. The picture they paint is of a crazed and wounded animal intent upon killing the officer, which then bolsters a state-of-mind narrative that the officer was scared for their life. I can honestly say that I have never personally reviewed a case where a suspect was shot either in the head or the heart and did not collapse almost immediately. The weapons and ammunition police officers carry are not designed for target shooting. They are designed to cause maximum damage and kill, and to do so with as few shots as possible.

In early November 2017, I received an email from attorney Ellin Gurvitch from the Geragos & Geragos law firm in Los Angeles asking if I would review a case. I had already worked a case successfully to settlement with another attorney from the Geragos firm, so I was more than willing to review the matter. The firm is after all headed by one of the most recognizable attorneys in America. I was not about to say no. But then the bad news; the case had already been working its way through the system for a couple years and was now less than two months away from trial. Assuming I agreed to take the case, I would be faced with a nearly impossible task—to completely reinvestigate a shooting involving nine police officers, including a police canine, at two different locations using multiple levels of force. It would not be easy sorting through the thousands of pages of statements, reports, and forensic analyses in such a short period of time, but I agreed to take a look.

The next day, Ellin emailed me a Dropbox link to the evidence. As I typically do, before looking at the evidence, I went to the internet to read the media accounts. The media typically reports the police version of the incident. I find it beneficial to begin there because the police are notorious for steering the media away from the problem areas of a case. Reading the press reports gives me an idea of what the police are saying about the matter, but more importantly, they tell me what the police are not saying. In the case of 19-year-old John Deming Jr., almost immediately I recognized a number of potential holes in the official account of what happened in the early morning hours of July 5, 2015, at a car dealership in Pleasanton, California.

John Deming Jr. was a recent graduate of Piedmont High School in San Jose, California. The son of a reserve police officer, by all accounts John was a normal kid who had never been in trouble and had no history of drug use. The police admitted early on that his toxicology tests were negative for all drugs. Yet for reasons that remain a mystery even to his family, on the night of the incident, while driving from his home in San Jose to see his father in Oakdale, a hundred miles to the east, John experienced some type of psychosis and ended up in Pleasanton. At approximately 2:30 a.m., the Pleasanton Police Department was notified of a burglar alarm at a classic car dealership at the intersection of First and Spring Streets. Within minutes, eight Pleasanton police officers and a police canine were outside the building, with an officer from neighboring Livermore responding to assist.

As the officers formulated a plan to enter the building, inside the well-lighted showroom they could see Deming Jr. jumping from car to car, obviously unconcerned about the officers arriving from all directions. He was making animal noises, and at one point climbed to the rafters of the showroom and began swinging. The officers could see that he had shot some of the vehicles with a fire extinguisher. Sergeant Eric Gora was the supervisor on the scene. He sent two of the officers, one of whom was Officer Daniel Kunkel, to the rear of the building to set up a perimeter. With the remaining officers still arriving, he formulated a plan to enter the building. Gora was the only Pleasanton officer with a body cam that was recording. On it you can hear him advise dispatch that Deming Jr. was either on drugs or a "5150," the police code for someone in need of psychiatric care. As Gora continued to assess the situation, Deming Jr. suddenly became agitated. He began yelling at the officers and heaved a floor jack through the glass door in their direction. Gora immediately instructed one of his officers to shoot Deming Jr. through the broken glass with a bean bag round. The round missed, and Deming Jr. retreated to the middle of the showroom.

With Officer Kunkel and another officer watching the rear of the building, including the broken window through which Deming Jr. had made entry to the building, Sergeant Gora instructed his other five officers to "stack up" and prepare to make entry through the front door. The Livermore officer, Sergeant Horton, was still minutes away. Gora's body cam was recording the events. What they found when they entered the building may not have been what they expected. Near the middle of the showroom, Deming Jr. was sitting calmly on top of a pickup truck. He had no weapons or other objects in his hands, and his first words were, "I have nothing . . . I mean you no harm." The six officers, armed with an assault rifle, a less-lethal shotgun, a semiautomatic handgun, and a Taser, surrounded Deming Jr. on three sides and began yelling commands at him to get off the truck and onto the ground. Mixed in with the chaotic sound of the officers yelling, the police canine began barking loudly and begging to be unleashed. All the while, Deming Jr. remained calm.

Each of the officers in the showroom that night had been through CIT training. The principles of de-escalation are uncomplicated. In this case, Deming Jr. was already de-escalated. The goal was to avoid escalating him. It was Sergeant Gora's responsibility to take command of the situation, and once Deming Jr. was found to be calm and unarmed, to shift the officers' response from a tactical arrest response to a crisis intervention, with the primary goal of getting Deming Jr. safely out of the building and to a hospital emergency room for a psychiatric assessment. To accomplish this goal, Gora's CIT training should have told him that three things needed to be done immediately. First, only one person should have been designated to communicate with Deming Jr. Gora should have immediately instructed the other officers to remain quiet. Second, since Deming Jr. was clearly unarmed, Gora should have instructed the officers to lower their weapons. At that point, every weapon in the building was pointed directly at him. And third, the canine should have been removed from inside the building. Police canines bark, bite, and subdue. At that point there was no need for any of the three. There is nothing that will escalate a mentally ill individual quicker than the presence of a police canine, especially when the officer holding him back is threatening to unleash him. The presence of the canine, along with multiple officers aiming an assortment of deadly weapons and yelling commands from three sides, was a recipe for escalation. Surprisingly, Deming Jr. remained calm. It was perhaps the first time I had ever witnessed a mentally ill individual trying to de-escalate the police, rather than the other way around.

Gora had certainly missed an opportunity for a peaceful resolution, and now things were about to get worse. Gora ordered one of the officers to deploy his Taser. By now, fearing the canine, Deming Jr. had slid himself from the hood of the truck to the top of the cab. To use a Taser in this situation would be a violation of policy and accepted police practices. A Taser represents an intermediate level of force and is designed to incapacitate a suspect long enough to secure him in handcuffs. It is not a weapon to be deployed against just anyone for the purpose of gaining their compliance. It requires that the person be actively resisting and presenting a level of threat to the officer or others that is significant enough to justify its use. It is not an appropriate force option when the person is only passively resisting—simply refusing to obey an officer's commands—and is not an imminent threat to the officer or others. It is also true that essentially all departments prohibit the use of a Taser against an individual in an elevated position. The reason for this is obvious; a person shot with a Taser loses muscular control for a five-second period, long enough to fall and suffer a significant injury.

The fact that Deming Jr. was on top of the truck did not prevent one of the officers from moving forward on Gora's command and firing the Taser. One of the darts hit Deming Jr. but stuck only in his shirt. The other hit the truck and bounced to the ground. The shot had no impact since a Taser requires that both darts hit the target to create a closed circuit for the electrical charge to arc. Surprisingly, Deming Jr. pulled the dart from his shirt and said, "Really?" Apparently believing the Taser was an appropriate course of action, Gora ordered a second shot. This shot, fired by a different officer, also hit Deming Jr. with only one dart. As he pulled the second dart from his clothing, now visibly agitated, Gora called out "less lethal shotgun!" This meant that a third officer would now take aim with a shotgun and fire a bean bag round at Deming Jr. To a civilian, and especially one dealing with mental illness, there is no difference between the sight of a less lethal shotgun being pointed at them and that of a real shotgun. Deming Jr. immediately leaped from the truck and ran into a hallway on the one side of the truck the officers left uncovered. That hallway led to the rear window through which he had entered the building. As he ran, the officer fired the less lethal shotgun and struck him on the back of one of his legs. The officers gave chase, but by the time they reached the window, Deming Jr. had exited the building and was being pursued on foot by Officer Kunkel who was covering the rear of the building. Within seconds, and before the officers even exited the building themselves, three rapid gunshots rang out. The shots came from a parking lot just to the west of the car dealership. When the officers reached that location less than a minute later, they found Kunkel lying flat on his back nearly unconscious. Deming Jr. lay nearby with gunshot wounds to the head and abdomen. He would not survive the encounter. After Deming Jr. jumped from the pickup truck and disappeared into the hallway, he would not be seen again on video until Gora rounded the corner of the parking lot with his body cam still recording. There were no witnesses to what happened in the parking lot except Kunkel, and he had failed to activate his own body cam. Kunkel was found with both arms outstretched, his pistol on the ground near his right hand and his Taser near his left. I could see in the video one of the Taser wires wrapped around Kunkel. Deming Jr. lay approximately 10 feet away, and although he can be seen on the video still moving, it was obvious he had suffered a traumatic head wound. Following protocol, two of the officers handcuffed him. He was pronounced dead at the hospital a short time later.

On July 6, 2015, Kunkel was interviewed by a detective and a deputy district attorney with his own attorney present. Kunkel stated that after Deming Jr. jumped through the broken window in the rear of the building, he immediately gave chase, commanding him to stop and get on the ground. Deming Jr. refused and ran toward the parking lot. Kunkel immediately attempted to deploy his Taser as he ran. One of the darts hit Deming Jr. in the back, but the other missed and fell to the ground with the wire still attached. According to Kunkel, just before reaching the parking lot he heard a "pop" and felt a pain shoot up his leg. He had torn a hamstring. Now he was chasing Deming Jr. with an injured leg and a Taser dart still in Deming Jr.'s back. He pulled the Taser trigger a second time, but again, because only one of the darts had hit its mark, the Taser had no effect. Kunkel believed he then tore his other hamstring, and at that point he could no longer keep up with Deming Jr. He stated that Deming Jr. then stopped and turned after snapping the Taser wire attached to him, ran back, and delivered what he described as a "karate kick" to his chest, knocking him to the ground. He stated that Deming Jr. then got on top of him in a top-mount position and began repeatedly striking him in the face. After attempting to use his Taser directly against Deming Jr.'s face, he stated that he drew his weapon and fired at point-blank range into Deming Jr.'s body. In his deposition of June 20, 2017, during which he provided essentially the same narrative, he described this first shot as a "retention" and muffled shot, meaning he held the weapon close to his own body and stuck the muzzle directly against Deming Jr.'s. He stated that the shot had little effect, and that Deming Jr. continued to strike him. Fearing for his life, Kunkel then fired a second time while Deming Jr. was still on top of him, this time causing the fatal head wound. Kunkel was clear that after this second shot, Deming Jr. fell to Kunkel's right and onto the pavement approximately at arm's length away. Kunkel was also clear that neither he nor Deming Jr. moved again. In fact, he stated that he personally was unable to move.

The police like to say that it is impossible to stage the perfect crime. It is equally impossible when they try to do the same. I had my suspicions about Kunkel's story. Like Officers Manney and Wilson, Kunkel had no apparent injury to his face, which had purportedly been struck multiple times by Deming Jr.'s closed fist. Immediately after the incident and the next day there was no redness or swelling apparent. In pictures taken a week later there was no bruising at all. There was, however, a large bruise on the back of his right leg close to the knee. I recognized this type of injury and began to construct in my mind a likely scenario.

To understand the sequence of events once Deming Jr. exited the building, I first conducted a timeline analysis. There is no quicker way to destroy a false narrative than with a proper timeline. In this case there were three data sources with time stamps—Gora's body cam, the Livermore officer's body cam, and Kunkel's Taser, each capturing different parts of the incident. My goal was to sync the three data sources in an effort to construct a complete sequence of events. Body cams and Tasers are notorious for "time drift," meaning their time stamps are seldom accurate. I first had to find a sync point to anchor each of the data sources to. The easiest point was the moment Kunkel's three shots rang out. The shots were heard on both Gora's and the Livermore officer's body cams, and thus I began the timeline by placing the moment of the shooting at an arbitrary point on the timeline. All other events were then placed on the timeline based on the number of seconds that elapsed either before or after the moment the first shot was fired. Once I had synced the three data sources, I then added an overlay of the recorded radio traffic that occurred during the incident, beginning with Kunkel advising that

Deming Jr. had jumped through the window and ending with him yelling "shots fired" over the radio.

Once I had completed the timeline, I quickly realized that Kunkel's version of events was simply not possible. When I reviewed the data report from Kunkel's Taser, I found that only eight seconds passed between the second and third deployments. The second deployment was a trigger pull before the wire snapped. I knew, because detectives recovered the green blast doors of the Taser, that the cartridge Kunkel was carrying was a 25-foot cartridge. So, that meant that Deming Jr. was 25 feet in front of Kunkel when the wire purportedly snapped. The third deployment, according to Kunkel, was a drive stun after Deming Jr. was on top of him. In order for the timeline to work, Deming Jr. had to turn back and run 25 feet toward Kunkel; kick Kunkel in the torso and knock him to the ground; jump on top of him in a top-mount position; then begin hitting him repeatedly in the face; and he had to do it all in just eight seconds. And this assumed Kunkel made no effort to defend himself prior to deploying the drivestun. Kunkel's narrative simply did not work.

Kunkel was clear that after the third Taser deployment he dropped the Taser, rocked to his right, drew his weapon, and then fired one shot into Deming Jr.'s torso. He said nothing about handling the Taser any further, and in fact, I could see it on Gora's body cam video still on the ground when the other officers arrived to find Kunkel nearly unconscious and on his back. Here Kunkel had a problem. Once I time-corrected the Taser's internal clock and placed it on the timeline, I discovered that it had in fact been handled after both shots were fired and before the other officers arrived. Seven seconds after the shots were fired, the Taser was placed in "safe mode." One second later Kunkel broadcasts over his radio, "Henry-11, shots fired." That meant only one thing to me: Kunkel had attempted to stage the scene.

Once I had the timeline constructed, I next reviewed the physical evidence. There were three types of evidence available for analysis: Kunkel's firearm (including the empty casings); Kunkel's Taser; and the relative positions of Kunkel and Deming Jr. when the other officers arrived, as well as their wounds. Regarding Kunkel's firearm, I found it interesting that essentially everyone involved—Kunkel, the investigating detectives, and the district attorney—seemed to completely ignore the fact that Kunkel fired three times in one second or less, as recorded by Gora's body cam. The investigative and summary reports all documented only two shots. Corroborating the body cam recording was the fact that three empty shell casings were found at the scene. Kunkel is clear that after this second shot, Deming Jr. fell to Kunkel's right and onto the pavement approximately at arm's length away. He was also clear that neither he nor Deming Jr. moved again. In fact, he stated that he personally was unable to move. The physical evidence refuted nearly every part of Kunkel's narrative. Deming Jr.'s wounds, particularly the head wound, were both bleeding profusely, even before the other officers arrived a few second later. It would have been impossible for Kunkel to have caused those wounds while Deming Jr. was still on top of him and not have a single drop of blood found on his uniform or weapon, which was purportedly held directly against Deming Jr.'s body. Both were tested for blood and DNA. None was found.

There were no powder burns or stippling (unburned powder) found on either Deming Jr.'s body or his clothes. Like the blood, this too was highly unlikely, if not impossible, if Kunkel's description of the shots were true and accurate. In fact, Kunkel's firearm was test-fired in the criminalistics lab against a test cloth, and it was determined that 24–36 inches was required before the test cloth was free of residue from the firearm. It did not surprise me that this critical piece of evidence was ignored by both the detectives and the district attorney. It alone disproved Kunkel's account of what happened. Also, Kunkel fired three shots in one second or less, as recorded by the body cam videos. His account of shooting once, then being beaten again for a period prior to shooting the second time simply did not happen.

Finally, Kunkel stated that he never moved from the spot where he fired his weapon. In fact, in his interview on July 6, 2015, he stated that he was unable to move. Given the known ejection characteristics of semiautomatic weapons, it was impossible for Kunkel's empty casings to have ended up where they did. If he did in fact hold his weapon tucked against his own body for the first shot with Deming Jr. on top of him, the casing would have ejected right back into his own body, or perhaps even Deming Jr.'s. Not only were the empty casings found a number of feet behind Kunkel, but at least one of them was found on the opposite side from where Kunkel's gun would have ejected it had the casing been unobstructed. The empty casings were simply not where they should have been if Kunkel's account were true and accurate. Given the physical evidence, as well as the timeline of the 28 seconds during which Kunkel used his Taser and then his firearm, I was able to determine the likely sequence of events once Deming Jr. exited the building:

00: Kunkel advised over the radio that Deming Jr. had exited through the window.

:01 Kunkel immediately deployed his Taser. One dart hit Deming Jr. in the lower back, while the other missed its mark. Kunkel then chased Deming Jr., and as he did, he ran through the second Taser wire, which became wrapped around his leg.

:08 As the two rounded the corner into the parking lot, Kunkel caught Deming Jr. and took him to the ground (Deming Jr. had by now dropped to the floor of the building from the rafters and had been shot in the back of the leg with a beanbag round. It is doubtful he was able to outrun Kunkel for long). Knowing the Taser would have been ineffective with only one dart in Deming Jr., Kunkel deployed it a second time in drive stun mode while his hands were on Deming Jr. This created a closed circuit. With one of the wires wrapped around his leg and the Taser itself pushed against Deming Jr.'s body, Kunkel inadvertently Tased himself. Deming Jr. too felt the effects of the Taser, and both likely fell to the ground. I had previously recognized the bruising on Kunkel's leg as a probable Taser wound rather than the visible signs of a pulled hamstring. Now it made sense.

:16 While both were still on the ground, Kunkel pulled the trigger a third time with no effect. Having broken contact with Deming Jr., there was no longer a closed circuit for the Taser to deliver its charge.

:18   As Deming Jr. began to get up, Kunkel yelled "get on the ground!" (as heard by a witness in a nearby house).

:20   Deming Jr. continued to get up and Kunkel drew his weapon and fired three times in less than a second from approximately 10 feet away, striking Deming Jr. twice and missing once. Immediately before the shots, Kunkel dropped his Taser (also heard by the witness). After the shots, and before any other officers arrived, Kunkel lay down on the pavement without holstering his weapons or making them safe.

:27   Kunkel laid his firearm on the pavement by his left hand without de-cocking it. Realizing the Taser wire was still wrapped around his leg, he then placed the Taser in safe mode and dropped it back on the pavement near his right hand.

:28   Kunkel broadcast "shots fired!" and waited for the other officers to arrive without moving further, giving the appearance of being knocked unconscious or nearly so.

It was the first case, though not the last, where I concluded that the shooting scene had been staged. I knew my report would cause some controversy. The trial was only a few weeks away. If the city of Pleasanton disagreed with it, they would surely seek a continuance and try to discredit my findings in a deposition. Their first response, however, was to submit reports from two local experts they quickly hired after getting my report. They both submitted what I like to refer to as "Hail Mary" reports. In such reports, they simply disagree with the opposing expert and offer up any justification for the shooting they can dream up, no matter how absurd and unscientific. Once received from Ellin Gurvitch, I provided her a written rebuttal to both reports that very effectively destroyed their opinions and methodology. A few days later, after Ellin submitted my rebuttal report, the city of Pleasanton threw in the towel and agreed to settle the case for $285,000.

What John Deming Jr. needed in those early morning hours was a group of CIT-trained police officers who recognized that he was in the midst of a mental health crisis and knew how to get him safely out of the building and to a hospital where he could get the help he needed. Instead, he got yelled at, threatened, called "dude," tased, shot with a less lethal shotgun, bitten by a canine, and then killed by two .45 caliber bullets to the head and torso. Essentially everything the officers did that night was wrong and opposed to their training. The minute they realized they were dealing with a 5150, they should have shifted their plans and protocols from a forcible arrest to a crisis intervention. But once again, like so many other cases before it and after, the idea of de-escalation took a second seat to arresting a young man they viewed only as a suspect in a burglary with whatever force was necessary. The case of John Deming Jr. only confirmed what I already knew, that whenever de-escalation is set aside in favor of confrontation, the outcome is usually deadly for the person in need of help.

A few years later, I found myself back in Pleasanton, California, investigating a case of suspected compressional asphyxiation. The officers involved were all cleared of wrongdoing despite the fact that the entire incident was captured on video. The victim, who was only passively resisting their efforts to handcuff him, was subjected to multiple Taser deployments, closed fist strikes, strikes from an expandable baton, and he had to endure having a knee pinning his head to the ground while the officers applied a full body wrap and spit mask after he was already handcuffed. Not surprisingly, the person died before they even got him fully loaded in the ambulance. It did not surprise me that the local prosecutor cleared the officers; after all they always do. My surprise came when I read the report of the internal investigation that was completed by the Pleasanton Police Department. Not that the investigation found nothing wrong with the officers' use of force, but rather, that the officer who conducted the investigation was none other than Sergeant Gora, the officer in charge during the death of John Deming Jr., and who had himself escaped any disciplinary action for having failed to properly respond to and de-escalate that matter. When a systemic problem, especially in law enforcement, is left unattended to, like an open wound, it is bound to fester and only get worse.

- CHAPTER 8 -

The Case of Anthony Soderberg

Pleasanton, California

Perceptual Distortion: How the Police Strategically See Things That Are Not There and Fail to See Things That Are

I learned early on that when an officer has no other explanation for shooting an unarmed individual to expect the perceptual distortion argument to eventually be offered up by the officer's lawyer or union representative. It allows the officer to simply deny seeing something that was right in front of them or to see something that was not even there. It is an easy way to argue that under the extreme stress of the moment, the officer saw a gun in what turned out to be an empty hand. Or, as in the case of Cedrick Chatman in Chicago, it allows them to assert that they misperceived an iPhone box for a gun, in spite of the fact that a square box has no resemblance to a gun.

I had dealt with the perceptual distortion argument a number of times and typically found it easy to dispute based on the officer's actions or statements following the incident. But I never imagined I would one day be confronted by a case in which an entire SWAT (special weapons and tactics) team purportedly experienced the same distortion. And not just any SWAT team, but the Metropolitan Division of the LAPD, the most elite SWAT team in the world. I must admit, I was a bit intimidated by taking on such a case. Even LAPD Chief Charlie Beck had become publicly involved in the matter by issuing a report detailing how his officers were justified in their actions. Following that, the case, which involved a homeless man who battled drug abuse and mental illness, quietly faded from the media's interest.

My involvement in the Soderberg case began with a call from Los Angeles attorney Greg Kirakosian. Greg had not yet agreed to take the case and needed to understand exactly what happened. It was indeed confusing and involved almost sixty police officers, including two helicopter-based snipers. Greg asked me to review some limited reports he had at that point and to provide him a summary, along with a basic chronology of what took place on the day Anthony Soderberg ended up with thirty-one bullet holes (entry and exit) in his body. When I finished my review, I concluded that it was possibly the worst case of excessive force I had ever seen and that the LAPD had to some extent engaged in a coverup.

The incident began at approximately 9:00 a.m. on May 8, 2017, when uniformed LAPD officers from the Foothill Patrol Division responded to a call of a "hot prowl" burglary on Alethea Drive. The 911 caller advised that she woke up to find a man later identified as Anthony Soderberg inside her house. She advised that Soderberg was talking to himself about Jesus and that when confronted, he told her he was looking for something to eat. The woman offered him some cookies and returned to her bedroom where she exited the house through a bedroom window and called 911. When the officers arrived, she advised them that Soderberg was polite and had made no threatening gestures toward her. The house was located on top of a hill and had a steep downward slope to the main road (Big Tujunga Road) directly behind it. It was later learned that Soderberg was living in a small homeless encampment at the bottom of the hill.

When the officers arrived, the woman advised them that there were three weapons inside the house—a handgun, a shotgun, and a rifle. The woman's partner arrived at the house and advised the officers that the shotgun was hidden in a closet; that the rifle was in a locked case with the key hidden inside a drawer; and that the handgun was on a shelf, along with a loaded magazine. At least two of the responding officers, Eriverto Montano and Cody Baumann, were able to peer in through the open bedroom window where all three weapons were located. Rather than maintaining visual control of the bedroom while other officers entered to take Soderberg into custody, they retreated and advised the command center that they had a "barricaded subject." They had missed an opportunity for a quick and peaceful resolution.

How a police department defines a threat will dictate their response to that threat. Definitions must be case-specific and fluid, and at times the police must adjust their response to confront a rapidly evolving situation. At times they must elevate their response, while at others, they must de-escalate. In this case the LAPD conformed their response to the definitions they imposed rather than to the threat they faced. The criterion-based definitions used included "hot prowl," "barricaded subject," and later, "active shooter." This progression almost guaranteed a violent outcome. I concluded that each was used inappropriately.

"Hot prowl" is a term used in law enforcement to describe a subtype of burglary in which the victim remains inside the residence. These are especially dangerous cases due to the possibility of a hostage situation or the intruder harming the caller. An example of a hot prowl is a woman who calls 911 while hiding under a bed or locked in a bathroom. The police response is rapid, with the primary goal of preventing harm to the victim. While this case certainly had the potential of being a hot prowl, the fact is, by the time the homeowner called 911, she had already exited the house and was safely outside. There was no one else in the house but Soderberg. The police therefore never responded to a hot prowl, but rather to an unlawful intruder who had committed no known crime inside the residence to that point. It was questionable whether Soderberg had even committed a burglary at all, as opposed to a trespassing. Burglary requires the intent to commit another crime once unlawfully inside. The only evidence of Soderberg's intent suggested that he was merely looking for something to eat.

Given that Soderberg possibly had access to weapons, and with no effort made to communicate with him, the decision was made at the scene to reclassify the case as a "barricaded subject." Not only had the LAPD improperly classified the case initially as a hot prowl, but now they were elevating it to an even higher threat level without any indication that Soderberg had gained access to the weapons. By doing this, it allowed for the Metropolitan Division's SWAT team to be deployed, complete with a two-man helicopter-based sniper team. Their arrival began a stand-off that would last all morning. It also meant that things were about to go from dangerous to deadly.

Even though I did not yet have all the evidence and reports, I was able to construct a basic chronology for Greg Kirakosian, now nearly two years after the incident. The picture I was beginning to construct of what happened that day was not a good one. There were at least three media helicopters that captured parts of the incident on video, and I was able to find pieces of their footage, along with the accompanying news reports, still posted online. What I watched was deeply disturbing. It did not surprise me that without exception the reporters were portraying Soderberg as a dangerous and armed home intruder who was refusing to come out. That after all was how the LAPD spokesperson was describing him during her hourly briefings throughout the morning. At least one of the helicopters had captured the final moments on the house's back patio. Even then, with the incident reaching its violent conclusion right in front of them, they praised the courage of the LAPD officers. What I saw was much different. I saw an unarmed and scared man, already seriously wounded, being shot by high-powered assault rifles from all sides, including from the helicopter, as he fell down the steep embankment behind the house. He was dead before he stopped rolling. As I would later describe it in my report, it had the appearance of a live fire training exercise.

My recommendation to Greg was that someone needed to take the case. It had mostly been forgotten by the press by now. It may have been forgotten completely had Greg not agreed to meet with Soderberg's mother. It is true that attorneys must weigh the potential rewards before committing their time and money to a case. Monetary judgments are based on things like lost wages, medical expenses, and financial support for the spouses and children left behind.

Perhaps the lowest potential for a sizeable judgment comes from a case where the police use deadly force against a homeless individual with no children who has a history of mental illness and drug abuse. It is a sad reality that some attorneys will not consider taking such a case. The good ones, however, the ones committed to seeking justice and improving their communities, will, even when faced with the risk of losing money. Greg agreed to move forward with the case, and I agreed to complete a full investigation once the LAPD released the investigative file to us.

Once I received the materials from Greg a few weeks later, I immediately began my review. The file included literally thousands of pages of reports, summaries, transcripts, and pictures. I began with the case summaries, especially those of Chief Beck and the Force Investigation Division (FID), the unit within the LAPD charged with investigating officer-involved shootings. It is easy for the general public, the ultimate consumer of such documents, to get overwhelmed by all the tactics and tactical jargon found in them. To some extent, that is the goal. The temptation is to assume that the actions of the officers were surely appropriate and reasonable under the circumstances. After all, these were highly trained LAPD SWAT officers who were being directed every step of the way by experienced commanders. When such summaries focus so heavily on the step-by-step tactics employed, especially those involving things such as helicopter-based snipers, high-tech robots, and sophisticated weaponry, it is easy to begin thinking of the incident as a complex military operation carried out against a faceless and nameless enemy. It is easy to lose sight of the big picture, which in this case was that a young, unarmed, homeless, and mentally ill man had entered a residence in search of food. And when the opportunity presented itself to attack or become aggressive toward the homeowner, he instead asked if she had any cookies.

I very quickly began to fill in the gaps of the chronology I had previously prepared. One thing that became immediately apparent was that the LAPD had overstated the threat posed by Soderberg, first in their decision to reclassify the case as a "barricaded subject"—this was required before a SWAT team could be deployed—and later, in justifying their use of a helicopter with the two snipers on-board. The factors that should have been considered when evaluating the threat included: (1) Soderberg stated to the homeowner that he was looking for something to eat; (2) he was obviously homeless and mentally ill, given that the homeowner overheard him talking to himself and acting in ways consistent with mental illness; (3) he had no apparent weapons when he entered the house; and (4) he did not become aggressive or make any attempt to attack the homeowner. This is not to suggest there was no threat at all. There was, especially with guns inside the residence. But these factors should have influenced the intensity of their response. Also, perhaps the single most important piece of information the LAPD had was from the second homeowner who advised that the rifle was locked up with the key hidden. Soderberg thus had access only to a handgun and possibly a shotgun that was hidden in the closet. This fact should have influenced the responding officers' evaluation of the threat. It apparently had no impact.

Regarding the inaccessibility of the rifle, I found it interesting that Chief Beck failed to mention this fact in his summary to the Board of Commissioners. He made no mention of the second homeowner advising officers that the rifle was locked up with the key hidden, and in fact he stated that there was a concern Soderberg would load the assault rifle and attempt to escape with it. It seemed obvious to me that Beck was attempting to influence the Board's perception of the threat level, and through them the general public's perception. He offered no discussion of the handgun or shotgun, knowing that neither is a significant threat against the assault rifles carried by most officers in their squads, especially when those weapons are in the hands of an untrained shooter.

Approximately ninety minutes after the incident began, the SWAT team responded. While en route to the location, the team commander, Lieutenant Lopez, requested that the helicopter-based aerial platform sniper (APS) team respond, a request that had to be approved all the way up the chain of command to Assistant Chief Beatrice Girmala. The primary reason given by Lopez was because of the terrain and Soderberg's elevated position with access to weapons. He advised command staff that the APS would be necessary to secure a tactical advantage from an elevated platform. In fact,

Soderberg never had a tactically superior position, or even an ele-vated advantage. By this time, he was contained inside a house with multiple officers on the perimeter and a SWAT team responding. In his summary, Chief Beck described the problem of the terrain and Soderberg's purported tacti-cal advantage in the following ways:

- A challenging position to contain due to Soderberg being in an elevated position at the end of a cul-de-sac in hilly terrain.
- In a tactical position of advantage due to elevation, with access to numerous ravines to escape into the surrounding community.
- Had a full advantage and a 360-degree view of the officers down below.
- In a position where it would be very dangerous for anybody to try to contain or engage him on foot.

The problem with these descriptions is that none of them were true. The fact was, the house was very easily contained, and none of the officers were ever in a tactically inferior position. In fact, on three sides of the house, including the side to which the responding officers initially approached, the officers were never even at a lower elevation. On the north side of the house was the only ravine avail-able for escape, but that terrain actually worked to the LAPD's ad-vantage. There is limited vegetation in that ravine, and at the bottom is the natural barrier of a major paved road (Big Tujunga Canyon Road). Two officers were able to easily contain the entire north side of the house, including the ravine, from that road. Other officers could also have taken an elevated position on the west side of the house, but it was not necessary since they easily contained that side of the house from the area of the driveway and a detached garage. At no time did Soderberg ever have a 360-degree view of the officers. That was simply a false statement. And at no time did he ever have a tactical advantage, especially with only a handgun and possibly a shotgun. The fact was, Soderberg was very quickly contained with no possibility of escape. It must be pointed out that Soderberg con-tained himself by remaining inside the house. With officers from the Foothill Patrol Division very quickly arriving and surrounding the structure, and with a non-APS helicopter overhead, containment had essentially been achieved with tactical advantage before SWAT officers and the APS helicopter even arrived. The terrain was an insignificant factor in this case.

During my review of the evidence, I discovered that in thirteen years, this was the first time the LAPD had ever deployed the APS. I wondered why they did so in this case, a case where the use of a helicopter was so unnecessary and unneeded. With the arrival of SWAT there were as many as fifty officers holding a perimeter around the house. The thought occurred to me that if the LAPD was at risk of losing their funding for the APS, given that they had never once used it in thirteen years, perhaps they were using this case as an opportunity to show the city's budget people some usage. There was very little risk involved, with Soderberg having access only to a handgun and possibly a shotgun. At no time in the recorded radio traffic did I hear the pilot being advised that Soderberg had access to an assault rifle. It was reasonable to conclude that the officers on the ground had no fear at that point that the rifle could be accessed.

At approximately 1:00 p.m., now four hours after the initial 911 call by the homeowner, the SWAT team deployed an ICOR robot with an on-board camera and speaker to the open bedroom window. An officer commanded Soderberg over the speaker to exit the house with his hands up. I questioned the use of the robot at that point, especially with someone diagnosed with schizophrenia, which is often accompanied by extreme paranoia. A crisis negotiation team accompanied by a staff psychologist had already made a minimal effort to make contact with Soderberg. They discontinued their efforts after less than fifteen minutes. The robot had just the effect I would have expected. Soderberg, who had by now found the handgun, fired five shots directly at the window where the robot was peering in. Almost immediately the on-scene commander ordered the introduction of gas into the house. At least 30 "Ferret" rounds were fired in through the windows. These are projectiles filled with either liquid or powder chemical agents that lack the high flammability of traditional gas cannisters. The SWAT team was elevating its level of force.

Approximately five minutes after the introduction of the gas, Soderberg exited the rear of the house with the handgun in his hand.

One of the SWAT officers who was posted behind a Bearcat armored vehicle in the driveway stated later that Soderberg leveled the gun and fired in his direction. The officer returned fire with six shots that all missed. Soderberg was then observed shooting three times at the helicopter before reentering the house. It did not surprise me that he fired at the helicopter, which like the robot, was no doubt escalating his level of paranoia significantly. He missed of course. There was almost no chance that an untrained shooter could hit a moving helicopter with a handgun. More importantly, when I reviewed the physical evidence, particularly the locations of the empty casings scattered about, I realized that none were found supporting the contention that Soderberg had fired at the officers behind the Bearcat. It did not happen.

The SWAT commander decided to escalate their level of force once again and ordered that "hot gas" be introduced into the house. This was the flammable kind, and before the cannisters were fired in, a Fire Department helicopter with water on-board was deployed. Without sufficient ventilation, a house full of CS gas has the capacity to literally blow up. If that were to happen, the entire area would be at risk of fire, given the dry California conditions. At 1:42 the gas was fired in through a window. By that time, Soderberg had put the handgun on a chair in the living room and never touched it again.

As expected, less than five minutes after introducing the gas, Soderberg again exited from the back, only this time with nothing in his hands. Four officers, including the two APS snipers fired a total of twenty-one times at him and hit him multiple times. They would all later say they saw either a gun or some other object in his hand. Their mass perceptual distortion was underway and about to get worse. Shot multiple times, Soderberg was able to crawl into a shed attached to the house through a large hole in the side.

At this point, one would expect that the team members would have simply gone into the shed and secured Soderberg before rendering medical aid. Instead, they sent the robot in while a team of three entered the house and observed Soderberg through a window in the living room. The shed had been added at some point after the house was already built, so while the window once looked to the outside, it now looked into the shed. The officers advised over the radio that Soderberg was lying in a fetal position in a corner and bleeding badly, and that he appeared to have something in his hand. It was later determined that he had nothing in his hand. Unbelievably, when I looked at the inside of the house where the officers were watching Soderberg, less than 5 feet away lay the handgun clearly visible on the chair. They knew he was unarmed, and instead of entering the shed to at least attempt to save his life, the decision was made to instead throw in a "stinger" grenade, an explosive weapon that is filled with small rubber pellets. It is typically used for riots and crowd control and can cause a great amount of pain. I was shocked to read that the grenade was thrown in and exploded within inches of Soderberg. He took the full force of the blast, and while it caused him to jump, he remained on the floor. One of the officers later provided the absurd statement that Soderberg looked like he was waiting to ambush whoever entered the shed. Unfortunately, they still were not finished.

After one of the officers manning the robot's camera advised that Soderberg appeared to have an object in his right hand and tucked beneath his body, Lieutenant Lopez ordered that a second stinger grenade be thrown in along with another cannister of the hot gas. This time the stinger exploded near Soderberg's face and caused him to sit up. Now it was plain to see that he was unarmed. But instead of saying so, now one of the officers watching through the window, with the handgun lying right next to him on the chair, advised that Soderberg was reaching for his waistband. Having endured multiple gunshots from high-powered assault rifles, two stinger grenades, and multiple gas cannisters and Ferret rounds, Soderberg still had the strength to crawl out of the shed and onto the patio.

What happened next was what I had watched on the internet, something so graphic that the video clips were eventually removed from the media websites. As Soderberg literally crawled toward a retaining wall at the top of the ravine, now shot multiple times and likely on the verge of dying, multiple officers began to fire on him. In the video you could literally see the bullets hitting him. He had just enough strength to lean over the retaining wall and fall into the ravine. Lopez then broadcast what amounted to a shoot-to-kill order. At least two officers later described the dispatch as "we cannot let this individual get to another structure or escape containment." In fact, the actual broadcast, which I was able to isolate, was "We're not going to let him get up in the community and break containment." To a police officer, such an order from a commander is exactly as described, a shoot-to-kill order. And that is exactly what the officers did. Additional shots were fired from long range after the command was given and while Soderberg was literally kneeling on the ground after stopping his roll down the slope. At that point, the officers were no longer evaluating the risk but were simply carrying out Lopez's order. A few more shots and it was over. Anthony Soderberg was dead. For good measure, prior to approaching his lifeless body, they shot him four more times with 37 mm sponge rounds, which are extremely painful at best and potentially fatal at close range. Lieutenant Lopez wanted to see if he would move, which of course he did not do. And then, in one last act of indignity, the officers released a K9 to sink its teeth into Soderberg's wrist to roll him over.

Each of the officers who used any type of force that day was interviewed following the incident. I had access to the transcripts of those interviews. I had never before, nor since, seen a case where essentially every officer involved misperceived the exact same thing while perfectly recalling every other aspect of the incident. It defies logic and science. The misperceptions in this case, which involved at a minimum fifteen officers, all had the same effect—they placed a gun in Soderberg's hand when there was not one there and had him shooting when he was not. The statements of these officers, all of which I was able to prove false with the physical evidence, had been included by Chief Beck in his summary report as evidence in support of the reasonableness of their actions, which was surprising to me given that Chief Beck had unrestricted access to the same physical evidence and forensic analyses that I had. The "misperceptions" were many, and included the following:

- Officers Joseph Goosby, Thomas Chinappi, and Mario Rios all stated that the first time Soderberg exited the house with the handgun, they observed him either with their own eyes or via the robot's camera come around the corner of the house and fire his handgun at the officers posted behind the Bearcat armored vehicle parked in the driveway. In fact, this did not happen. All of Soderberg's bullets and empty casings were accounted for, and none were fired from this location. It was Goosby who had fired six shots at Soderberg from behind the Bearcat and missed.

- Officer Chinappi stated that Soderberg emerged from the residence a second time with the gun in his hand after the introduction of the hot gas. This did not happen. Soderberg never reentered the house after this, and the handgun was later found inside. At this same time, Officer Pultz stated that he too observed a "dark object" in his right hand. Officer Pultz fired his rifle at Soderberg four times. Soderberg then took cover in the attached shed. There was no evidence of a dark object ever found.

- Officers Messinger and Gallegos, the two snipers on the helicopter, stated that while Soderberg was on the patio moving from the house to the attached shed, they could both see a gun in his right hand and feared that he was going to shoot at the helicopter. In fact, Soderberg was unarmed at this point and likely wounded. Officer Messinger fired 14 times, and Officer Gallegos once, as Soderberg took cover inside the attached shed.

- Officer Wong stated that after Soderberg crawled into the shed, he could see via the robot camera a "dark object" in his right hand. In fact, there was no such object ever found. Officer David Keortge stated that after a sting grenade was thrown into the shed right next to Soderberg (who by now was lying on the floor after being shot multiple times), he rolled out of the shed and into his direction. Keortge stated that at that time he observed the barrel of a gun in Soderberg's hand. In fact, Soderberg was unarmed, and Keortge fired one time from approximately 50 feet away.

- Officer Canaan Bodell stated that when Soderberg rolled out of the shed, he (Soderberg) raised his hand toward him holding a dark object. In fact, Soderberg was holding nothing, and Officer Bodell fired twice from approximately 50 feet away.

- Officer Isaac Moreno stated that after Soderberg rolled out of the shed, he observed Soderberg point a gun or some other object at the officers. He stated that he did not fire because there were other officers still inside the house.
- Officer Jerry Fritz stated that after Soderberg fell over the retaining wall, having by then been shot multiple times, he observed a dark object in his hand he believed to be a gun, and that he was pointing it back at the residence. In fact, Soderberg was holding nothing in his hands, and Officer Fritz fired three times as Soderberg literally rolled down the ravine's slope.
- Officer Juan Flores stated that he observed Soderberg fall over the retaining wall with a dark object in his hand. Officer Flores stated that Soderberg slid down the hill and appeared to be on the verge of escaping the containment area with the gun. This was one of the more blatantly absurd statements. By this time Soderberg was mortally wounded and falling down the hill. He had nothing in his hands, nor did he give any appearance of escaping. In fact, escape was not even possible with numerous officers on the paved road below. Officer Flores fired twice from 189 yards.
- Officer Cliff Chu stated that as Soderberg fell over the retaining wall, he could see a dark object in his hand. He stated that he believed Soderberg was of the "utmost danger," and that he was preparing to shoot it out with officers in an attempt to escape. In fact, Soderberg had nothing in his hands, was shot multiple times and bleeding, and was literally falling down the ravine already near death. Officer Chu fired twice from a distance of 189 yards.
- Officers Jeremy Escamilla, Gregory Martin, and Billy Lee all stated that after Soderberg fell down the hill, he raised himself on his knees in what they perceived to be a shooting position and feared for the lives of the other officers. In fact, by this time Soderberg was mortally wounded and bleeding from multiple gunshots, a number of which they would have witnessed. At no time could they possibly have feared for the lives of the other officers. The three of them fired a com-

bined seven times at Soderberg from a distance of 56 yards as he lay on the ground dying.

There is no doubt that a police officer may misperceive something in his or her visual or auditory field under moments of high stress, but those misperceptions are typically distortions of time and space. They typically do not involve seeing something that is not there, or failing to see something that is, except in the most stressful situations where the officer's ability to accurately perceive is overwhelmed by their sympathetic nervous system ("fight or flight"). This was not an especially high-stress operation for experienced SWAT officers. By their own accounts, when the above shots were fired, Soderberg was armed only with a handgun—notwithstanding the fact that for all but six of the forty-four shots fired he had no gun at all in his hand. For the most part, the distances these officers were firing from were well outside the effective range of a handgun. They were shooting at

will with little or no risk of being hit by return fire. Furthermore, if the officers are to be believed, then a number of them experienced perceptual distortion while viewing the happenings on a robot's camera. It leads one to wonder how experienced SWAT officers could possibly experience levels of stress high enough to alter their perception of reality when they were one step removed from it.

Anthony Soderberg, a homeless and mentally ill 29-year-old man who was living nearby in a makeshift encampment, entered a house without permission looking for something to eat. He was unarmed, nonaggressive, and made no effort to attack the homeowner when she discovered him in the house. In fact, the homeowner later described him as like a "guest" when he asked her about some cookies that were left out. She did not ask him to leave, but instead retreated to a bedroom to call 911 while he helped himself to the cookies. By the time the handcuffs were finally placed on his dead and bloodied body hours later, the LAPD had deployed the following:

- Approximately sixty police officers
- Three "Bearcat" armored vehicles and a smaller armored unit supplied by the sheriff

- Three police helicopters (and three APS snipers)
- Two ICOR robots
- Fifty-eight ferret rounds of CS powder
- Two canisters of CS/CN "hot gas" (highly flammable)
- Four 37 mm impact munitions
- Two sting grenades
- Forty-four rounds of 5.56 ammunition fired from thirteen
- high-powered assault rifles
- A police canine
- Fire Department assets (including a water-dropping helicopter)

The LAPD was so focused on response criteria, protocols, and command authorizations that they lost sight of the fact that what they really had was a CIT matter rather than a tactical barricaded-subject case. Soderberg needed services and possibly an involuntary commitment. Instead, he ended up with thirty-one bullet holes in his body (entry and exit), four large abrasions from the 37 mm projectiles, multiple smaller abrasions from the two stinger grenades (including on his face), and a bite mark from the K9. It was not determined the extent to which his lungs may have been damaged by the introduction of the hot gas.

About the time I completed my investigation and submitted my report to Greg, it was announced that Chief Beck was retiring. I next saw him in my own state of Illinois when he was asked to serve as the interim superintendent of the Chicago Police Department. I remember watching Mayor Lori Lightfoot proudly introduce him to the community and discuss the expertise he would bring to the department during their search for a permanent superintendent. All I could think about was Anthony Soderberg and how Beck had either lied in his summary to cover up the excessive force used by his officers or had blindly added his signature to someone else's lies. As for the officers, the Civilian Police Commission in Los Angeles agreed with me and ruled that all but a single officer who fired their weapon that day violated LAPD policy, a finding Chief Beck publicly disputed. It is unclear whether any of the officers were ever disciplined.

Once I submitted my report, the lawyers representing the LAPD subpoenaed me to sit for a deposition. I was expecting a tense exchange. After all, I was the deputy sheriff from rural Illinois calling out the world's most elite law enforcement unit. My department was too small to even have a SWAT team. But in the end, it was not tense at all. I was no longer intimidated. In fact, I was quite prepared for the fight. But the attorney questioning me seemed almost embarrassed by what he had to at least try to defend. We parted with a handshake, and a short time later the city of Los Angeles settled the case for $1,150,000. They knew I had uncovered the truth of what happened, and they knew there was no way to make such an egregious misuse of force appear reasonable. Anthony Soderberg, one of society's throwaways, and the type of person bad cops view as disposable, was used by the LAPD for what amounted to a live-fire training exercise and had offered the department a risk-free opportunity to finally use their helicopter-based sniper team for the first time in thirteen years. They have not used it since.

- CHAPTER 9-

The Case of Michael Dial

White County, Tennessee

The Vehicle Pursuit: Pavlov's Bell for a Deadly Ending

Before I was ever hired by Nashville attorney David Weissman to work this case, I had seen the video. It was broadcast across the country on every major network. But it was not the video of the shooting itself that was being broadcast. Rather, it was the aftermath when White County Sheriff Oddie Shoupe showed up at the scene moments after the shooting had ended. Not realizing that one of the deputies had unknowingly left his body cam activated and recording, the sheriff walked briskly from his squad car toward the spot where Michael Dial lay inside his truck with a bullet wound to his head and could be heard telling the deputy, "I love this shit! God, I tell you what, I thrive on it!" After working cases in places like Chicago and Los Angeles, I knew this case would offer an entirely different set of issues.

White County is a small rural county in Tennessee midway between Nashville and Knoxville. It is the type of county where the sheriff is often the most powerful person in the county. Oddie Shoupe was in his fourth term as sheriff. A tall imposing man with a close-cropped haircut, he had the appearance of an older Buford Pusser, Tennessee's most famous sheriff. During his sixteen years in office, he had been sued upwards of fifty times for everything from unlawful arrest to even offering jail inmates time off of their sentence in exchange for their agreement to get permanently sterilized, a practice a federal judge eventually stopped. He is the type of sheriff who is loved by one segment of the county's population as much as he is loathed by another. Having been a uniformed deputy sheriff in a small rural county, I felt that I was in my element working this case.

The pursuit of Michael Dial began in a neighboring county. His mistake was to enter White County. Even after the deputies from the neighboring county terminated their pursuit, which never exceeded 50 mph, the White County deputies continued. Sheriff Shoupe's boys were not about to let Dial get away. Within a few miles after passing through the town of Sparta, Dial was fatally shot at a time when he was no longer driving on the roadway and after a spike strip had flattened one of his tires. By the time Sheriff Shoupe caught up with the pursuit, Dial's dilapidated pickup truck, which was pulling a trailer loaded with junk, had rolled uncontrollably into a line of trees after Dial suffered the gunshot wound to his head. Making matters worse, the deputies at the scene misidentified Dial as another local man who had a troubled past. Word spread fast, and within a short time, that man's mother arrived at the scene believing her son was dead. As she approached Sheriff Shoupe, he very coldly told her, "He fired at us . . . we had to take him out." There was of course no truth to what he said. Dial was unarmed and never so much as even attempted to strike an officer's vehicle with his truck.

By the time I became involved in the matter, the local district attorney, Bryant Dunaway, had already cleared the two officers who had fired at Dial—Reserve Deputy Adam West and Sparta officer Charlie Simms—of any wrongdoing. The reason Dunaway gave was because of the reckless nature in which Dial was driving. Two things became clear to me rather quickly. First, it was obvious that Dunaway had cleared the two officers without even knowing which one had fired the fatal shot, something the Tennessee Bureau of Investigation (TBI) never determined. And second, I suspected that once I reviewed the dash cam evidence, his assertion that Dial needed to be shot because of his reckless driving would not be supported. Eventually, I was able to determine the former and disprove the latter.

The "pursuit" of Michael Dial on April 13, 2017, violated just about every tenet of police training on the issue of pursuits. Deputy Brandon Young's dash cam captured much of the pursuit once Dial entered White County, including his own efforts to catch up and deploy a spike strip. Young's driving was nothing short of reckless. At least three different times he forced oncoming traffic off the road and then passed in-between those vehicles and traffic moving in his same direction. Dial had not committed any serious or violent crime. He was suspected only of committing a minor shoplifting at the Walmart in Smithville, an allegation that was determined to be unfounded by a Smithville officer even before the chase began. While investigating the matter, the officer determined that Dial's license had expired—he was found parked in the Walmart parking lot—and eventually watched him pull away after telling him not to drive the truck. It was at that point when the pursuit began, still for a minor offense; however, it was terminated once Dial crossed into White County. The pursuit was then continued by Deputy Young, as other officers converged.

Vehicle pursuits are among the most dangerous activities the police involve themselves in. They are dangerous for the suspect, the officers involved, and the public at large, especially others driving in the vicinity. There are a critical few moments immediately after a suspect vehicle accelerates away when the officer must weigh the risks and rewards of pursuing it. They must evaluate whether an immediate apprehension is necessary and whether they have sufficient information to arrest the individual later. The most important variable that goes into their decision is the underlying crime the individual is suspected of committing. The days are long over when the police chase every vehicle that refuses to stop as if the suspect were a machine-gun-toting bank robber who had just shot up the town. In fact, most departments now have policies restricting their officers' ability to pursue a vehicle.

Unfortunately, the reality is that police pursuits, even those that should never have been begun or continued, are as common as ever. Police officers are trained in how to properly pursue a vehicle, but they receive little or no training in how not to pursue one. They are conditioned by their training and experience to believe that allowing a suspect to escape is unthinkable. When a suspect bolts away either on foot or in a vehicle, it is like Pavlov's bell. Once the fight-or-flight response sets in and the adrenaline surges, many officers lose their ability to think clearly and to properly evaluate their own actions in real-time. They simply react to the immediate circumstances, and suddenly they may find themselves driving 90 mph down city streets to stop someone who only ran through a stop sign or had an expired license plate. And if there is in fact a deadly outcome, especially if an innocent civilian is injured or killed, then like any other question-able use of force, the officer must create a narrative to bolster their actions. This is not to say that all pursuits are improper. Quite the contrary. There are many where immediate apprehension is critical to avoid more violence and innocent bloodshed.

The most common narrative used when there is a bad outcome is that the vehicle had to be stopped because their dangerous driv-ing was putting the public at risk. Notwithstanding the fact that the suspect would not have been driving in such a manner had they not been chased, such a narrative is used to justify not only the chase, but also the use of deadly force to stop the vehicle or to prevent the driver from taking off again. How many times have we seen on the nightly news a chase end with multiple police officers unloading their weapons into the vehicle? Some are justified, such as when the driver or a passenger points a gun at the officers. But in many, most in fact, there is no weapon, and the reasons given by the officers for shooting are either because the public would be in danger if the suspect were to get away and continue their dangerous driving or because they feared that the driver was going to run over them or ram their squad. It seems to matter little when they have the suspect vehicle completely boxed in with nowhere to go. In the case of Mi-chael Dial, the assertion that Dial would place the public at risk if he were allowed to drive away was the very justification offered by District Attorney Dunaway to clear the two officers who fired their weapons. It did not seem to matter that Dial was driving a truck that could barely reach 50 mph with an overloaded trailer attached, a trailer that had one flat tire, and by the time of the shooting, no tire at all.

I began my investigation by reviewing the dash cam videos from the neighboring county. Not once did Dial drive in the wrong lane of traffic or run someone off the road. In fact, it is not even clear that he was violating any traffic laws other than failing to stop for the four officers who were behind him. The only time a car in the opposing lane appeared to take defensive measures was when the squad cars were passing a semi truck, not Dial. He had already passed the semi and did so safely. When a pursuit enters another county, the pursuing officers broadcast one of two directives to the officers in the neighboring county. Either they broadcast "stop and hold" if the underlying crime was serious enough to bring the suspect back to their county to charge and book into jail there, or they broadcast "make your own case." When they do that, they are telling the officers who take up the pursuit that they are done with it and have no plans to bring the individual back to face charges. In that case, the new pursuing officers must find a reason to stop and charge the person in their county, or they can simply choose not to pursue the individual at all. When Michael Dial entered White County, the officers from the neighboring county had no intentions of pursuing the matter any further.

By the time Dial turned northbound onto Highway 111, now in White County and outside the town of Sparta, there still had been no contact between his truck and any police vehicle. By then, Dial had run over the spike strip deployed by Deputy Young and was barely able to maintain control of the truck and trailer, even at a low speed. His first contact with a police vehicle was captured by Young's dash cam. It occurred when Sparta officer Charlie Sims pulled to Dial's right and attempted to force him off the road. It was Sims who struck Dial, rather than Dial being the aggressor. On the video, Dial appeared to maneuver to miss the squad cars then and throughout the pursuit. At the same time Sims was striking Dial from the right, Deputy Lanny Wheeler was striking Dial's trailer on the left in a PIT (pursuit intervention technique) maneuver. His attempt was unsuccessful and caused his front passenger tire to go flat. This did not deter Wheeler from striking Dial's trailer from behind three more times without having full control of his squad car. He finally terminated his involvement once the flat tire had burned completely off the rim.

Because his vehicle became disabled, Wheeler was not present when the shooting occurred further down the road. The account he later provided of the incident was relatively accurate but for two things. In his report he described how Dial turned his wheels into his squad car when he pulled up alongside his truck. What he failed to point out was that Dial had no choice but to turn into him because Sims was on the other side forcing him off the roadway in his direction. The other issue with Wheeler's report was his description of Dial ramming the back of Sims's squad car after Sims pulled in front of him. He stated that he could see Dial ramming the back of Sims's squad multiple times as Sims attempted to force him to a stop.

In reality, I determined that Dial never once hit or rammed Sims in the rear of his patrol car. There was evidence of contact, and I could see the contact on Young's dash cam video. Sims did a good job of locking up end to end with Dial's truck as they traveled at the same speed. As Sims began to slow down, Dial broke the contact and moved to the side. Any opportunity for Sims to continue this effort was made impossible by Wheeler's erratic driving as he continued to strike Dial's trailer from behind. As far as I could tell, this was the only time Dial made contact with the rear of Sims's squad car, and it was initiated by Sims. Dial neither sped up nor purposely rammed the rear of Sims's squad car at this time, nor at any other time during the pursuit.

By this point in the chase, with Wheeler driving on his rim, it had become one of the most erratic and dangerous chases I personally had ever witnessed, either on video or in real life. I could not believe that Wheeler and Sims were both attempting a PIT maneuver on a trailer! Such a maneuver requires specialized training to carry out properly, and there are many restrictions on its use. Done properly, the officer positions their vehicle to nudge the rear driver side corner of the suspect's vehicle with their front passenger side corner. The idea is to cause the suspect vehicle to spin out of control without leaving the roadway and allowing the pursuing officers to box it in with their vehicles. Done improperly, especially by someone not trained and certified to use the technique, it can lead to a deadly outcome. The suspect vehicle can easily spin out of control in a way that causes it to leave the roadway and crash. Attempting the technique can also cause the officer to lose control of their own vehicle and crash. There is no training that advocates for attempting a PIT on a pickup truck pulling a wagon or on the wagon itself. I frankly could not believe I was seeing it. Things were about to get even more dangerous.

As Wheeler dropped out of the chase with his vehicle disabled, Deputy Young pulled up and began striking the trailer with his squad. Sims was still in front of Dial, and a Tennessee Highway patrolman joined the pursuit from the rear. Also joining the pursuit was Adam West, a White County reserve deputy. West was driving his own truck, which was equipped with a police radio and his own body cam. Reserve deputies are essentially untrained and unpaid deputies who in theory are used by a sheriff for things like parades and special events. In reality, they are a way for a sheriff to hand out badges to friends and political supporters, allowing them to carry guns and even have arrest powers in certain situations. In my experience, having reserve deputies without very tight controls on their power only increases the risk of significant problems. In this case, I could not believe I was watching on the dash cam videos a reserve deputy joining in the chase in his own private vehicle. What I truly found shocking was that he had actually taken a position ahead of the Tennessee Highway Patrolman in the pursuit. I was convinced that the highway patrolman could see the disaster that was unfolding in front of him and purposely held back. Once West joined the chase, having activated his body cam to show a gun in his hand, only one thing could have made the situation go from bad to worse . . . Sheriff Oddie Shoupe.

As I typically do in these cases, I took the time to listen to the recorded radio traffic between the officers involved and the White County dispatchers, as well as between the officers themselves. With Sims still in front of Dial and Young behind him continuing to strike the trailer with his squad, West obviously did not want to damage his truck, so he remained close behind without making contact. The following series of dispatches was broadcast:

Dispatcher:	*Per 59 (Sheriff Shoupe), take him out by any means necessary, including deadly force.*
Unidentified:	*10-9? (Police code for please repeat).*
Dispatcher:	*Per 59, use deadly force if necessary. Take the subject out by any means necessary.*
Deputy Young:	*10-4, Central be advised I'm fixing to ram him here.*
Dispatcher:	*County units, per 59, do not ram this subject . . . use your shotgun to end this pursuit.*

I had to listen again to make sure I heard what I thought I heard. It is unfathomable that a sheriff would give such an order without being on-scene and involved in the incident. There is only one time when such an order is given in law enforcement, and that is when a suspect is armed, has already killed, and has demonstrated or articulated their intent to continue killing. An example is an escaped murderer who has killed while on the run and who has made it clear they do not intend to be taken alive. But in this case, obviously none of those factors were present. Dial had committed no serious crime and was a threat to no one. A sheriff of any county certainly has a great amount of authority, but no sheriff has the authority to order their deputies to break the law, which is what Sheriff Shoupe was doing. It is quite telling that Deputy Young chose not to shoot at Dial. It is likely that as an academy-trained deputy, he knew that such an action would not be justified. West on the other hand lacked that level of training and experience. When the sheriff gave his order, there was no doubt that West was more than willing to carry out his command. On his own body cam video, West could be seen checking the magazine of his gun. He was preparing to shoot. Sadly, it was obvious to me that the sheriff's first concern was his fleet of squad cars, all of which were damaged because of the officers' actions rather than Dial's.

After striking the rear of Dial's trailer, Young pulled alongside Dial and executed a PIT maneuver, which turned the vehicle sideways and momentarily stopped its forward movement. West did not hesitate. He began to fire his gun through his open window. Dial accelerated into the grass and down a hill toward a row of trees. As he did, West exited his truck and continued to fire. By this time, Officer Sims, who was in front of Dial, stopped and exited his squad and began shooting as well. Dial continued driving erratically through the grass, and then, obviously hit by one or more of the shots, he removed his foot from the accelerator and idled into the trees. Deputy Young followed and ran his squad into the back of Dial's trailer, apparently to prevent him from leaving. It was not necessary. The pursuit was over. Dial lay in his truck with a fatal gunshot wound to the head.

Once I determined the sequence of events from the various body cam and dash cam sources, I next reviewed the officers' reports. I expected to see the deadly force script incorporated at every possible point. The deputies did not let me down. The reporting officer for the White County Sheriff's Department was Deputy Wheeler. He filed the original incident report, with West and Young filing supplemental reports. It was obvious from West's report that he was not a trained police officer. His report was incomplete, inaccurate, and misleading. It was also obvious that he knew enough—or he was being coached—to create a state of mind narrative that supported his decision to use deadly force. His report contained the following passage:

> He at that time hit unit 73, Sgt. Lanny Wheeler, hard enough to total his unit and took him out of the pursuit. At this time, I was in fear for my life and the other officers' and the general public's lives. I wondered if my Sgt. was okay. I witnessed the driver of the truck ram a City of Sparta officer with deadly force. I was so scared.

The biggest problem with this passage is that none of it was true. Wheeler's squad was not "totaled." It had a flat tire caused by Wheeler continually ramming Dial from behind, and not the other way around. It was the fact that Wheeler was driving uncontrollably on one of his rims that caused him to pull over. There was absolutely no reason for West to be concerned about Wheeler's welfare.

Also, at no time did Dial ram Sims. Once again, it was Sims who was striking Dial in an effort to run him off the road and into the grassy median. West's assertion that he was "so scared" during the pursuit was an absurd statement to include in a police report. He had covered all the bases when he suggested that Dial had used deadly force when he rammed the police vehicles; that he was a threat to the general public; and that he himself was scared for his life. West also fabricated his account of when he began shooting:

> I at that time removed my seatbelt, drew my weapon and kept driving. When the driver rammed another officer, I believe was Deputy Brandon Young, the driver of the truck went to the right of the roadway towards the grass. I immediately threw my truck in park, jumped out, and the driver of the truck was trying to get his vehicle back to the road, I believe to hurt and endanger the lives of the officers and public. I at that time fired my weapon towards the truck to try to neutralize this threat. I believe I fired ten times.

Not only did Dial NOT ram Deputy Young's vehicle—Young was actually behind him—it was Young who rammed Dial. It was Young who finally executed a PIT maneuver and stopped Dial's forward movement momentarily. It was then that West began shooting. West conveniently forgot to mention that he began shooting before he ever exited his truck. Not only would a trained police officer never do this, but West very dangerously fired from inside his truck when Young was potentially in his line of fire. West described the end of the pursuit as follows: "After firing I heard other gun shots, looked to my left and saw Sparta Officer firing at the side of the truck after I saw the truck ram into Deputy Brandon Young and then hit a tree."

This passage misrepresented what was clearly seen on the dash cam footage. Dial did NOT ram into Young before hitting the trees. Dial was already shot and unconscious when he hit the trees. It was Young who rammed into Dial's trailer after Dial had already come to a stop.

West's report really lacked any integrity at all and should have been dismissed in its entirety. What is amazing is that the report was approved by two different supervisors, one of whom was Deputy Wheeler. I assumed that the report had been reviewed and considered by District Attorney Dunaway. The report's inaccuracies and misrepresentations were obvious, and they should have been to him.

Deputy Young's report was also replete with inaccuracies. He provided a narrative that described Dial striking his and Wheeler's squad cars multiple times. Again, it was clear to see in the dash cam videos that it was Wheeler who repeatedly struck Dial's truck and trailer and did so in an extremely dangerous manner when neither the truck nor his own squad car was completely controllable because of the flat tires. Young then stated the following:

> Officer Sims, the Tennessee Highway Patrolman, and I attempted to box the subject in again. The subject then struck my driver side front and back door. I then began trying to snatch the trailer with my brush guard in an attempt to stop the subject. I hit the subject twice before he ran into the median. The subject acted as if he was going to pass Officer Sims while in the median. The subject then got back onto Hwy 111 North. I tried to approach the driver side of the trailer to get the subject off the roadway. I noticed that the subject had went down the side of the embankment. As I was bringing my vehicle to a stop, I noticed Officer Adam West begin to shoot at the subject.

At no time did Dial strike Young's vehicle. Rather, Young struck Dial's truck four different times and missed once. The final contact was a PIT maneuver which successfully turned Dial sideways and stopped his forward motion momentarily. This was the moment when West began shooting. In his report, Young said nothing about executing the PIT maneuver at this point. Also, at no time did Young attempt to approach the driver side of the trailer. Finally, Young said nothing in his report about West firing from inside his truck immediately after he turned Dial sideways with the PIT maneuver.

The reports filed by the officers in this case were reminiscent of the old joke where the boy in trouble for beating up another boy tries to convince his mother that the other boy struck him in the fist with his nose! Dial was never the aggressor in this matter, and never did he purposely try to ram any of the squad cars, as confirmed by the dash cam videos; yet in the reports we see just the opposite. Whenever a squad car is seen on one of the dash cam videos ramming Dial's truck or trailer, it was reported by the officers as Dial ramming the squad cars. None of the reports were accurate, and in the case of West and Young, there were several misrepresentations.

One of the most important questions I needed to answer was which officer fired the fatal shot? I knew with certainty that the two officers, Sims and West, fired a combined fourteen times at Dial's truck and that one of the bullets hit Dial and killed him. The bullet that struck Dial was not sufficiently intact for a determination to be made by the crime lab; however, I anticipated that I could make this determination through a proper analysis of the video and audio evidence, as I had done in other cases. One problem I immediately had was that Sims's dash cam footage was barely audible. I attempted to overcome this problem by boosting the audio portion of the footage to the point where Sims's four shots could be discerned. Once I was able to then sync Sims's dash cam footage with West's body cam footage, it became obvious that West fired the fatal shot.

I was also able to determine from West's body cam footage exactly when the fatal shot was fired. West began firing before he ever exited his vehicle. He fired two quick shots from the driver's seat, one of which passed through the hood of his own truck. He then exited and fired eight more shots at Dial's truck as he drove down the embankment and continued forward through the grass. Because the bullet struck Dial in the head and moved left to right, West had to have shot when Dial turned his wheels to the left to drive back up the embankment, thus exposing his left side to West's aim. I was able to isolate the point when this happened. Because I was able to sync Sims's dash cam with West's body cam, I was able to confirm that when West fired the fatal shot, Sims had not yet even exited his squad or fired his weapon. Further, by enhancing Sim's video, I was able to show that by the time he fired his weapon, the window of Dial's truck had already been shot out and Dial was slumped over the steering wheel. It was indisputable that West had fired the fatal shot.

The question must be asked why neither the TBI nor District Attorney Dunaway made a determination or public announcement regarding which officer fired the fatal shot. It was easy to determine using some basic investigative techniques. There were likely two answers to this question. I had to assume that they knew West fired the fatal shot, so the more appropriate question was why they chose not to identify him as the shooter. First, only one of the two shooters reported to Sheriff Shoupe, and that was West. Sims neither reported to the sheriff, nor was he beholden to his authority. If Sims had been the fatal shooter, then the orders given by Sheriff Shoupe to use deadly force would have had little relevance. That is not the case with West. And second, West was a reserve officer who should never have been involved in the chase in his personal vehicle, or in any vehicle for that matter. Furthermore, like any reserve officer, West was not appropriately trained to participate in such an action. He should have been ordered by the other officers to back off and follow, obeying all traffic laws in the process. So, by not naming West as the shooter, it made it more difficult to hold the sheriff and White County liable for Dial's death. And by leaving the door open to call Sims the shooter, a professionally trained and certified police officer, they also were leaving open the possibility of offering a qualified immunity defense. Once I determined that West was the shooter, that possibility was eliminated.

As abhorrent as Sheriff Shoupe's comments were when he arrived at the scene, they only got worse. While talking to the same deputy who did not realize his body cam was on, the following ex-

Sheriff Shoupe: *I told 'em, I said take him out.*
Deputy: *I heard.*
Sheriff Shoupe: *Damn, I don't give a shit!*
Deputy: *It wasn't long after that I heard shots fired.*
Sheriff Shoupe: *They said, we're ramming him. I said, don't ram him, shoot him! Fuck that shit. Ain't gonna tear my cars up. If they don't think I'll give the damn order to kill that motherfucker, they're full of shit. Take him out!*

change took place:

The use of deadly force against Michael Dial boiled down to two things: a sheriff who was too quick to authorize deadly force in order to limit the damage to his patrol vehicles, and an undertrained reserve deputy who was too quick to follow that directive without properly evaluating the situation. Both violated all accepted standards of police training and practice on the issue of deadly force. The sheriff should never have given such a foolish order, and West should never have interjected himself in the pursuit in his private vehicle. Both Deputy Wheeler and Deputy Young had the authority to order West to terminate his involvement, but both failed to do so. A police pursuit is a dangerous incident, in terms of potential accidents, but also in terms of the police themselves overreacting in the excitement of the moment. Any chase demands command and control by supervisory personnel. In this case, that would have been Deputy Wheeler, who held the rank of sergeant; yet he was the one driving the most erratically in a patrol vehicle he could barely control. The truth is, there was no command and control, and thus at the end of the day there were multiple damaged patrol vehicles, and one dead suspect whose only crime was driving on a suspended license.

I would like to say that this case was the first and last time I would ever hear anything out of Sheriff Oddie Shoupe. It was not. Just a few months later there was another pursuit of a minor traffic offender that started in a neighboring county. And just like the case of Michael Dial, once the neighboring county called off the pursuit when the vehicle entered White County, Sheriff Shoupe's boys took over and eventually rammed the side of the vehicle to bring it to a stop. The driver was injured by the impact. When the sheriff arrived, his first question to the deputy was: "You got your camera going?" After the deputy told him it was, Shoupe motioned for him to turn it off. Like something straight out of a television sitcom, in spite of the deputy's better efforts, the body cam remained on, and a few minutes later recorded Shoupe directing his deputies to change their stories to say that it was the suspect who had rammed the police vehicle. A few months later, after the story hit the press, Shoupe announced his retirement and quietly left office. It also hastened the county's decision to settle with Michael Dial's wife for $250,000.

As for Adam West, the reserve deputy who fired the fatal shot? In a normal world he would have been criminally charged, or at the very least precluded from ever again serving as a reserve deputy. But White County is anything but normal it seems. Before he left office, Sheriff Shoupe promoted West to a full-time paid deputy's position. He did so without conducting a proper background check. Had he done so, he would have discovered that West had been arrested multiple times in the past, including for assault and burglary, and had even spent time in jail. Quite a contrast to Michael Dial, whose most egregious crime on the day he died was having the audacity to drive his old truck into Sheriff Oddie Shoupe's county with an expired license.

- CHAPTER 10-

The Case of Nicholas Dyksma

Columbus, Georgia

Compressional Asphyxia: How the Police Conceal and Defend a Deadly Tactic

There is no police training anywhere that supports the tactic of multiple officers piling on top of a suspect's back to get him or her handcuffed. In fact, the training they receive is how to avoid using such a tactic. Yet still they do use it, and quite often. Until the advent of the cell-phone camera, and later the police body cam, compressional asphyxia, and the actions that lead to it, were relatively unknown to the general public. And if the pathologist performing the autopsy was not informed of the officers' specific actions, chances were that the autopsy report would indicate a cause of death that did not include the fact that multiple officers had pinned the individual to the ground for an extended period of time. I suspect a frightening number of individuals have died over the years from the asphyxiating actions of police officers that were never properly reported.

Today, when a case happens where police officers are videotaped piling on the back, neck, or head of a suspect who later dies, the officers will invariably justify their actions by stating that the suspect posed a significant threat by kicking, biting, spitting, or reaching for an officer's gun, even if no such behavior by the suspect can be seen on the videotape. The police are particularly good at describing a threat in subtle terms—a certain look, a sound, a slight movement of the hand. It becomes difficult to disprove, especially when the officers involved have a chance to view the videotape prior to offering their accounts of the incident to investigators. In many jurisdictions, the police unions have negotiated a mandatory "decompression" period before the officers involved must provide a statement to Internal Affairs investigators. While on the surface it may appear that such a requirement is designed to allow an officer to clear their mind and thus improve their recall by decompressing from the stress of the encounter, in reality, its primary purpose is to allow the officer time to construct a favorable narrative with the help of union representatives and lawyers.

Nicholas Dyksma was just 19 years old when he died while being arrested by deputies in Harris County, Georgia. The incident began on August 31, 2015, when a Columbus, Georgia, police officer attempted to check on Dyksma after receiving a report that he was asleep in his truck. It quickly evolved into a chase when Dyksma took off and attempted to elude the officer. The officer terminated the chase as they neared the Harris County line. But like Sheriff Oddie Shoupe's boys up in Tennessee, as Dyksma entered Harris County, deputies from that county were waiting. Deputies Tommy Pierson and Joe Harmon immediately took up the chase, while Deputy William Sturdevant set up a spike strip a few miles inside Harris County. Just a few short minutes later, Nicholas Dyksma was loaded into the back of an ambulance unresponsive and with two Taser darts embedded in his body. He was pronounced dead at a local hospital.

I was brought into the case by Georgia attorney Craig Jones, one of the leading civil rights lawyers in the South. I had worked other cases with Craig and respected his legal knowledge and abilities. He was one of the first lawyers in the United States I had worked multiple cases with. When he called me, he told me what he knew about the case and emailed me a partial dash cam video that had been released by the sheriff to the public. While it did not show what happened once Dyksma was pulled from his truck by the deputies at the conclusion of the chase, it did show the conclusion of the chase when Dyksma was forced into a ditch by Deputy Pierson. It further showed what appeared to be Dyksma dangerously accelerating when the deputies approached on foot. None of the deputies were struck by the truck, and with nowhere to go but deeper into the ditch, Dyksma let off the accelerator. At that point one of the deputies deployed a Taser through his window. Now incapacitated, the other deputies pulled him from the truck and the video ended. When the video was released, the sheriff pointed out to the media how Dyksma had tried to run over the deputies and how they were forced to use the Taser to stop him. One thing is true about dash and body cam video, things are not always as they seem.

One of the first documents I was able to obtain was the autopsy report. Georgia is unique because autopsies are performed by the Georgia Bureau of Investigation (GBI), the same agency charged with investigating the matter. I did not have a lot of confidence in the GBI based on other cases I had worked in Georgia. Sometimes in these cases the smallest of details can be the most important evidence. The GBI was notorious, in my experience, for missing those details and completing a rather superficial investigation that almost always favored the officers involved. The medical examiner who completed the autopsy recorded the cause of death as follows: "Sudden death during an altercation with law enforcement, after deployment of an electroconductive device, with prone position, compression of the neck and torso, and acute methamphetamine intoxication."

Additionally, the medical examiner found multiple abrasions on Dyksma's neck and face, as well as two puncture wounds on his left chest caused by the Taser darts. The first question I had was why Dyksma, who weighed just over 100 pounds, would ever need to have his neck and torso compressed to the ground by what turned out to be four large deputies, one of whom, Deputy Pierson, appeared from the video to top 275 pounds. And this after apparently being incapacitated by a Taser. The medical examiner's cause of death was not definitive that Dyksma had been a victim of compressional asphyxia, as I suspected he was.

Almost a year after the incident, Craig finally received the investigative file from GBI and forwarded it to me. Fortunately, the dash cam video that had previously been released was now provided in its entirety. The video, recorded by Deputy Heath Dawson, begins as Dawson was driving southbound on Georgia Highway 27 a few miles inside Harris County. He very quickly met Dyksma driving northbound on four flat tires and boxed in by Deputies Pierson and Harmon. Sturdevant had successfully deployed the spike strip. Dawson did a quick three-point turn to join the chase, but by the time he caught up, Dyksma's truck was in the ditch and the deputies were exiting their squads.

At first glance the video seemed to confirm the deputies' accounts of what happened. Harmon stated in his GBI interview that when he exited his squad after Dyksma lost control of his truck and went into the ditch, he was holding his firearm and giving Dyksma verbal commands to exit the vehicle with his hands up. Dyksma refused and had his doors locked. Dawson can then be seen breaking out Dyksma's driver side window with his expandable baton. Dyksma can then be seen accelerating in an apparent attempt to leave. Harmon stated that as Dyksma accelerated, he holstered his firearm, drew his Taser, and fired it through the broken window because he feared that Dyksma was attempting to run over the other deputies. Dyksma was hit on the left side by the Taser and appeared to immediately take his foot off the accelerator and lay down across the seat. This was the version of events given to the press before the deputies' reports were released.

On the video, Dawson can then be seen breaking out the passenger side window of the truck to unlock and open the door and, with the help of Pierson, violently drag Dyksma out of the truck and onto the ground. While he was being handcuffed behind his back—he was neither struggling nor resisting—three of the deputies applied their weight to Dyksma's back, legs, and neck. Dyksma can be heard on the video screaming as Pierson applied the full weight of his body to the back of his neck with his knee, and after he had already been handcuffed. Very quickly Dyksma became unresponsive, a circumstance the deputies failed to recognize until six minutes after he was handcuffed. Even then they waited an additional four minutes to begin CPR.

One of the first steps taken by Craig Jones was to seek a second opinion on the autopsy. On May 8, 2017, Dr. Kris Sperry, a board-certified forensic pathologist, reviewed the autopsy results and report. While the GBI pathologist had provided a more general conclusion about the cause of death, Dr. Sperry was very specific and concluded as follows:

> It is my opinion, to a reasonable degree of medical certainty, that Nicholas Dyksma died during the course of being restrained by law enforcement officers, and that the specific events that caused his death were repeated forcible compressions of his neck, torso, and back while the restraint was being effectuated. The failure to recognize that Mr. Dyksma was in extremis and that his clinical condition was deteriorating contributed to his death; by the time that the extremely serious nature of his deterioration was recognized, he could not be resuscitated. But for the chest and neck compressions which were applied during the restraint, it is my opinion that Nicholas Dyksma would not have died.

All four deputies involved in this incident submitted a written report. Those reports were eventually made available. Harmon repeated in his report that he had approached Dyksma's truck with his firearm in hand, and that he reholstered it and drew his Taser in an attempt to stop Dyksma from accelerating. I found this odd because if Harmon truly believed Dyksma was accelerating to run over the other deputies, two of whom were on the other side of the truck, then he would have been justified in using his firearm to stop him. Why would he use his Taser instead, which was not even guaranteed to hit him with the darts having to travel through a broken window, and if it did, there was a possibility that because of the short distance, the spread of the darts would be insufficient to incapacitate Dyksma. I decided to do what I always do and more closely review the video.

If there is one thing I have learned about reviewing video, especially the lower quality videos recorded by dash and body cams, it is that you must watch them many times over, even if you see nothing out of the ordinary initially. It is not unusual for me to lay in bed at night doing that very thing. I will watch videos forward, in reverse, in slow motion, and sped up. I will apply different filters and lighting settings. Eventually, as you watch while considering other theories about what happened, you may begin to see something for the first time. Such was the case here. I had done nothing special to the video in terms of enhancements. However, on what must have been my twentieth viewing I caught sight of something. It was a speck of white that momentarily appeared on Harmon's firearm. I immediately realized what it was and zoomed in and enhanced the video to confirm it. The white speck was the decal that is found on the side of the X26 Taser carried by many officers, including Harmon. I then zoomed in on his holster and sure enough, his firearm was still holstered. He had given an account in his report that was just the opposite of what had actually happened. After Dawson shattered the driver's side window, Harmon aimed his Taser, not his firearm, and then, as Dyksma accelerated, he reholstered the Taser and drew his firearm.

There are two types of muscle contractions. Concentric contractions cause the muscles to shorten, while eccentric contractions cause the muscles to elongate. A Taser causes the latter type. This is why when people are shot by a Taser they will straighten out like a board. It was obvious after seeing the Taser in Harmon's hand what had happened. Dyksma never voluntarily accelerated the truck. While he did quietly remain inside with the doors locked, after his window was shattered by Dawson, Harmon immediately reached up and shot him with the Taser, causing his leg to contract against the accelerator. I had a simple way of testing this. If it were true, then five seconds after accelerating and at the end of the Taser's cycle, Dyksma would go limp and immediately quit accelerating. That is in fact what happened, and with a little more enhancement of the video, I was able to actually see the two Taser wires leading into the window just before Dyksma accelerated.

The question I asked myself was why would Harmon submit a false and misleading report? With a little thought, the answer seemed obvious. In using the Taser, Harmon chose to use an intermediate level of force at a time when Dyksma was only passively resisting by not unlocking the door to his truck. He was not attempting to leave, nor was he using the truck as a weapon. Harmon's use of the

Taser when he did was inconsistent with accepted police training and standards of practice. Harmon had attempted to make his use of the Taser appear reasonable by portraying it as a reaction to Dyksma accelerating the truck forward and placing the officers at risk of harm. Not only had he fired his Taser when no threat was present, but he also shot Dyksma in an area of the chest police officers are trained to avoid due to the risk of death or serious injury.

While Harmon had been untruthful about a very important part of the incident, his report did not even compare to Dawson's in terms of its veracity, or lack of. It was a stroke of luck that I had noticed the white speck on Harmon's Taser, but in Dawson's case I only needed to watch his own dash cam video a single time to realize that essentially every part of his report was untruthful.

Deputy Dawson was positioned ahead of the other deputies as they pursued Dyksma in his direction. Dawson was driving southbound on Georgia Highway 27 when Dyksma, Harmon, and Pierson approached from the opposite direction heading northbound. In his report he wrote the following:

> As I was approaching in the South bound lane, the suspect vehicle went around Deputy Pierson's patrol vehicle and drove North bound towards me in the South bound lane. To avoid a "head on" collision with the vehicle at that speed, I went into the North bound lane allowing the suspect's vehicle to pass me on the passenger side.

There is essentially no part of this statement that is truthful. The dash cam video is indisputable. Dyksma did not drive toward Dawson. He did in fact pass by Pierson's vehicle, but then he returned to the northbound lane of travel immediately and before he was even close to hitting Dawson head on. Furthermore, each of the vehicles at that point was moving at a much slower rate of speed with Dyksma's tires flattened by the spike strip. What Dawson failed to report was that he was actually the one who had crossed into the wrong lane of travel. After Dyksma returned to the northbound lane, Dawson swerved into his lane apparently attempting to run him off the road. It was Dyksma who took evasive action. And Dawson's statement that Dyksma had passed by his vehicle on the passenger side was simply a fabrication. Dawson also stated that when they attempted to get Dyksma to unlock his door and exit the vehicle, his wheels were spinning, and it appeared that he was attempting to leave. This too was a fabrication. It was clear to see on the dash cam video that Dyksma's wheels were not spinning, nor was he doing anything to suggest that he was preparing to accelerate. His wheels did not move until Dawson broke the window and Harmon deployed his Taser. And then finally, Dawson stated the following in his report:

> I saw Deputy Pierson fall to the ground out of sight and immediately thought he had become trapped under the vehicle. I ran around the rear of the truck to aid Deputy Pierson. Once I made it to the tailgate of the truck (tires still spinning and throwing gravel in an attempt to gain traction), I saw Deputy Pierson regain his footing. Simultaneously, I saw Sergeant Harmon holster his duty weapon and retrieve his Taser. Sergeant Harmon deployed the Taser, striking Dyksma which immediately caused the vehicle and its tires to stop spinning.

Unbelievably, everything in this passage was false. On the video I could see both Pierson and Dawson when Pierson fell after kicking the truck. Dawson was already behind the truck with Pierson in full view. He never lost sight of Pierson, he never ran to Pierson's aid, and he did not see Harmon holster his duty weapon and stop Dyksma from accelerating further by deploying his Taser. Dawson's report, which he obviously coordinated with the other deputies, was intended to portray Dyksma as a significant risk throughout the incident, and to bolster Harmon's narrative that only his use of the Taser stopped Dyksma from running over the other deputies. Almost the entirety of Dawson's report was easily disproven by his own dash cam video.

Pierson was the deputy who attempted to make the initial stop of Dyksma once he entered Harris County. He was also the deputy who assisted Dawson in dragging Dyksma from the truck. Like the others, Pierson too misrepresented in his statement what had happened during the incident. He admitted that once Dyksma was pulled from the truck, he placed his knee on Dyksma's upper back after he was handcuffed to ensure that he did not struggle while Dawson double-locked the handcuffs. It was clear to see on the dash cam video that Dyksma was not struggling, and further, since he weighed only slightly more than 100 pounds, it would have been quite easy to control him if in fact he had been struggling. I could also see that Pierson did not place his knee on Dyksma's upper back, but directly on his neck. I could hear Dyksma scream when he did. Pierson left his knee on his neck for twenty-one seconds and then repositioned to the other side of Dyksma. Unbelievably, he then again placed his knee on Dyksma's neck for an additional seventeen seconds. It was obvious to me that by this time Dyksma was unconscious. Not surprisingly, Pierson omitted a full discussion of his actions in his report, especially relating to the neck compression. He also attempted to portray Dyksma as struggling. This was simply false. Dyksma was violently dragged from the truck after being incapacitated by the Taser, and then stepped on by three of the deputies while they handcuffed him. At no time did he struggle. In fact, the only time he appeared to even attempt to struggle was when he screamed after Pierson put his knee on his neck the first time.

The law enforcement community has long been aware of the dangers of applying weight to a person's neck or back while they are lying face down on the ground. Compressional asphyxiation can very quickly lead to death, not just by cutting off the person's ability to breathe, but also by restricting that ability while allowing the airway to remain open. The former leads to death by strangulation, and the latter, to death by hypoxia, or a condition in which the body simply does not get enough oxygen at the tissue level to sustain life. Death can occur rapidly in both instances. In the context of police practices, while it may be acceptable at times to momentarily apply pressure to a suspect's back to facilitate handcuffing, it is never appropriate to apply force to their neck unless deadly force is justified. This is the training all police officers in the United States receive, and have for at least the last three decades. Deputy Pierson did so twice, and both times after Dyksma was already handcuffed; the second time, after he was obviously unconscious.

Police officers are trained in first aid. Every police officer who graduates from a police academy is certified in CPR and basic life support. Most carry first aid bags. In this case, the medical response by the four deputies present was anything but fast and professional. CPR was not begun for nearly ten minutes after Dyksma was dragged from the truck and for six minutes after they first realized he was unresponsive. Before they finally began chest compressions, they seemed confused and unsure what to do. They did essentially nothing to keep Dyksma alive until EMS personnel arrived on the scene. They rubbed his back, shook him, told him to wake up, and even brought out an ammonia capsule and held it to his nose, obviously an ineffective technique when the person is no longer breathing. There is no way to tell definitively if they could have saved Dyksma's life. But if any of them were trained in basic life support, as I expected they were, then they ignored their training. And if they were not, then the Harris County Sheriff's Department failed to properly train and prepare its deputies. Whichever the case, any chance to save Nicholas Dyksma's life was likely lost by waiting six or more minutes to begin CPR.

In the report I submitted to Craig Jones, I concluded that not only had the deputies used excessive force, but that they also were attempting to obscure their actions by submitting false, misleading, and incomplete reports. Nicholas Dyksma was a teenager who had committed no crime prior to the initiation of the vehicle chase by the Columbus police officer. He had threatened no one and very quickly found himself driving at a slow rate of speed on four flat tires after the Harris County deputy successfully deployed the spike strip. When his truck finally came to rest nose down in a ditch, he was quickly surrounded by deputies Harmon, Dawson, and Pierson. The deputies, with no indication that Dyksma intended to actively resist, immediately became aggressive, pointing their weapons, kicking the truck, and yelling profanities. It is reasonable to conclude that Dyksma refused to unlock his doors out of fear, given how aggressively the deputies were acting. He was after all just a teenager.

Eventually, after I withstood a contentious deposition by a lawyer who is also an ex-cop, the case settled for $500,000. For me, the case represented just about every obstacle a family faces when they seek justice in an excessive force case involving the police. In this case, it began with a terribly bad investigation by the GBI. They failed to even recognize that Harmon had used his Taser before Dyksma accelerated, rather than after, and that it was the Taser that caused his acceleration. This was such an important piece of evidence, and no one involved in the investigation, neither from the GBI nor the Harris County Sheriff's Department, caught it. Also, and not surprisingly, when the deputies were interviewed, the GBI investigators conducting the interviews seemed more focused on facilitating their collective defense than confronting them about the many and obvious inaccuracies, inconsistencies, and outright lies in their reports.

And then there was District Attorney Julia Slater, who employed Harris County Sheriff Mike Jolly's son as one of her investigators and who refused to recuse herself from the Dyksma review because of that conflict. Unbelievably, both she and the sheriff concluded that the deputies had acted appropriately, and thus neither disciplinary action nor criminal charges were ever pursued against any of the deputies. Given the number of cases I had worked in Georgia up to this point, especially in the southern part of the state, it did not surprise me that the fix seemed to be in from the beginning. Nearly four years later, apparently under some public pressure to take action in the matter, Slater presented the evidence to a Harris County grand jury. A grand jury is only as good as the evidence they are provided. It is also true that a grand jury will only indict someone if the prosecutor asks for an indictment. There was no indication that Slater made such a request, nor that she presented expert testimony to ensure that the grand jurors fully understood the evidence they were reviewing. It is almost a certainty that she did not allow them to read my report, and since I seemed to have been the only person in the entire post-incident investigation who caught the fact that Harmon had lied about when he used his Taser—even the media, which had access to the dash cam video, missed it—without my report the grand jurors simply could not have reached an informed conclusion. Not surprisingly, in March 2019 they concluded that the deputies, even Tommy Pierson, had done nothing improper.

Most troubling of all was when Federal Judge Clay Land granted the sheriff and all the deputies except Pierson qualified immunity. It did not matter that the sheriff had ignored his own policies when he cleared the deputies of wrongdoing, or when Dawson shattered Dyksma's window and caused numerous injuries to his face. It did not matter that Harmon had caused Dyksma's acceleration when he inappropriately used his Taser, and then lied about it in his report to hide that fact. The Judge even ruled that the first time Pierson smashed his knee down on Dyksma's neck for twenty seconds was not even inappropriate. It did not matter that Pierson weighed nearly three times what Dyksma weighed. It did not matter that three other deputies were assisting in getting him in handcuffs. In the end, the judge released everyone from liability except for Pierson, and then only for the second time he placed his knee on Dyksma's neck.

In my mind, Pierson was sacrificed for one simple reason. Not long after the death of Nicholas Dyksma, Pierson was indicted on multiple counts of sexual assault while in uniform and on duty. By the time Judge Land ruled on qualified immunity in 2018, Pierson was convicted and sentenced to seventeen years of prison and probation. As of the publication date of this book, he remains an inmate at Long State Prison in Ludowici, Georgia. It was an easy out for the judge because no one cared about Pierson. I was convinced that he ruled that Pierson was not liable for the first knee to the neck because it would have made the argument that the other deputies did not have time to intervene more difficult to make. Pierson's criminal conviction made it easy to throw him under the bus while giving the other deputies, including the sheriff, a pass. As is so often the case, Craig Jones was left with a case against a deputy who had no way of ever paying a judgment except for whatever liability insurance he carried.

Even with Pierson in prison and the dash cam so clearly showing how Nicholas Dyksma died, the attorney representing Harris County still appealed Judge Land's decision in an effort to get even Pierson released from liability. Fortunately, the Appellate Court disagreed, and the case was settled for $850,000 nearly three years after Nicholas Dyksma died. But for Pierson, the deputies involved— Harmon, Dawson, and Sturdevant—remained in their positions. And while this case should have sounded the alarm on the deadly tactic of police officers putting their weight on a suspect's back or neck, sadly it did not. A few months later I found myself back in southern Georgia for yet another suspected case of compressional asphyxia just a short distance from where Nicholas Dyksma had died. It would eventually take a 2020 case in Minneapolis, Minnesota for the public's awareness, and their intolerance, of this deadly tactic to finally take root.

- CHAPTER 11-

The Case of Isaiah Murrietta

Fresno, California

The Waistband Defense: When the Police Reach for an Excuse

How many times have we heard in a news report that a suspect was shot by the police after reaching for his waistband? It is one of the most often used elements of the deadly force script, and one that is difficult, if not impossible to disprove. Bringing the hands close to the waistline is one of the natural consequences of running. And if a suspect happens to be a young man who chooses to wear loose-fitting pants, it is guaranteed that he will reach to his waistband just to keep his pants up. So, whether captured on video or not, the waistband defense is an especially effective tactic, especially when the suspect is found to be unarmed.

The case of 16-year-old Isaiah Murrietta was in fact caught on video by a security camera pointed at the schoolyard where he was shot and killed as he ran from Fresno police officers. The incident was covered by the national media. The attorney representing the Murrietta family was Stuart Chandler, a local attorney who had recently completed another high-profile case in Fresno and with whom I had previously had discussions over the telephone. I contacted Stuart and asked if he needed an expert for the Murrietta case. At the time I was working another Fresno case with attorney Bill Schmidt, a friend of Stuart's. Stuart agreed to bring me into the case and forwarded the evidence and case files so I could begin my review.

The chain of events that led to Murrietta's death at the hands of the police began on April 14, 2017 when he and his older brother, Israel, were identified as having been involved in a shooting on a Fresno street after an exchange with a group of young men outside a pizza establishment. The older Israel was identified as the one who had fired a handgun into their vehicle as it drove away. The shots caused the driver to lose control of the vehicle and crash into a tree. The driver was pronounced dead at the scene and was later found to have suffered a torn aorta, among other injuries. The other three occupants of the vehicle were transported to the hospital with serious injuries.

The day after the incident, multiple units from the Fresno Police Department were conducting surveillance on a residence believed to be the home of Israel and Isaiah Murrietta. Even though Isaiah was not the shooter, they intended to charge him with assisting in the murder. Their goals were to execute a search warrant of the residence and effect an investigative detention of the two brothers to hopefully question them. They also wanted to get a current picture of the younger Isaiah to show to witnesses. At some point, a vehicle occupied by a driver and two passengers arrived at the house. One of the passengers, a male, exited the vehicle and entered the house and returned shortly after with some clothes. The surveillance officers were not able to positively identify the individual as one of the Murrietta brothers. After leaving the residence, an investigative traffic stop was carried out in a retail parking lot by multiple officers. The front passenger, who was in fact Isaiah Murrietta, exited the vehicle and ran. He was pursued by officers on foot and in vehicles.

What happened next was caught on the security video. Within a few blocks and while still being pursued, Murrietta climbed over a six-foot wrought iron fence into an empty schoolyard and continued to run. As he did, Sergeant Ray Villalvazo braced his hand against a fence rail and from the opposite side of the fence fired a single shot at Murrietta from a distance of 30 feet. Murrietta was hit in the back of the head and immediately collapsed. He was pronounced dead a short time later at the hospital. It did not surprise me that Chief Jerry Dyer almost immediately took to the microphones and announced that Villalvazo fired out of fear for his life after Murrietta reached for his waistband. The game was on.

Of course, I knew that the waistband defense is generally used to defend the indefensible. In this case I was able to watch the shooting on video. It is a defense that has no basis in fact. I had actually conducted a small research project on the issue. I wanted to see just how prevalent the practice was among suspects, especially those attempting to flee on foot and concealing a firearm in their waistband. Asked another way, was there a correlation between a fleeing suspect reaching for their waistband and the presence of a firearm? First, I had to define exactly where my focus lay. In the context of foot pursuits where the officer fires their weapon and the suspect is killed, there are three possible sets of circumstances:

1. The officer knows before firing their weapon that the suspect is armed. This would include cases where the suspect fires at the officer pursuing them; where the suspect does not fire but has the gun visible in their hand as they run; and where the pursuit is part of an ongoing incident involving the use of a firearm.
2. The officer shoots and kills a suspect without knowing for certain if a firearm is present, and a firearm is in fact found on the suspect's person.
3. The officer shoots and kills a suspect without knowing for certain if a firearm is present, and the suspect is found to be unarmed.

Only one of these categories was of interest to me. Regarding category no. 1, if the officer has foreknowledge that the suspect is armed, then reaching for the waistband is likely a legitimate defense. These cases tell us little about a correlation between reaching for the waistband and the presence of a gun, since a gun will be present either just before or during the pursuit 100% of the time. And regarding category no. 3, we already know there is no correlation here between reaching for the waistband and the presence of a gun, since there was no gun in 100% of the cases. Category no. 2 then cuts down the middle between those cases where there is always a gun and those where there is never a gun. Here is where my focus was directed. My research question was this—in those cases where the officer shoots and kills a fleeing suspect, and their only reason for shooting was because the suspect reached for their waistband as they ran, in how many such cases was a gun later found on the suspect's person? The answer to this question would tell me much about the validity of the waistband defense, and whether police officers should be using deadly force in response to that action when it is unknown if the suspect is armed, and where the foot pursuit is not part of an ongoing incident involving the use of a gun by the suspect.

I reviewed all fatal police shootings for the year 2017 (n = 986) to identify those that met two criteria. First, the suspect was shot and killed during a foot pursuit; and second, the suspect was found to be armed with a gun. Once those cases were identified, then an internet search was conducted to review available media accounts and press releases related to each case. The final step then was to identify from those sources which cases fell into category no. 2, as described above (where the officer had no foreknowledge of the gun, and thus made a correct decision regarding the threat based only on the suspect reaching for their waistband as they attempted to flee). A second part of the analysis included those cases where the officer shot and killed an unarmed suspect during a foot pursuit to identify the reasons the officer gave for using deadly force.

For 2017, I was able to locate seventy-nine cases that met the two criteria. Six of those cases were later found not to have involved a foot pursuit by the police. One case, which listed the victim as "unidentified," could not be located based on the date and department indicated. For the remaining seventy-two cases, the suspect's use of the firearm was categorized as follows:

- Thirty-three suspects fired at the officers during the foot pursuit.
- Nineteen pointed the gun but did not fire.

- Sixteen displayed the gun but did not point.
- Four did not display the gun but had used it in an ongoing
- felony incident.
- Zero neither displayed nor used the gun in an ongoing incident, but the suspect reached for their waistband during the foot pursuit.

Additionally, a total of thirteen cases were found where an unarmed suspect was shot and killed during a foot pursuit. In seven of those cases, including the case of Isaiah Murrietta, the officers reported firing after the suspect reached for their waistband or pocket. Four cases involved a physical struggle with the suspect during which the officers fired, while one case involved a suspect who had previously stated that he would kill any officer who tried to arrest him. Finally, there was one case where the officer reported the presence of a gun on the suspect's person; however, it was later disputed by a security video. No weapon was found, and the officer was criminally charged.

Not a single case was identified where the officer fired their weapon only in response to a suspect reaching for their waistband during a foot pursuit, and a gun was later found on the suspect's person. I concluded that by itself there is no correlation between a fleeing suspect reaching for their waistband and the presence of a gun. Stated another way, in those cases where an officer shot and killed a fleeing suspect for no other reasons than because they reached for their waistband, those officers were wrong 100% of the time. All were found to be unarmed.

Furthermore, when an officer shoots and kills an unarmed fleeing suspect, I found that it is likely the waistband defense will be invoked. For 2017, in 53.84% of the cases where an unarmed fleeing suspect was killed, the officers offered the waistband defense, or a variation of it, to justify their actions. If you remove the cases where a physical altercation occurred between the officer and suspect during the pursuit, that percentage increases to 77.77%. The bottom line is this: a fleeing suspect who is armed with a gun will almost certainly use it in some manner (shoot, point, display), and the officer who shoots and kills a fleeing suspect for no other stated reason than because the suspect reached for their waistband, as in the case of Isaiah Murrietta, will likely kill an unarmed person.

At the time Murrietta's vehicle was stopped by the surveillance team (he was a passenger), there was no warrant for his arrest. During their pre-operation briefing, the lead detective in the murder case, Detective Mark Yee, had advised them that they lacked sufficient probable cause at that point to arrest Murrietta for the murder committed by his brother. It was clear they were making only an investigative stop of the vehicle. This type of detention allows the police to detain only temporarily someone for questioning and limits their authority to put them in handcuffs or to conduct a search of their vehicle or person. In this case, it was questionable whether they even knew for certain that the vehicle's passenger was Isaiah Murrietta. Villalvazo later claimed that he did recognize the passenger to be one of the Murrietta brothers, someone he admitted to having had no previous contact with. Other officers gave statements that disputed Villalvazo's claim.

- Officer John DeLuca stated during his interview that Villalvazo drove by the house but was unable to identify Murrietta because his back was to him. He stated that he then did a drive-by but also was unable to make a positive identification.
- Sergeant John Hoagland, who also participated in the detail but was not part of the surveillance team, stated during his interview that one of the detectives who had eyes on the house, Detective Williams, advised him at the time that they could not say for certain that the individual getting in and out of the car was either Isaiah Murrietta or his brother.
- Detective Rick Williams later filed a report in which he admitted that they were unable to identify the individual as one of the Murrietta brothers. Interestingly, he stated that he did in fact direct Officer DeLuca to do a drive-by and that DeLuca was unable to make an identification. He says nothing in his report about Villalvazo doing a drive-by, nor does he say Villalvazo advised him at any point that he personally had made an identification.

The radio traffic leading up to the shooting confirms that no positive identification of Murrietta had been made by any of the officers, including Villalvazo. When the vehicle pulled away from the house, Williams pulled alongside it in the next lane of travel. He is heard broadcasting to the other team members, "Uh, a lookalike in the passenger seat and maybe in the back, uh, seat, so . . . two for sure, possibly three." Following this transmission, the vehicle stop was made one minute later, and two minutes after that, "Shots fired!" was called out. It is clear that Murrietta had not been positively identified prior to being shot. Villalvazo had thus made the decision to use deadly force—a decision he based in part on the fact that he viewed Murrietta as a dangerous homicide suspect—against someone who had not even been identified. The fact that it turned out to be Murrietta, though not the brother who had fired the weapon the day before, did not absolve Villalvazo of his duty to base such a decision on what was known at the time, especially when that decision was to knowingly shoot in the back a teenage suspect who had no weapon in his hand and was running away. Sadly, Villalvazo seemed to have put into practice an oft-repeated joke among cops—"Kill them all and let God sort them out!"

No piece of evidence in this case was more powerful than the video itself. I will typically watch case videos, whether from a body cam, dash cam, or security camera, many times before reaching my final conclusions. I clip them, re-color them, slow them down, zoom in on things, and even watch them in reverse. Often I do not spot or make sense of a critical piece of evidence until I have viewed the video many times and in many different ways. In this case, I needed to view it only once. There was no part of the video that was ambiguous or open to interpretation. It very simply and clearly showed Villalvazo aim his gun at an unarmed 16-year-old kid who was running away and fire, ending his life with a single shot to the back of his head. What I observed was not a case of a police officer who misread the situation or experienced some level of perceptual distortion in the stress of the moment. What I saw was nothing short of a cold-blooded killing by an experienced police officer, a killing that both Chief Jerry Dyer and the district attorney, each with a straight face and apparently a clear conscience, had called "justified." I was committed to do my part to not allow them to get away with it.

In the video, one thing that immediately caught my attention was that Murrietta's pants fell almost to his knees after climbing the fence, clearly exposing his red underwear. With his baseball cap held in his right hand, he used both hands to pull up his pants as he ran from the officers, one of whom was climbing the fence in pursuit. Villalvazo, who had pulled up to the spot in his police vehicle, made no effort to climb the fence but instead drew his firearm and braced it against the fence to fire. He had a clear view of Murrietta the entire time and could see that his pants had fallen, the pants he later told detectives he believed concealed a handgun in the waistband.

Villalvazo was interviewed by detectives the day after the shooting. There and in his later deposition he made a number of statements that were clearly disputed by the security video. The first statement involved the manner in which Murrietta looked back in his direction after crossing the fence. In his interview, Villalvazo described a single "look and reach" by Murrietta. This description changed in his deposition over two years later. He then stated that Murrietta had gotten "target lock" on him at the same time he reached for what he thought was a gun on his left side. He repeated his description of Murrietta's glance as "target lock" multiple times during the deposition.

In reality, neither of the descriptions provided by Villalvazo was consistent with the video evidence. There was nothing about Murrietta's actions that was even remotely consistent with "target lock," as that term is used in firearms training. Target lock refers to the various steps that a shooter takes prior to reaching the point of pulling the trigger. It includes capturing the target in your field of view, raising your weapon to a firing position, and then obtaining a proper sight picture of the target. When target lock is achieved, there is nothing left to do but to pull the trigger. It is absurd indeed to suggest that someone who was not even holding a weapon, and who glanced momentarily behind them, could somehow have achieved target lock. Furthermore, in both descriptions, Villalvazo described how Murrietta glanced back and reached for his waistband with his left hand simultaneously. This did not happen. At the moment

Murrietta glanced back toward Villalvazo, a glance that lasted less than a second, he was using both hands to lift up his pants. He then looked forward and took six more running steps before being shot and collapsing.

The second issue regarding Villalvazo's statements related to which of Murrietta's hands he perceived as threatening. In his initial interview he stated that Murrietta was grabbing at his right side the entire time he was running from his vehicle toward the school. In response to the question, "What were you thinking at that moment?" Villalvazo answered:

> Well, at that moment, you know, we were, um, in a chase of a homicide suspect. Uh, I knew that the homicide suspect had been in possession of a firearm prior to the murder. Uh, I believed he was carrying a firearm by his movements, uh, by the way he was running from the officers, what I had seen in the parking lot, that he was armed. Um, he wouldn't let go of that right side. He was kind of awkward too in that way, as you're holding your hip, um, and then when he ran to the daycare, uh, I was concerned for the daycare and the kids being inside as he went over, uh, and then him not, uh, complying with my commands to stop from the officers and to myself. Uh, I was in imminent danger at that time when he looked and reached that he was gonna fire and shoot at me.

Notwithstanding the fact that Villalvazo did not know for certain who he was even chasing, he stated that he based his decision to shoot primarily on Murrietta's movements with his right hand. The obvious problem is that just before the shooting, Murrietta reached back to hold his pants up with his left hand. In his deposition he was confronted on this point and gave the following answer:

> Because I lost sight of him from the time he went in front of the van to the bus and I don't know what he did in that transmission period when I picked him up again. So, for me it was probable and reasonable that he moved that gun to

the other side.

In an effort to correct the problem he created for himself, Villalvazo offered here his purported belief that in the few seconds during which he lost sight of Murrietta, for some unknown reason Murrietta decided to remove the fictitious gun from his pants only to place it in the other side of his waistband and continue running. While it may be commonplace for suspects to throw guns as they run from the police, it would be difficult indeed to find a case where Villalvazo's scenario had actually happened. The absurdity of his statement did not surprise me. It is commonplace that as time passes, the officer involved in a questionable shooting will adjust and change their narrative as they are confronted with new questions. Villalvazo was struggling to make the waistband defense work. When he realized that in his initial statement he had described the wrong hand reaching, he had to find a way to get the gun from Murrietta's right side to his left. As expected, he then added a "just-in-case" defense.

During his deposition, Villalvazo testified that shooting Murrietta was necessary to protect the kids at the daycare (the school), as well as people in the neighborhood. This seemed a stretch given that Villalvazo did not have a positive identification of the person he was chasing. Further, at no time during the traffic stop and foot pursuit did anyone call out on the radio that a gun had been spotted on Murrietta's person. At the time of the shooting there were no children outside the building, something Villalvazo admitted to knowing. If anyone put the children at the school at risk, it was Villalvazo. When I eventually visited the shooting scene, I was able to determine his line of sight when the shot was taken. I found that from the spot where he had braced his hands against the fence, which I was able to determine from the video, to where Murrietta was shot and collapsed, ends directly in the middle of one of the school's windows. Had he missed the shot, there is a high probability that the bullet would have entered the school. Also, Murrietta really had nowhere to go. To enter the neighborhood, he would have needed to scale a concrete block fence even higher than the metal fence he climbed over to enter the schoolyard. Given the number of officers involved in the pursuit, there was essentially no possibility of Murrietta climbing that fence and escaping into the neighborhood. He was perfectly contained.

An investigation of the matter was conducted by the Internal Affairs Bureau of the Fresno Police Department, and a final report was forwarded to Chief Jerry Dyer on November 30, 2017. There was one crucial fact that was absent from the report, and that was the distance between Murrietta and Villalvazo at the time of the shooting. I was able to determine the distance to be approximately 30 feet. The distance is important in a police officer's decision to use deadly force. Almost all police departments in the United States train their officers at 9, 15, 21, 30, and 45 feet. Some will include minimal shooting at 75 feet. The majority of qualification rounds are fired from less than 10 feet because most police shootings occur within that range. All police officers know that the accuracy of a handgun becomes increasingly less with distance, and that at 30 feet, an untrained shooter will likely be unable to even hit their target. To do so while running with your back turned is impossible. This should have been an important consideration in Villalvazo's decision to shoot. The distance is never even mentioned in the investigative materials.

After completing my report, I submitted it to Stuart Chandler with the following conclusions:

- At the time of the shooting, Murrietta had not been positively identified by any of the officers, including Villalvazo. Although he testified that he did at least identify Murrietta as one of the Murrietta brothers, notwithstanding the fact that such an identification falls short of a positive one, the evidence disputed that Villalvazo made any identification at all.
- At the time of the shooting, there was no outstanding arrest warrant for Murrietta, and no probable cause sufficient for an arrest. The officers' plan was to effect an investigative stop and detention, and possibly a probation hold, for the purpose of questioning Murrietta, and to secure a better picture to be used with witnesses from the day before. The officers knew that Murrietta was on probation only for a misdemeanor offense. The officers knew that Isaiah Murrietta had not fired the gun the day before and that it was his older brother, Isra-

el, who had fired it at the moving vehicle.

- Prior to the Villalvazo shooting, Murrietta had demonstrated no behaviors consistent with being armed with a gun, and no other officers reported seeing a gun as he ran. While Villalvazo later attempted to color Murrietta's actions by referring to his momentary glance as "target lock," there was absolutely nothing about his glance that is even remotely consistent with that terminology. Furthermore, Villalvazo attempted to reconcile the problem of which hand Murrietta was clutching his waistband with by offering a bizarre theory that in the 2–3 seconds he lost sight of him behind a bus, Murrietta had made the decision to pull the gun from his right waistband and for some unexplainable reason transfer it to his left waistband. It is important to note that other officers in the foot pursuit never lost sight of Murrietta, even when he passed behind the bus. None of them warned via their radio that he was armed, something they surely would have seen had Murrietta switched the gun to the other side of his waistband.

There is a danger that comes with every case for a plaintiff's expert, especially those with pure intentions who are fighting to level the playing field and improve things. It is the danger of simply giving up and quitting. When I first watched the video of Murrietta being shot, I was as stunned as I was when I watched Anthony Soderberg get shot by nearly every member of an LAPD SWAT team while he crawled unarmed on his hands and knees. In the case of Murrietta, it sickened me to hear Chief Jerry Dyer and District Attorney Lisa Smithcamp call it a justified shooting. I wondered how any intelligent person could possibly watch the video and call it that. The fix was in. There was literally no chance that Villalvazo would be criminally charged or even disciplined. Unfortunately, Isaiah Murrietta, a 16-year-old kid who had not even fired the gun the day before, had no intrinsic value when weighed against a veteran officer's career and pension. The thought occurred to me that had the incident not been captured on videotape, Murrietta would have quickly been forgotten by everyone, including the local press.

I nearly quit providing expert witness services after this case. I wondered if I was having any impact at all. I did not necessarily wish to see police officers sent to prison, but I knew nothing would change, especially in cities like Fresno, until a few were. I knew they would eventually settle the Murrietta case. I also knew the city would condescendingly say that while they did not believe Villalvazo did anything wrong, they felt it best for the taxpayers to settle the matter to avoid a costly trial. It is all so predictable. In the end they did settle the matter in April 2021 for $4.9 million. Israel Murrietta went to prison for the murder the day before his brother was killed. And Ray Villalvazo simply went back to work. As for me, I decided not to quit just yet. Instead, I deleted the case file from my computer as I typically do once a case is completed and moved on to the next one.

Every now and then I go back and watch the video of Isaiah Murrietta being shot. It is easily found now on YouTube.com where it will undoubtedly reside for many years to come. Some of the best cops I have known were troubled teenagers. A few even had juvenile arrest records sealed or expunged prior to seeking employment as a police officer. Ultimately, it may have been one of the things that made them good cops. I have thought about Isaiah Murrietta often since working the case. I have even wondered if perhaps he too might have become a police officer someday. Even troubled 16-year-olds have dreams and aspirations. He may very well have been a good one.

- CHAPTER 12-

The Case of
Drew Edwards

Maquoketa, Iowa

Excited Delirium: A Popular Excuse with Deadly Consequences

I never met Drew Edwards, but I knew him well. Every small town has their own version of Drew. He is that one guy in town who is a constant thorn in the side of the police when intoxicated or doing drugs, but then can be a perfect gentleman when sober. Always one step from homelessness, he typically has a long rap sheet, beginning as a juvenile, of mostly misdemeanor offenses such as driving under the influence, public intoxication, and minor drug offenses. The police dread arresting him because they know he will be intoxicated and will resist every time, typically without attacking the officers trying to arrest him. In the small town of Maquoketa, Iowa, 22-year-old Drew Edwards was definitely that person.

On the morning of June 15, 2019, Officer Mike Owen of the Maquoketa Police Department (MPD) and Chief Deputy Steve Schroeder of the Jackson County Sheriff's Department were dispatched to a domestic disturbance. Owen found three people standing in the front of the apartment building with personal belongings strewn about the yard. The three individuals were Drew Edwards, his nephew, and the nephew's girlfriend. There was no physical altercation taking place when Owens arrived, with Schroeder arriving immediately after Owens. The nephew told Owen that Drew had moved in with them the day before, and that after going fishing the night before, arrived back at the apartment under the influence of some type of drug. A fight ensued and Drew was told to leave with his belongings.

Following some limited discussion with the nephew, Owen made the decision to arrest Drew for misdemeanor assault. The exchange was captured on Owen's body cam. Drew remained calm but refused to get on the ground. It was obvious Owen had been through the routine with Drew before. He became immediately stressed and his voice raised. Owen can be seen on the video drawing and pointing his Taser and yelling, "Drew, you do this every time! Now get on the ground!" Drew remained calm and continued gathering his belongings and saying he did not do anything. The more he ignored Owen's commands, the louder Owen's voice became. At the same time, Schroeder positioned himself to apply the handcuffs.

After a few minutes of back-and-forth, Owen deployed his Taser without warning and struck Drew in his abdomen area. Drew immediately went to the ground and yelled in pain, but then got back to his feet and ran with Owen and Schroeder in pursuit. Owen continued to pull the trigger on his Taser and deployed a second set of darts to Drew's back. Drew again went to the ground, now half a block away from the apartment. Once he was on the ground, the two officers held him down and attempted to handcuff Drew but were able to get only one wrist secured. Drew struggled and yelled at the top of his lungs. They were barely able to hold him down. Drew was now demonstrating the obvious signs of excited delirium—excessive strength, irrational speech, extreme agitation. The officers held Drew to the ground, including by applying their weight to his head, until help arrived. While they did, Owen continued to deploy his Taser. Eventually Assistant Chief Brendan Zeimet arrived to assist. Once they got the second handcuff secured, they rolled Edwards over and found that he was unresponsive and aspirating. He was later pronounced dead.

I was contacted to review the case by Cedar Rapids attorney

Dave O'Brien, an experienced civil rights attorney with whom I would eventually work numerous cases. Dave sent me the body cam video as well as the data report from Owen's Taser (Schroeder did not fire his Taser). He had a serious concern, and rightly so, about Owen's overuse of the weapon, especially given that Drew had a known heart condition, which was discovered and known to the police following his hospitalization after a previous Taser incident. I found the body cam video shocking but unfortunately not unusual. What I found more egregious than the use of the Taser was the way they held Drew to the ground for a significant period of time before Zeimet arrived to help. I advised Dave that the Taser use by Owen was certainly a problem, but that in my opinion the bigger issue was how they restrained him. I viewed it as an asphyxiation case more than an excessive Taser use case. Dave agreed and sent me a retainer agreement to work the case.

There is no accepted medical or psychiatric diagnosis called excited delirium. The symptoms it describes, however, are very real. It is a panicked response by the person being restrained, a response that is associated with both drug use and mental illness, and when it occurs, the possibility of sudden death is greatly increased. The person experiencing excited delirium simply cannot stop resisting and will demonstrate bizarre, paranoid, and even violent behaviors. A deadly cycle occurs where the more the suspect resists, the more weight and pressure the officers will apply to their body, which in turn only increases the suspect's resistance. A number of physiological changes will take place if the struggle is not stopped, and the suspect taken out of a prone position. Changes will include an increase in body temperature, an intense activation of the sympathetic nervous system, and arrhythmia of the heart.

The law enforcement community is well aware of this potential outcome, and all officers receive training to recognize it when it is happening and to respond properly. First, and regardless of the reason for the arrest, it is to be treated as a medical emergency. EMS personnel are to be immediately dispatched to the scene. And second, officers are trained to get the individual restrained quickly, and if they are unable to, then to stop what they are doing, relieve the pressure on the suspect's body, and allow them to sit up or roll to their side while they attempt to calm and de-escalate them. Simply maintaining their weight and pressure on the suspect until more help arrives is unacceptable. In addition to the risk of sudden heart failure, the risk of asphyxiation is greatly increased. The purpose of police training on this issue is to prevent that deadly outcome from occurring.

Police officers are so often incapable of backing down once their efforts to restrain a suspect have begun. The training provided to law enforcement on how to respond to a case of excited delirium seems to have had limited effect. When the "pile on" begins, more often than not, the officers will escalate their level of force until the handcuffs are applied. It is not uncommon to see Tasers, OC pepper spray, expandable batons, and even closed fist strikes used—the police like to call these "distraction" blows—in addition to applying their weight to the suspect's back, neck, and head. Not only will they ignore the signs and symptoms of excited delirium, but in cases where the suspect dies during the effort to restrain them, then it is common for the police to actually place blame for the death on the very thing they ignored in the first place. It is not unusual to read police reports where the officers involved admit to recognizing the excited delirium, but then make the case that they struggled so aggressively to get the suspect detained in order to keep them from dying from the effects of the excited delirium. It is as if excited delirium has the ability to kill independent of its cause, which of course is an absurd proposition.

I began my review of the matter with the autopsy report. The autopsy was completed on June 18, 2019, by Dr. Kelly Kruse of the Iowa Office of the State Medical Examiner. The cause of death was determined to be "sudden cardiac arrest during restraint in the setting of acute drug (methamphetamine) intoxication." Given what I saw on Owen's body cam video, it did not appear to me that Dr. Kruse was given correct information by the Iowa Department of Criminal Investigation regarding the use of the Taser. This information would have been important given the number of times the Taser was deployed. The combination of a Taser and the effect excited delirium has on a person's heart creates a perfect storm for sudden death. Dr. Kruse's narrative indicated far less Taser use than what actually happened. It did not surprise me. After reviewing the Taser data report that Dave O'Brien provided, which had been given to him by one of the DCI investigators, I quickly realized that it did not match what I could clearly see and hear on the body cam video. Dave had been given a bogus report that showed a lot less Taser use.

While Dave worked on getting the correct report for the correct Taser, I continued my review of the case and switched to Drew's arrest. The appropriateness of his arrest was an important question because if the arrest were unlawful, then all force used by the officers except that amount necessary to protect themselves or others was unavoidably excessive. The officers made a probable cause arrest for assault. Probable cause, as all police officers know, requires some amount of evidence. Mere suspicion is insufficient to meet that burden of proof. At the time of the arrest, the following information should have been pertinent to their decision:

- Drew was the complainant's uncle; however they considered themselves brothers. This relationship was known to Officer Owen, as demonstrated by his comments overheard on the body cam video when he was attempting to convince the nephew to file a complaint: "I get where you're at, he's your brother, whatever . . ."
- Part of the nephew's complaint was that Drew had forced himself into the apartment. However, he also admitted that Drew was living at the apartment and had brought his belongings there the day before the incident.
- Both Edwards and the nephew appeared to have signs of a physical altercation. Owen acknowledged that Drew had blood on him. There was no clear description of this altercation provided by either individual.
- When Owen arrived at the scene, both individuals were outside on the sidewalk and noncombative.
- Both individuals had just gotten out of jail.
- Neither Owen nor Schroeder inspected the apartment prior to deciding to arrest Drew to confirm the nephew's story or to look for evidence that a crime had been committed.
- At least twice during the nephew's exchange with Owen, he

stated his desire only to have Drew removed from the scene. On the body cam video, the nephew is heard saying, "just get him the fuck out of here," a comment he repeated a few minutes later. During this time, Owen repeatedly made comments obviously intended to convince the nephew to sign a complaint. Owen is heard saying, "It's your call. Personally, I'd rather see the fucker go back to jail."

- The policies of the Maquoketa Police Department allow its officers to issue a citation to a misdemeanor offender without making a custodial arrest. In this case, not only did both officers personally know Drew, a consideration in making this decision, but he was also calm and noncombative in his exchange with the officers.

There were two questions related to Drew's arrest. First, did the officers have sufficient probable cause for an arrest? And second, was a custodial arrest the proper course of action to follow? To the first question, my conclusion was no. The officers had not properly investigated the complaint prior to their decision to make a custodial arrest. They had not inspected the apartment; they had not been provided an actual description of the physical altercation by the nephew or his girlfriend; they had not asked Drew for his side of the story; and they had not fully inspected either Drew or the nephew for injuries or wounds.

In terms of accepted police training and practices, the officers had cause only to conduct an investigation, and even to detain Drew while doing so, but they did not yet have probable cause for an arrest. Officers are trained that when detaining an individual pursuant to an investigation, the person cannot be handcuffed unless there is a reasonable suspicion that the individual is armed or is preparing to run. Fear alone is not sufficient. During the exchange between Drew and the officers, there was no indication at all that he was either armed or intending to run. He was calm and noncombative, and he appeared to be preoccupied with collecting his belongings from the ground. No explanation was given by the nephew or his girlfriend as to how Drew's belongings had gotten strewn across the yard. The nephew could be heard on the video denying that he or his girlfriend scattered the belongings, and Owen failed to follow up with any questions to get to the truth of that particular matter.

I next shifted my focus to the use of the Taser by Officer Owen. As discussed elsewhere in this book, the Taser is a weapon of intermediate force that is used by the police for self-defense and defense of others. It is designated as an intermediate force weapon due to the risk of injury it poses. It is not to be used merely to force compliance. The weapon is uncomplicated. When the trigger is pulled, a gas cartridge propels two darts outwards as much as 25 feet. At the same time, the weapon's battery pack sends an electrical charge to the end of the weapon. If the darts hit their target and complete a circuit, meaning there is a path of conductivity between them, then the charge will leave the weapon and travel down the wires to the darts. The Taser delivers as much as 50,000 volts of electrical charge; however, because the amperage is so low, it is designed to avoid any lasting damage to tissue. The Taser is effective when there is sufficient spread between the probes to have its effect on a large muscle mass. When that happens, neuromuscular incapacitation (NMI) is achieved and the person contracts uncontrollably. If the probe spread is minimal, NMI will not be successful. The Taser can also be used in "drive stun" mode by simply pressing the end of the weapon into the suspect's body and pulling the trigger or the "arc" button on the side of the weapon. Because the electrodes at the end of the weapon are only a few inches apart, there is little chance of achieving NMI. Police officers are instructed to use caution when using a Taser in drive stun mode because it will not incapacitate the subject and they will immediately repel away from it. There is no failsafe mechanism that prevents an officer from delivering too much of a charge to a suspect through repeated trigger pulls. The charge will continue until the battery is depleted.

The Taser model used by Owen was the Axon X2. At the time, it was a newer model Taser that includes a cartridge with two sets of probes. It is designed to provide the officer a second set of probes if the first set misses their mark. In this case, Owen deployed both sets of probes. Like all Tasers, before an officer can carry the X2 on duty, he or she must complete training. This training is provided by the Axon Corporation using police officers who are certified by them to provide such training.

Once Dave O'Brien was able to secure the correct data report for Owen's Taser—no explanation was given for why an incorrect report was provided initially—I was able to determine that Owen delivered a total of fifty-five seconds of electrical charge to Drew. Neuromuscular incapacitation was not achieved by the Taser deployments. However, Drew's reaction throughout the encounter indicated that he was receiving painful shocks, most of them while he was on the ground with the two officers on top of him attempting to apply the handcuffs. And while Drew continued to fiercely resist, at no time did he attempt to attack or strike Owen and Schroeder.

I had already concluded that because the officers lacked probable cause to arrest Drew, and because he had demonstrated no threat toward them, the use of the Taser by Owen was excessive and inappropriate. But so too was the amount of electrical charge Owen delivered during the struggle. Since 2011, the principles guiding the law enforcement community's use of Tasers have been those established jointly by the U.S. Department of Justice (DOJ) and the Police Executive Research Forum (PERF). Regarding the level of threat necessary to deploy a Taser, the guidelines state the following:

- Electronic control weapons (ECWs) should only be used against subjects who are exhibiting active aggression or who are actively resisting in a manner that, in the officer's judgment, is likely to result in injuries to themselves or others. ECWs should not be used against a passive subject (guideline no. 25).
- Fleeing should not be the sole justification for using an ECW against a subject. Personnel should consider the severity of the offense, the subject's threat level to others, and the risk of serious injury to the subject before deciding to use an ECW on a fleeing subject (guideline no. 26).

Clearly, Drew was only passively resisting by refusing to get on the ground initially. All police training identifies this behavior as passive resistance when there is no active or implied threat to the officers. Drew was not being combative, nor was he even threatening to be. He was not even challenging the officers with his actions.

Notwithstanding the issue of probable cause, by the standards identified above, it was not appropriate for Owen to deploy his Taser when he did. Furthermore, when Owen deployed his second cartridge, Edwards was running away. He still had not actively resisted nor demonstrated any threat toward the officers or anyone else. The second cartridge deployment, like the first, violated these standards.

The second issue relating to the Taser, notwithstanding the fact that the arrest may have been unlawful to begin with, is the duration of Owen's multiple deployments. The same DOJ/PERF guidelines state that officers should use an ECW for only one standard cycle (five seconds) and then evaluate the situation to determine if subsequent cycles are necessary. They go on to state that officers should consider that exposure to the ECW for longer than fifteen seconds (whether due to multiple applications or continuous cycling) may increase the risk of death or serious injury and that any subsequent applications should be independently justifiable.

The MPD's own policies and procedures mandate that any individual who receives more than fifteen seconds of Taser charge be transported to a hospital for medical evaluation regardless of their outward condition. The MPD policies also mandate that if the first Taser cycle is ineffective, the officer should consider certain factors before applying additional charges. One of those factors is whether the need to control the individual outweighs the potential danger of multiple Taser deployments.

It is important to note that Officer Owen was well aware of what was going to happen when he deployed the Taser. On his body cam video, before deploying his Taser, he can be heard telling Schroeder, "You can Tase him a hundred times and it doesn't fucking stop him." And then, just before the officers approached Drew to place him under arrest, Owen is heard asking Schroeder, "It's gonna be a fight . . . you ready?" Both officers had a history with Drew, and both knew that Tasing him was not going to accomplish the goal of getting him under physical control. Drew had no history of actively resisting arrest. His history was entirely consistent with what he did in this case—freeze up and refuse to cooperate without being combative toward the officers.

Even if there had been probable cause to arrest Drew, the officers had the ability to issue a citation without making a custodial arrest. Given that they knew they would likely not be able to physically subdue Drew by themselves and that the Taser would only cause him to resist, they clearly had a compelling reason—Edwards's safety as well as their own—to avoid a physical confrontation. This was especially true given that Drew was accused only of a minor offense by his own nephew. I determined that the MPD policies allowed for the issuance of a citation for this very reason and others.

One additional consideration in evaluating Owen's decision to use his Taser was the fact that the officers chose not to call for additional officers to assist. Notwithstanding the problems noted with arresting Drew without first completing a proper investigation, the fact is, they had plenty of time to call for help. The officers were at the scene for twenty-eight minutes before Owen deployed his Taser. As in all such cases, less manpower means more force will likely be used against the individual being arrested. Even when Drew ran after the first Taser deployment, neither officer requested assistance. It was almost two minutes into the struggle before Owen finally requested it. It is clear from the body cam video that Owen's deployment of the Taser was motivated more by his impatience and anger toward Drew than by proper tactical judgment.

Once the two officers had Drew on the ground, they attempted to handcuff him. During this process, Drew's left ulna (wrist bone) was fractured. This likely occurred when Schroeder jerked hard on his left wrist to get it behind his back after one handcuff had already been applied. The manner in which he did it, using the handcuffs as leverage to force his arm backwards, is well known in law enforcement as a technique capable of snapping wrist bones. Police officers are trained to be cognizant of this danger when handcuffing a suspect. Also, police officers are trained to know that an individual being Tased may have difficulty submitting to being handcuffed due to the effects of the Taser, even when full NMI is not achieved. Schroeder did not appear to consider this when performing the action that likely caused the broken wrist. It was inappropriate to continue to force his arm behind his back by the single handcuff at the same time Owen was repeatedly deploying the Taser. The two actions were counterproductive.

In the video, Owen can be seen placing his right knee on Drew's head and neck. Shortly after, and after the sixth pull of the Taser's trigger by Owen, Drew's breathing became noticeably labored and continued to get worse from that point. It is clear from the sound of his muffled voice that his face was being forced into the ground. I was able to corroborate this later in the video with an indentation in the ground where his face was pressed against it. A few minutes later, Assistant Chief Zeimet arrived and immediately placed his right knee on Drew's shoulder. His entire body was now pinned to the ground, and Owen had now pulled the trigger on his Taser nine times. There is a point in the video when it is obvious that Drew has become unresponsive with sporadic breathing. Owen is even heard saying, "Drew, take some breaths. Relax man, relax." Owen finally removed his knee, and the officers rolled Drew over onto his side almost four minutes after the handcuffs were both applied. By then, Drew's complexion was blue and there was mucus coming out of his mouth.

Owen kept his knee(s) on Drew's head and neck for over twelve minutes. This is a violation of police training and accepted standards of practice. All police officers are trained to know the dangers of positional or compressional asphyxia. Additionally, officers are trained to be aware of the risk of sudden death when using a Taser in combination with physical restraint, especially when the signs of excited delirium are present. In the above-discussed DOJ/PERF standards, which have guided all Taser training since 2011, there is a guideline that states, "Personnel should be aware that there is a higher risk of sudden death in subjects under the influence of drugs and/or exhibiting symptoms associated with excited delirium." By the time the officers rolled Drew over he was unconscious and aspirating. He died a short time later.

Officer Owen made the decision to arrest Drew without first completing even a minimal investigation to determine if probable cause existed for the arrest. Chief Deputy Schroeder inappropriately went along with that decision. They never first inspected the apartment, the condition of which turned out to be inconsistent with the nephew's account of what happened. They never waited for the nephew to complete a written statement, nor did they even obtain a true verbal description of what had happened. The nephew was vague in his description, as was his girlfriend. He also provided no account of how Drew's belongings became strewn across the front yard, nor did Owen bother to ask.

Owen and Schroeder's haste in deciding to arrest Drew seemed motivated more by their past history with Drew than by the current situation. It was clear that the nephew did not wish to pursue charges until Owen essentially convinced him to do so. After the nephew decided that he just wanted Drew removed from the premises without charges, it was Owen who is overheard on his body cam video saying he would rather see Drew go back to jail. It was enough to convince the nephew to agree to file a complaint. Notwithstanding the question of probable cause, Owen and Schroeder had three options: a custodial arrest; the issuance of a citation without taking Drew to jail; or to simply remove Drew from the premises and seek a misdemeanor arrest warrant after a proper investigation. They unnecessarily chose the most dangerous option and recklessly put themselves and Drew at risk of personal injury. The combination of Drew's drug use, the multiple deployments of the Taser, the extended period of physical restraint—including Owen applying his weight to Drew's head and neck—and the failure to timely provide first aid after getting the handcuffs locked in place, all created a perfect storm for Drew's sudden death, an outcome made even more likely by his history of heart problems. Sadly, it was an outcome that was avoidable and unnecessary.

Typically, once I submit a completed use-of-force analysis and report to the attorney who hired me, who in turn submits it to the court, I next prepare for the fight to come. There will be motions to disqualify me as an expert, attempts to discredit me in the press, opposing pro-police experts writing rebuttal reports alleging I have no clue what I am doing, and depositions that often devolve into shouting matches laced with insults by the opposing attorneys. The fight is expected when you do battle against the deadly force industry. The trick is to not allow yourself to be intimidated and to remain mindful of the fact that the most powerful weapon in the fight is the truth.

In the case of Drew Edwards, the truth prevailed. In fact, there was no fight, not even a deposition. After submitting the report to Dave O'Brien, he took the fight to the City of Maquoketa and their attorneys by releasing the report to the media for the public to see. And then Owen's body cam video was released. While the public often misinterprets what they see on such a video, especially with a lack of understanding of the laws governing the use of force, now they were able to watch the video with my report in hand to help them understand what they were seeing. They were able to see why the arrest was unlawful, how the Taser was overused, and how easy it is to asphyxiate an individual even when they appear to be breathing. And they were able to see the tragic and painful reality of excited delirium play out in front of them. Most of all, they were able to see that in Drew's case it was all avoidable and that the presence of excited delirium in no way relieved the officers of their duty to protect and preserve life. Rather, it demanded it.

Eventually, the case settled for $4.5 million. It was the largest settlement I personally had ever seen involving a small-town police department. As expected, Owen, Schroeder, and Zeimet were all cleared of any wrongdoing by the local prosecutor. There is no disputing the fact that Drew was anything but an upstanding and productive member of society, but he was much too young to devalue his worth completely. I took a special interest in his case, I think because of my years as a deputy sheriff in a small rural county not far from Maquoketa, Iowa, and because I had spent those years dealing with my own Drew Edwards from time to time. In fact, I had a number of them over the years in the small towns around the county. I have no idea what happened to most of them, but some I still see from time to time sitting at a high school football or baseball game watching their grandkids play. They are as far removed from the days of running from the police as I am from chasing after them. A few have even thanked me for changing their lives with a small gesture I had long forgotten about. I am constantly reminded by such encounters that the most powerful and effective weapon in a police officer's arsenal is not to be found hanging from their duty belt. It is the instinct to show a little compassion and tolerance when they are needed most, even when that need is not readily apparent in the actions of the suspect.

- CHAPTER 13 -

The Case of Jorge Ramirez

Bakersfield, California

Contagious Fire: When One Shoots, They All Shoot

Have you ever found yourself standing on a street corner waiting patiently for the light to change, and then without giving it a conscious thought follow someone else into the intersection to cross? How many times has someone who would never dream of committing a crime found themselves in the back of a police paddy wagon after breaking windows and setting cars ablaze following a Super Bowl game? In a recent and well-publicized matter, law-abiding citizens who traveled to Washington, D.C., to participate in peaceful demonstrations suddenly found themselves climbing through the broken windows of the U.S. Capitol and creating havoc. And finally, how many times have we watched the violent conclusion of a police chase when a single officer fires their weapon and sets off a chain reaction of police gunfire?

The phenomenon of psychological "contagion" is not new. It has been studied for decades and is well understood. In law enforcement, it occurs when an officer bypasses their training and rational decision making and simply fires their weapon because someone else does. It is not a conscious decision on the part of the officers who succumb to its effect. Some psychologists argue that it is a behavioral mechanism that has evolved in humans for self-protection, a mechanism that compels us to seek safety by following the group rather than acting as an individual. The law enforcement community dislikes the term contagious fire because it implies that an officer may use deadly force without properly evaluating the threat as required by their training, their department policy, and the law. They prefer to use the term synchronous fire. But the fact is, law enforcement trainers endeavor to train the possibility of this phenomenon occurring out of their officers. They do this through repetitive and lifelike training designed to reduce the level of stress an officer may experience in a deadly force encounter. With less stress, the officer's ability to think rationally and maintain a strong presence of mind is increased and the possibility of contagious fire is decreased or eliminated.

The phenomenon of contagious fire was on full display on the night of September 15, 2013, when officers from the Bakersfield Police Department, consistently ranked as one of the deadliest departments in America for police shootings, attempted to serve a high-risk arrest warrant on 32-year-old Justin Harger, an individual known to be violent and wanted for a recent shooting. The officers were being led to Harger by 34-year-old Jorge Ramirez, a confidential informant who had recently been arrested on a drug charge. Ramirez had been in trouble before for various nonviolent offenses and had been in and out of rehab. His family later stated to the press that he was finally making a serious effort to get his life in order, and this contributed to his decision to assist the police. With charges hanging over his head, Ramirez began working with Detectives Lerry Esparza and Patrick Mara. It was and continues to be a common tactic in law enforcement: allowing an arrestee to "work off" the charges by acting as a confidential informant. It is a tactic, however, that is fraught with potential problems.

On the day of the shooting, Ramirez notified Detective Esparza that he would be with Harger that evening. The information was passed on by Esparza to Sergeant Eric Lantz, who assigned a team of officers to help serve the warrant. At around midnight and after having missed Harger at two other locations, a vehicle driven by Harger, with Ramirez occupying the passenger seat, pulled into the parking lot of the Four Points Sheraton Hotel at 5101 California Avenue in Bakersfield. On information provided by Ramirez, the officers were parked in positions around and near the hotel. As Harger pulled in—he was driving a vehicle different from the information they had received—a single squad car occupied by Officers Daniel Brewer and Rick Wimbish followed and came to a stop behind Harger when he pulled into the parking spot. In the chaotic minutes that followed, Harger exited his vehicle and fired a gun at the officers. Both returned fire. Officer Brewer was struck once and received a grazing wound to the side of his head. Hearing the shots, the other officers quickly arrived on the scene. A total of sixty shots were fired by the officers. Harger fired three times before his gun jammed and became inoperable. When it was over, both Harger and Ramirez were shot multiple times and pronounced dead at the scene. The police had killed their own informant.

I was first contacted about the case by Attorney Alex Alercon from the Geragos law firm in Los Angeles. He was well into the case by the time he contacted me, and time was running short to get an expert report drafted and submitted to the court. I had no concerns about the officers using deadly force against Harger. After all, he had fired at Brewer and Wimbish first. My focus was on Ramirez, and on trying to understand how the police could possibly shoot and kill their own informant. When I looked at his autopsy report, it was immediately apparent to me that he had not been killed accidentally. In fact, he was shot ten times in nearly every part of his body, including a straight-on shot to his face. It had the appearance of a coup-de-grace type shot. I noticed that Harger suffered a similar wound. I advised Alex that I would work the case and immediately began digging into the evidence. The case was already scheduled for trial, so I had to work quickly.

My first task was to figure out who fired their weapons and how many times. A total of sixty shots were fired by five officers. Of those shots, fifty-nine of the empty casings were recovered by investigators and documented. The number of shots fired by each officer was determined by detectives who personally inspected the officers' weapons and spare magazines immediately after the shooting. It was determined that Wimbish and Brewer each fired fifteen times. Officer Chad Garrett fired twice. Officer Ryan Vaughn fired his weapon once. And Officer Jess Beagley fired a total of twenty-seven times, which required him to reload once and continue firing. Two other officers who were present did not fire their weapons.

Officers Wimbish and Garrett were not unknown to me. They were involved in another shooting I had worked in Bakersfield involving a young man named Jason Alderman who broke through the glass door of a Subway sandwich shop late one night with a car jack and looked for money in the register and tip jar. Alderman was very intoxicated and ended up leaving a few minutes later without taking anything. Unfortunately for him, Garrett and Wimbish were waiting outside, and as he bent over to exit through the same broken glass door, Garrett fired multiple times from just a few feet away and killed him instantly. He was cleared of wrongdoing after telling investigators that he thought the car jack was an AK 47 assault rifle. It seemed a bit absurd that an experienced police officer could possibly mistake a car jack for an assault rifle from just a few feet away. In that case, the perceptual distortion tactic was used very effectively, and Garrett was cleared of any wrongdoing, notwithstanding the fact that the city settled the civil case a year later.

After plotting the empty casings, I next reviewed the officers' statements to investigators to determine if their accounts were consistent with the locations of the casings. I specifically focused on what they had to say about Ramirez's location and movement during the encounter. There was only one consistent thing about their statements, and that is none of them admitted to seeing anything related to Ramirez. Only Beagley, the one officer who admitted to actually shooting Ramirez, had anything to say about his movements and location. For the other seven officers, it was as if Ramirez had either disappeared or become invisible. Even Beagley's account was inconsistent with the physical evidence. It was obvious to me that the officers were making a concerted effort to avoid sharing any specific details regarding Ramirez, something they were quite willing to do with regard to Harger.

The first two officers to see and have contact with Ramirez were Wimbish and Brewer, both of whom were only a few feet away from

Ramirez when he exited the passenger side of the vehicle. Wimbish stated that as they were approaching Ramirez, Harger exited the vehicle, walked to the rear, and then fired two shots in their direction. Wimbish stated that he never saw Ramirez again. We know Ramirez had not retreated to the front of the vehicle because Wimbish described in detail taking a prone position behind his squad car and seeing Harger moving around at the front of his vehicle as he and Brewer returned fire. He said nothing about Ramirez and admitted to finally seeing Ramirez lying on the ground only after the shooting had ceased. Throughout the shooting incident, Wimbish would have had an unobstructed view of the location where Ramirez collapsed.

Brewer's statement was similar to Wimbish's. He too was within a few feet of Ramirez after Ramirez exited the passenger side of Harger's vehicle. Like Wimbish, he stated that once Harger fired his weapon, he never saw Ramirez again. Although Brewer had been injured, he was able to fire his weapon fifteen times and was in a position the entire time that would have provided a clear view of the location where Ramirez fell. For these two officers, Ramirez seemed to have simply vanished.

Garrett and Vaughn approached the shooting scene from the southwest corner of the building. Their statements were consistent that as they took cover behind a vehicle in the parking lot, Harger was still firing his weapon. And while both officers had a clear view from the south of Harger's vehicle, even being able to see Harger as he took cover in front of the vehicle, neither admitted to initially seeing Ramirez lying in plain view directly in front of them. Both stated that after firing their weapons at Harger, they did notice Ramirez on the pavement. They were also consistent that when they and Beagley moved forward to approach the vehicle, they (Garrett and Vaughn) moved toward Ramirez to secure him in handcuffs while Beagley moved toward Harger. Neither of the officers admitted to shooting Ramirez or having any knowledge of who did.

Sergeant Lantz was the third squad car in line behind Wimbish and Brewer and a second two-man unit occupied by Beagley and Officer John Otterness. Strangely, Lantz never mentioned Ramirez in his account of the incident. He never admitted to even seeing Ramirez during the shooting, nor having knowledge of who shot him. Otterness also denied seeing Ramirez throughout the encounter. He also denied even seeing Harger. He described a chaotic scene where shots were being fired in his direction, yet he said nothing about trying to ascertain how many people were in the vehicle and where they were. And like the others, he stated that he had no knowledge about who shot Ramirez, and that he never saw Ramirez on the ground until after the shooting had ceased and he approached the front of Harger's vehicle.

Only Officer Beagley admitted to seeing Ramirez once the shooting began and was the only officer who admitted to actually shooting Ramirez. But his account veered dramatically from parts of the other officers' statements that were consistent. Beagley stated that he first saw Ramirez during the shooting when Ramirez, unknown to him at that time, walked out from the front of Harger's vehicle and "advanced" on his location in front of Wimbish's squad car. Beagley stated that as Ramirez walked toward him, he reached toward his rear waistband. He stated that Ramirez refused to show him his hands, and so he fired his weapon multiple times. He described Ramirez falling forward after he was shot, and that as he fell, his right hand came forward in a manner consistent with someone drawing a gun. At that time, according to Beagley, he shot Ramirez at least two more times. Beagley stated that he then rendered aid to Brewer and that it sounded like a gun battle was still going on with someone positioned at the front of Harger's vehicle. Beagley stated that he became angry and decided to end the threat. He admitted to advancing to the front of the vehicle, and upon seeing Harger, shot him multiple times until he quit moving. He did not recall knowing Vaughn and Garrett were behind him until after he finished shooting.

There was essentially no part of Beagley's statement that was consistent with the evidence or the statements of the other officers. By the time Ramirez purportedly advanced on him near Wimbish's squad, both Vaughn and Garrett had already observed Ramirez lying on the pavement where his body was photographed. Also, Otterness, Garrett, and Vaughn all described Beagley moving forward with Garrett and Vaughn in a group "wedge" formation. And finally, had Ramirez actually advanced on Beagley, and had Beagley stopped that advance with multiple gunshots while yelling commands at

Ramirez, every officer at the scene would have been in a position to witness that part of the incident. Not a single officer corroborated Beagley's account. Furthermore, Beagley described Ramirez advancing toward his position near the squad car and falling forward after being shot multiple times. This was simply impossible given the location where Ramirez's body was found and photographed.

Though not expecting it, it really did not surprise me that the waistband defense was invoked by at least one of the officers, in this case by Beagley, the one officer who admitted to shooting Ramirez. The fact is, they had killed an unarmed confidential informant. It was my opinion that the officers attempted to obscure the facts with their statements. For the most part, they denied even seeing or recognizing each other during the incident. It was obvious to me that they had made a concerted effort to put forth a single account of Ramirez's actions that would justify his killing. That justification, as provided by Beagley, was Ramirez advancing on him and reaching for his waistband. Once again, the deadly force script was being deployed to defend the indefensible.

As I dug into the evidence to complete my analysis, there were three pieces of evidence I was particularly interested in exploring: the grazing wound sustained by Brewer, Harger's firearm, and the wounds sustained by Ramirez. Regarding Brewer's wound, it was a particularly bad grazing wound to the right side of his face above the eye. It was important to understand Brewer's wound because it marked the beginning of the shooting sequence. The wound could perhaps tell me something about Harger's location. Brewer and Wimbish both stated that Harger was the shooter; however, their descriptions of his location when Brewer was shot differed. Wimbish stated that Harger exited the driver's side of the vehicle and fired around the corner of the left rear quarter panel. Brewer stated that Harger fired from inside the vehicle, and that when he heard the shot ring out, he could see Harger still inside the vehicle on the driver's side.

According to published scientific literature, there are two types of evidence that can assist in determining a bullet's direction of travel when the wound is a grazing wound. The first are the skin tags found on the outer edge of the wound. These skin tags will point in the direction of the bullet's direction of travel. And second, the skin tags nearest the weapon will appear as lacerations with irregular margins, while the skin tags farthest away from the weapon will have simple abraded edges. When I looked at the pictures of Brewer's wound, I was able to see both types of evidence. The skin tags were clearly pointing forward, indicating that the shot came from behind. This was further confirmed by the fact that the skin tags eventually became a smooth abraded surface closer to the front. It was reasonable to conclude that while there was no doubt that Harger had fired his weapon, in reality, Brewer had been accidentally shot by Wimbish from behind as he returned fire at Harger. Both officers confirmed in their statements that Wimbish was positioned behind Brewer. It was my opinion that after Harger fired the first shot, Brewer immediately stepped back and directly into Wimbish's line of fire.

The second piece of evidence I focused on was Harger's gun, a Heckler and Koch 9mm semiautomatic pistol. It was found next to his body with the slide locked back by a jammed round. On the ground near him were two empty shell casings and one live round, with a third empty casing found under the front driver's side tire of Wimbish and Brewer's squad car. From these various pieces of evidence, I was able to conclude the following:

1. Given the location of the empty shell casing under the front of the police vehicle, it was reasonable to conclude that Harger fired his first shot from a position near the rear of his own vehicle, likely using the vehicle for cover.

2. Harger fired two additional shots from a position near the front of his vehicle, likely after retreating to that location after his first shot. These were his only shots.

3. The presence of a live round on the ground indicates that Harger's gun jammed after one of the three shots and that the live round ejected when he manually cleared the weapon of the obstruction.

4. The gun was found in a unique condition. There was a live round in the chamber and a second live round in the magazine obstructing the gun's slide, thus making it inoperable.

This is a very uncommon type of malfunction in a semiautomatic pistol. It is caused by neither a "failure to extract" nor a "failure to eject." The detectives incorrectly labeled it a Level 3 malfunction (failure to extract), but that would have required that the gun be found with an empty casing in the chamber rather than a live round. In reality, it was a Level 1 malfunction. The type of ammunition found in Harger's gun was an inexpensive type with a documented history of failing to fire due to defective primers.

It is clear that Harger manually ejected one live round after that round failed to fire. He then had a second misfire with another round. This time, however, he was no doubt gravely wounded, and when he attempted to manually clear the round, he was able to get the slide back only far enough to grab the next round, but not to eject the chambered round. As the slide moved forward then, the new round was obstructed from clearing the magazine but was protruded far enough forward to push the round he wanted to eject back into the chamber, which prevented the slide from closing. At that point, the gun was inoperable, and this is how it was discovered by the officers following the shooting.

So, we know with certainty that Harger fired three shots. He fired the initial shot at the rear of his vehicle and then retreated to the front. As he did, he either fired a second shot and then cleared a misfire, or he cleared the misfire and then fired two additional shots from the front of the vehicle before the second misfire. Given that Harger was obviously prepared to die, it seems unlikely that he would fire only a single shot at the rear of the vehicle when he likely had a tactical advantage with Wimbish and Brewer approaching Ramirez on the passenger side. It is a reasonable conclusion then that the gun misfired after the first shot. As he retreated to the rear, he cleared the misfire and then fired the other two shots.

This scenario, which is supported by the evidence, does not reconcile with the accounts provided by the officers, all of which were different in significant ways. Wimbish described at least eight shots taken by Harger. He stated that Harger fired twice from the rear of his vehicle and that he actually saw the muzzle flashes from those shots. He believed that Harger was firing in his direction through the windows of his vehicle. Wimbish described two more shots by Harger after Harger retreated to the front of his vehicle and he (Wimbish) retreated to the passenger side of his squad car. He stated that while he continued to fire from that location, Harger fired twice more from the front of his vehicle. He then observed Harger reach around the front of the vehicle and fire two final times, for a total of eight shots. Brewer did not describe a specific number of shots by Harger but stated that Harger continued to fire throughout the exchange. He stated that he first heard "multiple" gunshots coming from inside Harger's vehicle. Realizing that he had been shot, Brewer retreated to a position of safety behind a vehicle on the opposite side of the parking lot. He stated that after taking cover, he observed Harger continuing to fire his weapon from the front of his vehicle, and that after Officer Beagley arrived on the scene, Harger again started firing his weapon after momentarily stopping.

Beagley also did not describe a specific number of shots by Hargerbut gave an account much different from the other officers. He took credit for killing Ramirez and identified no other officers who shot him. Beagley arrived on-scene after the shooting had already begun, so a significant period of time passed before he killed Ramirez. He stated that after doing so, he retreated to Brewer's location, thinking the threat had ended. It was then, according to his account, that Harger began shooting again from the front of his vehicle. He denied knowing that there was a second person until then. At that time, he moved to the front of Harger's vehicle and shot Harger multiple times, including one shot to the head. He stated that he did so because Harger was reaching for the gun that was lying on the ground next to him.

The fact is, Harger fired only three times. Given that his initial shot was likely what set off the exchange of gunfire, his last two shots were likely fired quickly upon retreating to the front of the vehicle as Wimbish and Brewer returned fire. It is reasonable to conclude that Harger was done firing the three shots before Beagley and Otterness even arrived on-scene. This would also mean that as Wimbish and Brewer continued to fire toward and underneath Harger's vehicle; as Garrett and Vaughn each fired from the south upon exiting their van and running around the southwest corner of the hotel; and as Beagley fired at both individuals a combined twenty-seven times, there were no shots being returned. At that time and thereafter, Harger's gun was inoperable. Beagley admitted to approaching within 5 feet of Harger before delivering an execution style shot to the head. This would have been long after Harger's gun had jammed. The gun at that time was lying in a pool of blood on the pavement with the slide clearly locked back. Any police officer would have known immediately that the gun was either jammed or empty of ammunition.

The final piece of evidence I wanted to understand was the totality of Ramirez's wounds. The locations and trajectories of those wounds indicated three separate groupings of shots. First was the single shot to the back of his body in the left buttock. This was likely an incapacitating shot. Either it took Ramirez to the ground as he turned to escape a crossfire, or he was already lying on the ground and the bullet ricocheted off the pavement before hitting him. The second grouping of shots included two shots from a distance to Ramirez's legs, as indicated by the sharp angles. These two shots could have been taken by Brewer, Wimbish, or Beagley from their positions of cover. And the third grouping included seven shots that showed a pattern consistent with a "walk-up" as the shooter fired. These shots were no doubt fired by Beagley. The pattern showed the angles becoming progressively less pronounced with each shot until the final shot to the face. That shot appeared to have been taken from directly above Ramirez.

Based on the physical evidence, and to a lesser extent the very few consistencies in the officers' statements, I formed the opinion that the following sequence of events took place once the two vehicles came to a stop in the hotel parking lot:

1. Wimbish and Brewer immediately exited their vehicle believing Harger to be the passenger. They both moved to the passenger side of Harger's vehicle. Had they suspected otherwise, or were not certain, it is inconceivable that both officers would have moved to the same side, leaving the other side of the vehicle, as well as its occupant, uncovered.

2. As they moved to the passenger side, with Brewer in front, both Harger and Ramirez exited the vehicle. Wimbish immediately commanded Harger, believing him to be Ramirez, back into the vehicle. Instead, Harger moved to the rear of the vehicle, and using the vehicle for cover, fired one shot in the officers' direction. This casing ejected to the right and ended up by the front driver's side tire of the squad car.

3. With Harger's first shot, the situation turned to chaos. Brewer moved back from Ramirez just as Wimbish fired multiple times through the vehicle's windows and accidentally struck Brewer in the head, causing the grazing wound.

4. Still believing Ramirez to be Harger, and now having been shot, Brewer likely believed Ramirez fired the shot and fired once at Ramirez, who was now turning to get away from the line of fire. Ramirez no doubt expected that the officers knew he was the confidential informant and likely saw no danger in running some distance to safety. Brewer's shot hit Ramirez in the back hip area (left buttock), causing him to fall to the ground. This is the only shot from behind that Ramirez received. It must also be noted that this shot entered the body in three pieces, indicating that it may have ricocheted off the pavement. If this were the case, then it would support the argument that Ramirez was already on the ground trying to avoid a crossfire.

5. Harger fired a second shot as Wimbish and Brewer retreated, both continuing to fire in Harger's direction. Harger was likely wounded by this point. Harger fired a third time, but the gun malfunctioned. He immediately "racked" his slide to disengage the unfired round and then fired a third time. This was the final time he fired. When he attempted to fire again, the gun again failed to fire, and when Harger attempted to eject this round, he was unable to do so, and a new bullet from the magazine pushed the unfired bad bullet back into the chamber and jammed the weapon for good. This was how it was found. I could say with certainty that Harger fired only three times and likely did so before any other officers arrived. In his interview with detectives, Wimbish admitted

that at least two of Harger's shots were fired before the other officers arrived. So, the statements by the other officers that shots were continuing to come from the front of Harger's vehicle, or that it sounded like an ongoing "gun battle," were simply not consistent with the evidence.

6. Wimbish took a position behind his squad car and Brewer, bleeding badly, retreated behind a vehicle on the opposite side of the parking lot. Wimbish fired at least twice underneath the vehicle toward Harger who was likely wounded in the initial exchange of gunfire, while Brewer fired three more times from his position of cover. Ramirez was now on the ground and badly wounded by the first shot to his back.

7. Beagley and Otterness then arrived to Wimbish and Brewer's left, and Garrett and Vaughn approached from their right. There was no gunfire from Harger. The gun was jammed and inoperable. Beagley took a position next to Wimbish and fired multiple times until his magazine was empty (fifteen rounds). He then reloaded. At the same time, Garret fired twice and Vaughn once as they moved forward. Neither fired at Ramirez.

8. Beagley then moved forward toward Ramirez, who was wounded and on the ground and began firing as he approached. He hit Ramirez multiple times as he walked up on him, and then took a final shot from directly above him, shooting him in the face and likely killing him instantly or near instantly.

9. Beagley then turned and moved toward Harger, who was also wounded and on the ground. The inoperable gun, which had not been fired since Beagley's arrival, lay next to him in a pool of blood. Harger was on his back with his left side exposed to Beagley. Beagley fired at and struck Harger multiple times on his left side and then moved to a spot directly above him and administered a single shot to his face, likely killing him instantly or near instantly just like Ramirez.

It is a certain fact that executing the arrest warrant on Harger was a "high-risk" operation, especially given his history of violence.

This is precisely why Sergeant Lantz had his entire team involved. A highrisk warrant is never attempted without first developing a tactical plan. It also involves gathering as much intelligence as possible. It is inconceivable, especially since Esparza knew Ramirez, that Lantz and his entire team would not have had that information, including a picture of both Harger and Ramirez. Yet during the interviews that followed the incident, not a single officer admitted to having any information at all about Ramirez—not his name, whether he was in the vehicle with Harger, nor even his gender. Lantz assigned his entire team to the operation, deployed an undercover van, and held a team tactical meeting at a staging area near the Bakersfield Airport, yet the team knew absolutely nothing about Ramirez. Esparza later denied providing any information to Lantz about Ramirez, although on the day of the incident, including while Ramirez was with Harger, Esparza acted as the go-between while off duty and at home. Ramirez updated Esparza as to their location, who in turn relayed the information to Lantz. When I reviewed those text messages, it was clear to me that Ramirez was becoming increasingly nervous as the day wore on. He was in a dangerous situation, and when the police, especially Esparza, should have recognized his fear and taken steps to extricate him from the situation before attempting to arrest Harger, even if it meant letting Harger slip away, they chose instead to leave him on his own while a group of officers, who later claimed to have no information about Ramirez and who were already primed for a gun battle, confronted the two in a parking lot without even knowing for certain which was Harger.

When Wimbish and Brewer pulled up behind Harger's parked car, they should have executed a felony traffic stop, and then only after the other officers arrived. Instead, they left the cover of their vehicle and made contact with the occupants. In fact, there is no evidence they even called in the traffic stop over the radio. What happened next was chaotic. While they focused on Ramirez, likely after being told that Harger would be the passenger, Harger exited on the opposite side and fired in the direction of the officers. Wimbish returned fire, striking Brewer in the head, and then Brewer, likely believing Ramirez to be Harger, opened fire on Ramirez. The other officers responded only after hearing gunfire and someone announced over the radio the code for shots fired. In the end, either we can believe the officers and conclude that they very recklessly attempted to make such an arrest with essentially no information, or we can look at the facts and conclude that they did have the information but lacked the planning and communication to execute the warrant, with Ramirez's safety being the most important consideration.

As much as the thousand-yard stare and waistband defense are part of the deadly force script, so too is a denial of the contagious shooting phenomenon. The law enforcement apparatus in the United States tries diligently to train this potentiality out of its officers, but the fact is, it is one of the most powerful psychological forces on human behavior. When multiple police officers start shooting, it becomes difficult to get them to stop. Even the officers who fire first will at times be susceptible to the contagion effect of those who fire later. In this case, but for the initial three shots by Harger, multiple officers continued to fire when no shots were being fired in return. In fact, Harger had already finished firing his weapon before most of them even arrived at the scene. And at some point, the fact that a confidential informant was in the vehicle doing exactly what he said he would do—lead the officers to Harger—was no longer even a consideration.

Once I completed my report, I forwarded it to Alex Alercon with the recommendation that he get an expert opinion from a pathologist about Brewer's grazing wound. It is entirely possible that the officers had no idea that Wimbish may have fired the shot that struck Brewer, given the chaos of the moment. But certainly, the detectives charged with investigating the matter should have at least considered that possibility and analyzed the wound for themselves. To this day, the Bakersfield Police Department has never discussed the wound. Beagley's own words indicate that he may have been compelled to make such an aggressive approach to Harger and Ramirez, shooting both multiple times, including a coup de grace shot to the face of both from directly above, by his anger over Brewer being shot. At the time, Beagley would have had no idea that Wimbish may have fired the shot, but what he certainly would have known was that neither Harger nor Ramirez had fired a single shot from the moment of his arrival until he ended both of their lives. Further, notwithstanding the fact that Beagley stated that Ramirez was standing upright and reaching for his waistband when he fired, something no other officer reported seeing, the truth is, Ramirez was already injured and on the ground when Beagley moved forward and shot him multiple times.

There was no trial in this case. Shortly after submitting my report, the city of Bakersfield settled the matter for $400,000. All of the officers were cleared by the district attorney of any wrongdoing. Jorge Ramirez became a statistic in one of the deadliest cities in the United States for police violence. But what the statistics fail to show is that Ramirez was unarmed, had committed no crime, and had neither resisted nor attempted to escape. One can only wonder what he said to the officers as he was being shot ten times, especially as Beagley approached. It is reasonable to conclude that he must have been yelling loudly that he was their own confidential informant. But the police live by a simple rule when it comes to informants— they all lie, and none are to be trusted. Jorge Ramirez was nothing more than a means to an end. Had they simply stopped shooting once they realized Harger was not firing back, Ramirez may still be alive. Instead, he was shot as many as nine more times while he lay unarmed and on the ground, likely screaming at the top of his lungs that he was their confidential informant. It provides a clear example of why the police get so little cooperation from citizens in the community when it comes to identifying and locating criminal suspects. People tend to know when they are expendable.

- CHAPTER 14-

The Case of Tommy Le

Seattle, Washington

How the Police Can Turn Anything (Even an Ink Pen) into a Deadly Weapon

When I was first contacted by Seattle Attorney Jeffrey Campiche, I found the story a bit hard to believe. A King County sheriff's deputy had shot a high school kid in the back, alleging that the kid was threatening him with an ink pen. The victim, 20-year-old Tommy Le, a 123-pound Vietnamese kid, was killed the day before his high school graduation. For reasons that were never understood, Tommy had taken a hallucinogen on the day he was killed and was having a "bad trip" when the police were called by people in the neighborhood where he lived. Jeffrey also informed me that before Tommy was shot, he had been Tased by two deputies who were twice his size, one of whom was the deputy who then transitioned to his firearm and shot him twice in the back. Based on the limited information Jeffrey had at the time, I agreed to take the case. I could see no possible scenario where such a shooting could be justified, although as expected, the King County Sheriff's Department's internal affairs unit would eventually clear the two deputies of any wrongdoing.

The shooting occurred on the night of June 14, 2017, after deputies responded to the area of 136th and 3rd Avenue in Burien, Washington, on a report of an individual attacking someone with a knife. The individual, later identified as Tommy Le, left the area after one of the individuals retrieved a firearm and fired a warning shot into the ground. Before leaving, the witness went back inside and Le purportedly followed and struck his front door with a knife. Prior to deputies arriving, one of the individuals allegedly attacked advised the 911 dispatcher that the object Le had in his hand was possibly something other than a knife. This information was dispatched to the responding deputies. There were no reported injuries. According to official police reports, upon arrival, the deputies approached the alleged victims. As they did, one of the deputies, Cesar Molina, observed Tommy walking southbound on 3rd Avenue back in their direction. Molina confronted Tommy in the intersection and ordered him to the ground. According to Molina, Tommy was noncompliant and had a dark object in his hand. Molina deployed his Taser, but Tommy was not incapacitated and continued to walk forward. Molina quickly dropped the Taser, drew his firearm, and fired six times, striking Tommy with three of the shots. At the same time, Deputy Tanner Owens, who had approached on Molina's left side, deployed his Taser but missed. Tommy collapsed on the street and a short time later died from his injuries. Not surprisingly, the King County Sheriff's Department quickly circled the wagons and issued press statements indicating that the deputies had feared for their lives and the lives of the other officers and civilian witnesses, and that Molina had no other choice but to end the threat.

I have worked many cases where the police have attempted to portray the most ridiculous items as deadly weapons. It is part of the deadly force script to do so, no matter how absurd the argument. I have worked cases where officers shot and killed people who were holding things like a plastic bucket, a water-logged stick that broke into pieces as soon as it hit the ground, cell phones—a cell phone is almost a death sentence for a young Black kid running from the police—and even a shoe. But an ink pen? I could not imagine how a trained and experienced police officer could possibly view an ink pen as a deadly weapon, especially when carried by a 123-pound high school kid.

I began my review with an analysis of the physical evidence. There was no question that Molina fired at Tommy after he had already walked past him. He fired his weapon six times. Three of the shots, as well as a shot that hit Tommy in the hand, all struck a house on the opposite side of the street. When I compared the locations of the bullet strikes to the location of Molina's empty casings, I was able to determine the trajectories of the shots. I was also able to determine Tommy's path of travel from the location of the two sets of Taser blast doors. Assuming both deputies fired their Tasers directly at Tommy, which was the case, then the trajectories of the Taser shots showed me Tommy's location when each shot was taken. The picture that emerged was obvious. Molina had fired his Taser, striking Tommy with both darts in the chest and abdomen but not incapacitating him, likely because of his low muscle mass, and then zeroed in on him with his firearm, pulling the trigger as he did, as Tommy walked past him and toward Owens. I concluded that Tommy was either walking fast or running to get away because Molina had fired behind him with the first three shots. He then struck him with the next three as he moved with Tommy and zeroed in with his aim.

When I reviewed the autopsy report, including the pictures taken by the pathologist, I found an interesting piece of evidence. One of the two bullets that passed from Tommy's back to the front of his body was sticking partially out of the exit wound in his abdomen. The bullet had hit with enough force to lacerate his skin wide open from the inside, yet it remained in the wound. In my mind, the only possible explanation was that Tommy was already on the ground with his torso pressed against the pavement when the bullet passed through his body. The pavement then stopped the bullet's forward motion after it pierced through his skin. I immediately informed Jeffrey Campiche of my opinion, who in turn sought the services of a medical expert, Dr. Wilson Hays. Dr. Hays agreed and concluded that "the ballistic evidence demonstrates that Mr. Le was shot at least once while he was on the ground." So not only was Tommy shot in the back, but one of the shots struck him after he had already collapsed, likely from a combination of the other two shots that struck him and the effects of the Taser strike. When I later inspected pictures of this bullet after it was removed from Tommy's body, and after Jeffrey subpoenaed the pictures, I almost immediately recognized that the bullet had been manipulated. The copper jacket from the bullet had been manipulated to look less flattened, obviously, at least in my mind, to hide the fact that Tommy had been shot while on the ground. Even the lead detective on the case, Detective Johnson, admitted rather reluctantly during a deposition that the bullet in the picture did not look like the one taken by the pathologist during the autopsy.

I realized early on this case that the King County Sheriff's Department was not going to make it easy for us. Unbelievably, not a single official document, including Molina's own report, indicated that Tommy was shot in the back. Instead, the documentation indicated that he was shot in the "torso." While that description may have been technically correct by some standard, it was my opinion that it was a subtle attempt to obscure the fact that Tommy was shot in the back. There was no discussion in the investigative file about Tommy's body position when he was shot, and not a single mention of the bullet protruding from the exit wound in his abdomen.

I also found the investigative file lacking when it came to the two Tasers, particularly Owens'. I wanted to know if Owens had attempted to deploy his Taser after Tommy was already on the pavement. There are ways of determining this, but unfortunately, it appeared that Owens' Taser darts somehow disappeared from the scene before the investigating detectives arrived. If Owens missed his target, then the probes would have remained attached to the lead wires, which in turn would have remained attached to the cartridge. I was able to find pictures of the spent cartridge in the file. There were no darts attached to the wires, and there was no discussion of their disappearance in any report or interview. Had they missed their mark, assuming the Taser was fired while Tommy was on the ground, then the darts would have hit the hard pavement and the barbs at the end would have been bent upward.

There is another reason I wanted to see Owens's darts. In his report he stated that he actually struck Tommy with the Taser shot and that it had no effect. But I already knew from the Taser's data report that he had missed. I could also prove that with the darts in multiple ways. First, there would be no DNA material on the barbs. Second, there would be no signs of electrical burn inside the dart where the wire attached since the charge would not have left the end of the Taser body without a closed circuit to travel across. And finally, if both barbs were bent, then it would be proof not only that Owens had fired while Tommy was on the ground, but also that he had missed. Owens perhaps did not realize that there was a data report that could be retrieved from his Taser. It is not something street-level officers typically have access to. He may have believed that by removing the darts from the scene of the shooting, he could make it impossible to prove that he had missed. I felt that Owens was attempting to portray Tommy in the most negative light by stating that even after being hit by both Tasers, Tommy was able to continue moving forward in a threatening way with the ink pen in his hand. A variation of the superhuman strength defense was rearing its ugly head. Owens would even state during his internal affairs interview that after his Taser had no effect, he too was preparing to shoot Tommy out of fear for his life but ultimately did not need to. Molina had already gotten the job done. I was a bit befuddled by how Owens, 6 feet 7 inches and nearly 300 pounds, could possibly fear for his life against a 5 foot 4 inch, 123-pound high school kid with an ink pen.

One of the most troubling pieces of evidence I reviewed was the door Tommy was purportedly striking with a knife when the homeowner called 911. I knew instantly that whatever it was that Tommy had used to strike the door, it was not a knife. There were no sharp gouges. The marks were obviously caused by a blunt-edge object. One thing I immediately noticed was the presence of black marks on the door, and also what appeared to be ink lines in and around some of the gouges. Although it would still be quite a leap to make an ink pen a deadly weapon, it did at least support the deputies' story that Tommy had a pen in his hand when he returned to the scene. That is, until I found a second picture of the same door where the ink lines were strangely absent. The second picture had a time and date stamp, indicating that it was one of the pictures taken by crime scene personnel immediately after the shooting. Someone had added an ink mark after the fact. Jeffrey would later confront Detective Johnson about this issue during his deposition. Johnson had no good explanation. He admitted that they had tested an ink pen on the bottom of the door to determine if it could make the gouges, and that the test failed. But he could not explain how the ink marks got on the door in the actual gouge marks on the upper half of the door. Clearly, someone had manipulated the evidence to bolster the story of the ink pen.

For me, one of the central questions in this case was what Tommy was holding in his hand during the initial encounter with the homeowner. The homeowner first said during his interview that Tommy was holding a knife, but then said he was not sure it was a knife, but rather, a pointy object. Molina stated that at the time he fired his Taser and his gun, he could see a black pointy object in Tommy's hand. And Owens stated that after Le was shot, he was able to somehow kick an ink pen out of his hand and have it land 9–12 feet away. Interestingly, the pen's cap landed right next to it. Aside from the fact that police officers do not kick evidence out of people's hands when they are on the ground mortally wounded—the more accepted method is to simply reach down and pick it up—by then, assuming it were true, he would clearly have seen that he was kicking an ink pen. It is an absurd notion that Owens would have felt the need to kick an ink pen for his own safety and that of the other deputies.

I returned to the hundreds of pictures turned over by the King County Sheriff's Department to attempt to determine what Tommy had struck the door with. Whatever it was, it had to have a blunt edge and the capability to make the black marks that were visible on the door. Whenever I work a case, I always spend a lot of time looking at the hundreds of pictures typically taken by crime scene personnel. I look at them multiple times and sometimes weeks apart after I have developed new theories about what happened. In numerous cases I have been able to find things in the pictures that even the detectives at the scene missed. It happened again with this case.

It was a single picture that solved the mystery: a wood chip approximately 6 inches in length with a sharp but blunt end that was burnt approximately 2 inches on one end. It was unknown why the crime scene photographer chose to photograph the wood chip. I was able to identify its location using landmarks visible in the picture. It was lying on the ground between the intersection where Molina confronted Tommy and Tommy's apartment a few blocks away. There was no discussion of the wood chip in any of the documents, and it was not even clear if the detectives knew about it beyond the fact that the photographer had snapped a picture of it.

The picture of the wood chip immediately sparked a memory of two other pictures I had seen. One was of the homeowner's front yard on the opposite side of the intersection from where the burnt chip was photographed. There were other similar wood chips in the yard. And the second was a somewhat confusing picture from the autopsy. The picture was of Tommy's right hand. On his pinkie and ring fingers near the inside of his knuckles was a black substance. It was too good to be true. I was able to superimpose the picture of the wood chip over the picture of Tommy's hand. It was a perfect match. The charred end of the wood chip perfectly matched the location of the black substance on Tommy's hand if his fingers were wrapped around it. It was indisputable in my mind that Tommy had struck the door with the wood chip after picking it up in the homeowner's front yard. But what about the ink pen? Jeffrey Campiche answered that question himself when he met with detectives at the King County Sheriff's Department to gain access to the evidence. Lying right there in front of him on the table was the same type and color ink pen purportedly used by Tommy as a weapon. It was the type purchased in bulk by the Sheriff's Office.

At this point I was confident that I knew exactly what had happened. But like I did in all cases, I needed to find the holes in the officers' statements. The police like to say it is impossible to commit the perfect crime. I find it impossible to commit the perfect unjustified use of deadly force. The physical evidence almost always gives up the truth, but the statements of the officers involved—their inconsistencies, improbabilities, and even impossibilities—typically create a corner the officers cannot get out of. It is nearly impossible to provide such a statement that is perfectly consistent with the physical evidence and the statements of the witnesses and other officers involved. I began with Deputy Molina.

Molina's first account of the incident was a written statement he provided the day after the shooting. He described seeing Tommy approach the northeastern corner of the intersection from the north on 3rd Street. This is the same location where the burnt piece of wood was later photographed. He stated he could see Tommy holding a dark pointy object but could not recall which hand it was in. He also stated that after refusing to get on the ground, Tommy made a movement toward him with the dark pointy object raised to his chest. This was beyond the point where the burnt piece of wood was found on the ground, so I knew Tommy was likely unarmed at that point. Molina then deployed his Taser and hit Tommy. He stated that the Taser had no effect and he started backing up, at which time Deputy Owens came up on his left and fired his Taser, again having no effect. He further stated that after both Tasers failed to stop Tommy, he became fearful for the lives of his partners and the other witnesses, so he holstered his Taser and then drew his firearm and fired three to five times as Tommy continued moving forward (we know he fired six times). He stated that Tommy still had a pointy object in his hand as he fired at him.

I determined that the timeline made Molina's account impossible. After reviewing the time stamps on Owens's Taser deployment, the time required for Molina to fire six times, and the radio dispatch announcing, "shots fired," I determined that Molina would have had at best just three seconds to perceive that Owens's Taser shot had missed, and then holster his own Taser (with the probes still in Tommy), draw his firearm, and then take aim and begin to fire. There was simply no way Molina had sufficient time to shoot six times after Owens's Taser shot and before the "shots fired" dispatch. It was clear to me that Owens and Molina had essentially fired at the same time.

Molina never really described the threat he was confronting at the time he fired both his Taser and his firearm. He admitted that Tommy did not swing at him, physically attack him, or even tell him he was going to attack or kill him. Tommy was guilty only of walking toward Molina with a clenched fist and a pointy object in his hand being held near his chest, at least by Molina's account. Given that he could not recall which hand the pointy object was in, that the burnt piece of wood was now lying behind Tommy somewhere in the grass, and that the evidence clearly showed that Tommy walked around Molina rather than toward him, the only reasonable conclusion was that Molina fired his gun six times absent a threat. And finally, it bordered on absurdity for Molina to suggest that he feared for the other officers' lives, all of whom were armed and well trained, and that he needed to protect them and the civilians around them. Tommy was hardly an imposing figure. It seemed equally absurd that both deputies would use any amount of force against a young man holding only a "pointy object" and making no effort to attack either of them with it. At no time in his statement did Molina say anything about seeing an ink pen in Tommy's hand. When Tommy passed by with his back to Molina, Molina had the opportunity to use nonlethal force and should have simply grabbed him and taken him to the ground.

On July 24, 2017, Molina submitted to a videotaped interview at the Sheriff's Department's headquarters in Seattle, Washington. Although his narrative was essentially the same as his written statement, there were a couple of issues worth noting. First, Molina's description of the object in Tommy's hand had now changed from a "dark pointy object" to just a "dark object." One thing is for certain: when Molina came face to face with Tommy, he would have illuminated him and his hands with a very bright flashlight. That is standard practice and training in law enforcement. At such close range, it would have been literally impossible for Molina to have seen an object in his hand and not be able to identify it. Also, during the interview, Molina stated the following:

> I didn't have any other option to try to stop him. Given the fact that he had already tried to stab someone, he didn't stop at anything, and a neighbor had already shot at him and it didn't stop him, so I was in fear that he was going to try to hurt myself, Deputy Owens, MPO Paul, or any of the other individuals who were still on the street.

In this passage Molina essentially provided his justification for using deadly force. Every part of the passage was problematic. The most striking part was his assertion that he had no other options.

Even more striking was the fact that the investigators interviewing Molina did not follow up on this comment. At no time did he state that he commanded Tommy to drop whatever was in his hand. He stated only that he ordered him to get on the ground. This was significant. As for his options, he had multiple options available to gain Tommy's compliance. Again, he had the option of simply grabbing Tommy and taking him to the ground. Further, the Taser probes were still in Tommy. Notwithstanding the fact that the use of the Taser was also excessive under the circumstances, he could have simply pulled the trigger a second time to administer a second shock. Even though it may not have incapacitated Tommy, it would have been very painful, and a second shock could possibly have led to his compliance. And finally, Molina could have used his OC pepper spray, which at such a short distance would have been effective.

Owens provided a written statement on June 15, 2017. He admitted that when Molina deployed his Taser, and although Tommy was well illuminated, he was unable to see anything in his hand. He stated that after Molina fired his Taser, Tommy ran south toward him (Owens) and that when he was 5 to 7 feet away, he could see "something" in his hand but did not specifically say what. He stated that based on the original dispatch, he feared it was a knife. Like Molina, it seemed quite improbable that Owens could have seen "something" at such close range, but still be unable to see the shape of a knife or ink pen. The fact was, by then Tommy's hands were empty.

Owens stated that he deployed his Taser and that the Taser did not stop Tommy; however, he failed to point out that he completely missed Tommy. He stated that Tommy then pivoted to his southwest and ran in the direction of the other officers and civilians still holding "something" in his hand. Like Molina, not surprisingly, Owens stated that when Tommy pivoted, he feared for the lives of the other officers and civilians and at that point made the decision to shoot. He went on to describe how he holstered his Taser, drew his firearm, and prepared to shoot when he heard Molina's shots ring out. I concluded that his account was simply impossible due to what I knew about the timeline. I knew Owens fired his Taser at essentially the same time Molina fired his gun. By the time he holstered his Taser and drew his own gun, Molina was already done shooting. Furthermore, at least two other officers reported that after the shooting was done, Owens covered Tommy with his Taser—he was carrying a double cartridge Taser—until Tommy was handcuffed.

Owens then provided his account of the ink pen. He stated that after determining Tommy was no longer a threat, and while standing directly over him, he put on a pair of gloves and began rendering aid to Tommy. That reportedly was the first time he saw the ink pen in Tommy's hand, still being held like a knife. By this time, Tommy had been tased, had received a bad gunshot wound to his wrist and hand as well as two fatal shots to his back, and, according to Owens' own account, was continuing to roll around on the ground and attempting to stand even though mortally wounded. Yet throughout it all, he somehow maintained his grip on an ink pen? It was then, according to Owens, when he kicked the pen out of Tommy's hand. The obvious question was why he did not simply reach down and take it. I never bothered to work out the puzzle of exactly how to kick a pen out of a person's hand.

The central issue in this case was the question of what Tommy had in his hand when Molina, and then Owens, fired their weapons. There were two things neither of the deputies could admit to. First, neither could admit to seeing nothing in Tommy's hand, notwithstanding the fact that that was likely the case because then they would both be admitting to using force against an unarmed person. Second, neither could admit to seeing an ink pen before the use of force, because then they would be admitting to using force against a person holding only an object that in no way could be construed as a deadly weapon. Thus, Molina created the narrative of the "dark pointy object" to bolster, and be bolstered by, Owens's narrative of seeing the ink pen only after Tommy was already shot and on the ground. They avoided having to admit that they saw nothing in Tommy's hand, and the addition of the ink pen by Owens allowed them to say they saw something, but without being specific enough to prove a deliberate use of excessive force. Another attempt at the perfect crime. However, there was no way to reconcile the deputies' stories with the story the physical evidence was clearly telling.

By the time I submitted my report to Jeffrey Campiche, I was certain the King County Sheriff's Department would move quickly to settle the case to avoid the embarrassment of having their investigation fully exposed for the public to see. In fact, I had never seen such a compromised investigation. Evidence had disappeared from the scene or was left lying among the blood and medical debris for the streets department to clean up. Other evidence had been obviously altered. And still other evidence, namely, the ink pen, had been conveniently used to create a false narrative. Molina and Owens had been questioned by investigators in a way that was obviously designed to facilitate their defense rather than seek out the truth. And it appeared that not a single person involved in the investigation saw any problem with shooting a kid in the back for at most holding an ink pen that he was attacking no one with, and more than likely holding nothing at all.

Unfortunately, I was wrong about an expected willingness to settle the matter. The Sheriff's Department decided to fight, and they did so for the next two years. They filed motions to have the case dismissed and argued that Molina should be granted qualified immunity. They filed another motion to keep an independent report that was critical of the investigation from being used as evidence at trial. And of course, they hired their own expert who issued a report concluding that the deputies did nothing improper. Not unexpectedly, the expert they hired was associated with the Force Science Institute, and his report was full of pseudoscientific research and conclusions. Eventually, I wrote an affidavit in support of a motion to exclude the expert's testimony. He was precluded from testifying to most of his report because of a lack of qualifications and sound scientific methodology.

The motions continued but finally, one month prior to the trial, King County threw in the towel and agreed to settle the case for $5 million. Although I was looking forward to testifying and laying out the case for the public to see, I was happy that Tommy's family would not have to sit through the trial. The settlement ended one of the most blatant cases of excessive force I had ever been involved in. Deputy Molina of course was never disciplined for killing Tommy. The Sheriff's Department ruled that he did nothing improper. I was not surprised when I discovered that he had been promoted to detective. Promotions often follow unjustified shootings.

Perhaps the thing that troubled me most was a statement put out by King County Sheriff Mitzi Johanknecht following the announcement of the settlement:

> The King County Sheriff's Office was ready and willing to try this case in a court of law. Although the parties do not agree on the fundamental facts of this case, we are pleased the settlement will allow everyone to avoid a difficult, and likely painful, trial.

The one thing sadly missing from her statement was any mention of Tommy Le. She had relegated him to little more than a piece of evidence to be presented at trial; a 123-pound Vietnamese kid on the night before his high school graduation who, in her mind apparently, was justifiably shot in the back and killed by a police officer twice his size for merely walking down the street with an ink pen in his hand. And that is assuming we accept Molina's account. She could have perhaps reestablished some of the public's trust in law enforcement in the Seattle area had her statement simply said, "I'm sorry." Unfortunately, it was not to be.

- CHAPTER 15-

The Case of Bryan Carreño

Santa Barbara, California

Suicide by Cop: The Perfect Justification for a Perfectly Unjustified Shooting

The law enforcement community in America has used the suicide by cop argument to its advantage for decades. The police know that in certain situations where a questionable use of deadly force occurs, the easiest way for the officer to avoid responsibility is to place it square on the shoulders of the victim. By arguing a case of suicide by cop, it changes the complexion of the encounter from one where the victim was being confronted by the police to one where the police were being confronted by the victim. By making the victim responsible for their own death, it takes the focus off the police and puts them almost beyond scrutiny.

What the police never point out is that they are trained to deal with this type of situation without using deadly force and that the standard of reasonableness by which their use of force is evaluated will always be applied from the perspective of the officer and not the victim. The constitutional restraints on their use of force do not go away simply because the person they are confronting wants to die. Unfortunately, it seems that as soon as the police identify a case as a suicide by cop, the public, the press, and even the prosecutors join together in a collective "Welp, I guess that's that!" It is as if they suddenly lose sight of the fact that just because a person wants to die does not relieve the police of their professional and moral duty to keep them alive.

If you peel back the layers on this issue, you will find that many, if not most, of the people who have been killed by the police while purportedly committing suicide by cop really did not want to die but were emotionally overwhelmed by the moment. Others, when they yelled at the officers to "SHOOT ME, SHOOT ME!" were challenging the police rather than begging them. Yet the police have always lumped these cases into the same category. Dr. Kris Mohandie, a nationally recognized police and forensic psychologist who has worked as a crisis responder with the LAPD—he was present when O. J. Simpson holed up inside his house following the infamous white Bronco chase in 1994—is one of the foremost researchers in the United States on the issue of suicide by cop. Regarding a 2009 study on the prevalence of this phenomenon, he stated the following in an article published in the *Journal of Forensic Psychology*:

> Dig a little deeper into that 2009 study, however, and you see that the term is incredibly slippery. Only 30 percent of the shootings classified as suicide by cop were found to be preplanned by those who were ultimately shot by police. The remaining 70 percent were determined to be the product of a spontaneous decision made during an encounter with police. If we're considering all of these shootings to be suicide by cop, that means there is no difference between a person who, in the moment, refuses to surrender and someone who actively seeks out the police as a means to end his life. That's a distinction that absolutely has to be made. Otherwise, the phrase suicide by cop serves as a blanket excuse, a shrug of the shoulders when confronted with the worst possible outcome. In reality, these are the police encounters that need to be examined the most closely: ones in which a life may have been saved if officers made a different decision.

I was confronted with the question of whether someone truly wanted to die at the hands of the police in the case of Bryan Carreño, age 26, from Santa Barbara, California. I got the call from Attorney Bill Schmidt from Fresno. I had worked other cases with Bill and considered him one of the best. He sent me a body cam video which captured Carreño being shot at twenty-seven times by five Santa Barbara County deputies while holding a knife. Carreño was hit by twenty of the bullets. I immediately recognized it as a case of contagious shooting. The first deputy fired, and then the others immediately followed suit. Bill asked me specifically about suicide by cop and expressed a concern about moving forward if that were the case. I advised him that at first blush, especially after reading the various press accounts of the incident, the case did not appear to fit the criteria outlined in Dr. Mohandie's research, something I confirmed after reviewing the investigative file.

The case began on February 12, 2017, when the Santa Barbara County 911 Center received a call from Bryan's father reporting that Bryan was acting strange and appeared to be under the influence of some type of drug. He advised dispatchers that Bryan was hallucinating and tripping really bad. Additional calls were received from residents in the neighborhood reporting that Bryan was jumping fences, running through peoples' yards, and entering neighborhood homes without permission. Multiple Santa Barbara County deputies, as well as officers from the California Highway Patrol, arrived and set up a perimeter to begin searching for Bryan using a police K9. Additionally, a Sheriff's Department helicopter was overhead participating in the search.

The search eventually led the deputies to a house on Russell Way, where the owner, who was not at the house, reported that neighbors had called and advised her that an unknown individual was inside her house. The officers converged on the house, and while some of the officers watched the front, at least five others moved to a rear patio. Two of the deputies, Ken Rushing, a K9 officer, and Ken Moore, announced their presence and entered with the K9 through a sliding glass door. Almost immediately they were advised by others watching through the windows that Bryan was in the house and that he was holding a knife. The two deputies and the K9 retreated back out the door and joined the other deputies—Joshua Cockrell, Robert DeBarge, and Dustin Winebrenner—around the perimeter of the patio. At that point Bryan exited the patio door with a knife held down at his side. This part of the encounter was captured by Deputy Rushing's body cam. As he stepped off the concrete steps, with all the deputies yelling commands, the shots rang out and Bryan immediately fell to the ground dead. Just before being shot, he could be heard yelling, "SHOOT ME!"

The first thing that was apparent to me was that Bryan was neither attacking the deputies, nor was he charging them. It was also obvious from the video that Bryan began to collapse after the very first shot. The shots that followed occurred while he was falling to the ground. The medical examiner later reported that he was hit twenty times (twenty-seven total shots), which also caused seven exit wounds. The shots were grouped into three general clusters. The first included eleven shots to the front of Bryan's body with a slightly upward or downward trajectory. Most occurred while Bryan was still standing or just beginning to fall. The second cluster included six shots to the front of Bryan's body with a very pronounced downward trajectory, indicating that he was bending over and facing the deputies when those shots were fired. And finally, the third cluster included two shots to his back, which is consistent with Bryan rotating to his left and exposing his back as he fell. A final shot struck his hand. When detectives conducted a bullet count following the incident, it was found that Deputies DeBarge and Cockrell had each fired their weapon eight times; Deputy Moore, five times; Deputy Rushing, four times while holding back his K9; and Deputy Winebrenner, a trainee officer, two times.

The nature of any police response is determined by the information the responding officers have in advance of their response. In this case, the responding deputies clearly had information to indicate that a crisis intervention was the appropriate course of action rather than a criminal investigation. They had sufficient information to indicate that the outcome would be an involuntary psychiatric commitment or medical intervention rather than an incarceration for a criminal offense. Not only did they have the information provided by Bryan's father, but Bryan himself was known to at least two of the responding deputies. Deputy Rushing, the first officer to respond, had previous contact with Bryan. On May 21, 2016, he and another deputy responded to a domestic disturbance between Bryan and his girlfriend. In the course of that investigation, a case in which the girlfriend was the one who allegedly committed the criminal offense, Rushing became aware of the fact, as evidenced by his own report of the incident, that Bryan had attempted suicide in the past by cutting his wrist. On another occasion, Deputy DeBarge responded to a 911 call by the same girlfriend reporting that Bryan was threatening suicide. While no involuntary commitment was pursued by the deputies in either case, DeBarge indicated in his report that Bryan admitted to making suicidal comments to his girlfriend via email and that he requested information from the deputies relating to a psychiatric referral.

Apart from these earlier cases, the responding deputies also knew that in the current case, Bryan had come in contact with multiple people in the neighborhood and had committed no aggressive acts or other significant crimes. The deputies should have known from their crisis intervention training that the most important consideration when they located Bryan would be to avoid emotionally escalating him. This made it necessary to have a plan in place that should have included designating one properly trained deputy to engage Bryan in an attempt to build rapport and to have at least one deputy armed with a less lethal weapon ready to deploy if necessary. The deputies should have been reminded at the outset of their search that their goal was to safely engage and detain Bryan for a psychiatric and/or medical intervention. Prior to engaging him, the deputies had information that Carreño was hallucinating. Further, as stated above, just before the shots rang out, Carreño could be heard on the video yelling, "SHOOT ME!" This should have reinforced the idea that Carreño was emotionally escalated and in the throes of a mental health crisis.

The five deputies who fired their weapons all provided statements to detectives shortly after the shooting. It is accepted protocol throughout the law enforcement community that when multiple officers are involved in a shooting, they are separated, and another uninvolved officer remains in their presence until evidence technicians can search their uniforms and duty belts for potential evidence. In his later deposition, Deputy Rushing admitted that the officers involved in the incident were left unattended and together in the same room prior to being interviewed. He confirmed that a sergeant was initially present but left and that the officers were alone together for nearly two hours. In the context of accepted police practices, this was inappropriate. It provided the officers the opportunity to discuss the incident prior to being interviewed, which can lead to memory contamination, or inaccurate memories that have been influenced by someone else's recollection of the incident. It can also lead to evidence contamination.

I was able to review the transcripts of the deputies' interviews. I specifically focused on Bryan's movements and actions prior to being shot. Not surprisingly, the script was on full display in the deputies' accounts. Deputy Rushing told the detectives that Bryan was so close to one of his partners that he thought he was going to stab and kill him. He offered this as the reason he chose not to release his K9. Aside from the fact that Bryan did not advance on any of the deputies, and likely could not even see them with multiple ballistic lights shining in his eyes, the deputy's statement pointed out another problem I have seen many times in these cases, and that is the inability of a K9 officer to release their dog against an armed suspect. In this case, the dog was trained to attack Bryan's arm and immobilize him, but such a move would have brought with it the possibility of the dog being stabbed. It is a strange paradox in policing. K9 officers are trained to use their dogs as tools of de-escalation and to sacrifice them if necessary for the sake of the mission. Unfortunately, K9 officers become so attached to their dogs, and understandably so, that it becomes difficult to put them in harm's way. The officers who are most likely to seek such positions are often the officers least apt to voluntarily endanger their dogs. It was clear to me in this case that if Deputy Rushing had released his dog when Bryan exited the house, he would be alive today with little more than possibly a scar from a dog bite.

Deputy Moore told detectives that Bryan was waving the knife in weird motions and advancing on the deputies. I was not surprised when he also shared with detectives that Bryan seemed to have a thousand-yard stare. There it was, right on cue. Aside from the fact that Bryan was neither advancing nor waving the knife, I wondered how anyone with multiple high-powered ballistic lights shining directly in his eyes could possibly have demonstrated any kind of stare. And like Deputy Rushing, Moore told the detectives that he feared Bryan was going to kill one of his partners. It is a standard part of the deadly force script that when an officer knows they cannot justify shooting a suspect to protect themselves, if other officers are involved, then the default position is to state that they fired to protect the other officers, notwithstanding the fact that those other officers are, without exception, well-trained and well-armed officers.

Deputy DeBarge also invoked the thousand-yard stare, as did Winebrenner, though the latter spoke only about seeing the look of anger in Bryan's eyes. Both talked about his motions with the knife and his advancement on the deputies. Both stated that they had no doubt Bryan intended to stab one of them. I found this a bit absurd when Bryan's only words when he walked out through the door was "SHOOT ME!"

Deputy Cockrell was the senior deputy at the scene. He painted a picture of Bryan walking down the steps almost zombie-like. He too invoked the thousand-yard stare and stated to detectives that Bryan continued to walk toward the deputies with the knife in his hand and ignoring his commands to drop the knife. It did not surprise me that he said nothing about the multiple ballistic lights shining in Bryan's eyes. Ballistic lights are designed to blind a suspect. I found it preposterous that Bryan would have any look on his face other than the look of being blinded by the bright lights. Also, the video clearly showed that Bryan did not walk toward the deputies. He stepped off the concrete steps with his right foot first, and as soon as his left foot hit the ground the shooting began. He made no further forward movement toward the deputies, and even prior to being shot, there was no indication that he was preparing to lunge or charge toward any of them. His demeanor was mostly unremarkable. He simply lowered the knife to his side, stepped off the concrete steps somewhat casually, and was immediately shot twenty times.

One of the inexplicable issues in this case is why at least one of the five deputies on the patio did not simply deploy their Taser and bring the crisis to a quick end with no one getting hurt. There was no legitimate reason for not at least attempting its use. I found it interesting that there was no mention of the Taser issue in any of the deputies' interviews or reports, the investigators' comments and questions, nor even in the district attorney's summary report. The lack of a Taser deployment was a failure on the part of the senior deputy at the scene, Deputy Cockrell. Once they were in position on the patio, Cockrell should have immediately called out "contact and cover" and designated one deputy to position himself for a Taser strike. With that many deputies in such close proximity, being able to provide sufficient cover was not an issue. Distance was also not an issue. Using the Sheriff's Department's own measurements, I was able to approximate the distance from the steps to the closest deputies at 10–15 feet, and 25 feet to the deputy positioned farthest away from the steps. Given that police officers carry 25-foot cartridges in their Taser weapons, it was an ideal situation to deploy a Taser, both because there was sufficient cover and because at no time did Bryan charge or move aggressively toward the deputies. Time also was not an issue. A review of the video shows that there clearly was sufficient time to prepare for the possibility that Bryan might exit the house. At least three of the deputies were in position and watching him through the window while Deputy Rushing attempted to clear the house with his K9. They maintained those positions until the shooting incident ended. Making use of the Taser even more viable, with the ballistic lights essentially blinding Bryan, had one of the deputies moved forward to deploy his Taser, it is likely Bryan would not have seen him.

If there was one issue I was certain would find its way to the surface in this case, it was the notorious 21-foot rule. The thousand-yard stare defense allowed the deputies to transform Bryan into a zombie incapable of obeying commands, and the 21-foot rule allowed them to argue that it was too dangerous to do anything but shoot him. It was Deputy Cockrell who invoked this rule, both in his report and his later deposition. He obviously had not gotten the memo that the 21-foot rule had by then been discredited and all but removed from police training. Cockrell went so far as to testify during his deposition that because Deputy Winebrenner was within the 21-foot death zone, as soon as Bryan stepped onto the patio, Winebrenner could have justifiably shot him right then and there. Nothing was further from the truth. Cockrell's reliance on the outdated 21-foot rule was something I have seen in my cases, especially among older and more experienced officers who were trained prior to the rule being discredited. Traditionally, the law enforcement community has done a wonderful job training its officers, sometimes to the point of over-training them, but it has done a terribly bad job of untraining them when methods and techniques are discredited, replaced, or ruled to be unreasonable under the law.

Deputy Cockrell was also asked during his deposition about why the deputies chose not to deploy OC pepper spray. He offered the following testimony:

> So it goes back to the distance that I was at between him—between myself and Mr. Carreño. It would be unsafe for me to holster my firearm, pull out my OC, then spray it on him. Just because by that time, he would have, more than likely, already been at me or my partner. Even with OC, it doesn't— it can incapacitate people to the point where they can't see, but they still have the movement of the knife. And that was also a concern that I had, is even if he couldn't see, the knife—he could still use the knife to slash or to stab. (Deposition transcript, page 54)

There is essentially nothing about this statement that is consistent with accepted police training. Not only did Cockrell have the ability to deploy OC spray with his weak hand while maintaining the grip on his firearm, but there were multiple other officers available to provide lethal coverage. Also, if pepper spray could have potentially blinded Bryan, then that would have created the perfect opportunity to then deploy a Taser or the K9. And that is assuming Bryan did not drop the knife after taking a shot of OC spray to his face. None of the available less lethal options were considered, and Deputy Cockrell, as the senior on-scene deputy, took no steps to direct any of the other deputies to deploy those weapons.

By the time I finished my investigation, I was quite confident that Bill Schmidt had a strong case to move forward with. What was clearly seen on the video could not be disputed. As expected, the attorneys representing both Santa Barbara County and the deputies hired their own expert, an individual I had faced before. Also as expected, given that this particular expert was in my mind a "hired gun" whose only purpose it was to twist and distort the facts of the case any way necessary to support the defense, he issued a report concluding that the deputies had been justified in shooting at Bryan twenty-seven times. I felt confident that Bill Schmidt could get most of his report disqualified based on the lack of a factual foundation and the proper qualifications to discuss issues like "suicide by cop." As I was preparing an affidavit to support such a motion, the defense threw a curve ball I was not expecting.

As I was preparing for my deposition in the case, Bill Schmidt called and asked if I had ever heard of a Dr. Kris Mohandie. I instantly knew that the defense was going to argue that Bryan had committed suicide by cop. I also knew that Dr. Mohandie was likely serving as their expert on the issue and that we suddenly had a major fight on our hands. Jurors tend to believe witnesses who have the letters "Ph.D." behind their names. Not only would we have to overcome that obstacle, but we would also have to deal with the fact that Dr. Mohandie was one of the major researchers studying the phenomenon of suicide by cop. It was not going to be easy.

Once I received Dr. Mohandie's report from Bill Schmidt, I studied it with Mohandie's own research in front of me. I knew there was little to no evidence that Bryan intended to die at the hands of the police. I was quite familiar with the subject and had written about it myself in the past. Being already familiar with Dr. Mohandie's research, I could not figure out how he could reach the conclusions he did. I knew it would not be enough to simply argue that I was right and he was wrong. I had to find an effective way to rebut his conclusions. I decided to use his own research against him. Dr. Mohandie's first conclusion read as follows:

Mr. Carreño committed suicide by cop during this incident. Suicide by cop is a method of suicide that occurs when an individual engages in threatening (actual, apparent, and/

or feigned) behavior to cause law enforcement to use deadly force against them as part of their intent to commit suicide. Mr Carreño purposely and deliberately provoked his death at the hands of law enforcement. His death is clearly subject precipitated by definition and fact patterns.

My first reaction to this conclusion was that Mohandie had violated a basic ethical principle that guides the work of a behavioral science expert. He made a definitive statement about the intentions and motivations of an individual he had never met. Furthermore, such a definitive statement would likely be inadmissible anyway. Dr. Mohandie could certainly educate the judge and jury about the issue of suicide by cop, and even discuss behaviors demonstrated by Bryan that were perhaps consistent with this phenomenon, but he could not offer opinion on the ultimate issue of whether Bryan did or did not pursue this outcome, especially when there was little evidence in support of that conclusion. In Dr. Mohandie's own research, published in the Journal of Forensic Science, he cited a study involving all deputy-involved shooting cases handled by the Los Angeles County Sheriff's Department between 1987 and 1997 (437 cases). In the cases classified as suicide by cop, the study found the following precipitating behaviors by the suspect/victim:

- 50% pointed a firearm at deputies.
- 26% lunged at deputies with a knife.
- 15% fired their weapons at deputies.
- 4% threw a knife at deputies.
- 4% continued to assault civilians with a lethal weapon after
- being ordered to drop their weapon.

A simple viewing of the video footage in this case supported the fact that Bryan demonstrated none of these behaviors. At no time did he "lunge" at the officers. He never threw the knife, which was lowered to his side, and he assaulted no civilians, even when he had the opportunity to do so. He simply took one step off the porch, no doubt blinded by five ballistic lights pointed directly at him, and was fired upon twenty-seven times.

Dr. Mohandie also cited the work of E. S. Shneidman, author of The Suicidal Mind (1998). In that publication it was pointed out that in 90% of actual suicide cases, people had given verbal or behavioral clues to their intent within the week or so before committing suicide. The indicator of "preplanning" is well known to behavioral researchers who study the phenomenon of suicide. Even Dr. Mohandie himself provides a list in his study of historical indicators that the person might be considering suicide. They include:

- Has killed a significant person in their life.
- Has killed a pet or destroyed personal property.
- Has recently disposed of money/property.
- Faces arrest for a crime they perceive as serious.
- Faces a life situation they perceive as embarrassing or shameful.
- Has left a suicide note.
- Clinical depression
- Terminal diagnosis
- Two or more traumatic losses
- Previous police contact around suicide or violent risk issues.

None of these indicators were present in the case of Bryan Carreño. In his report, Dr. Mohandie was providing a post-incident evaluation of Bryan's behavior and intentions, yet he was ignoring his own research and the research of others. One additional factor that Dr. Mohandie ignored, and yet again, one discussed in his own research, is the contrast between a truly suicidal individual and one simply caught up in the moment with anger and frustration, or even one temporarily impacted by some type of substance abuse. In his own research, Mohandie found that only 30% of the shootings classified as suicide by cop were found to have been preplanned. The remaining 70% were determined to be the product of a spontaneous decision made by the victim as the incident was unfolding.

Dr. Mohandie also offered a conclusion related to the crisis intervention techniques, or lack of, employed by the responding deputies. In his report, he wrote the following:

> The crisis management techniques by first responders were appropriate. There were a number of high-risk indicators present in this case that indicated a low likelihood of a successful verbal outcome, the most significant being Mr. Carreño being unwilling to talk, having no demands, and being under the influence of methamphetamines and other substances. His intoxication made him not capable of being reasoned with, unpredictable, and uncommunicative in any meaningful fashion that was likely to lead to a peaceful resolution. This is further complicated by his history of defiance and acting out. In fact, he continued to manifest evidence of his ongoing drug-induced violent impulses, as demonstrated by arming himself with another knife he obtained from the house he broke into, and almost immediately attacking the officers when they found him in that residence. A willingness to talk and desire to live are essential factors for a peaceful resolution, and these factors dwell within the suspect. Given the dynamic nature of Mr. Carreño's behavior, special resources such as CARES or deploying a mental health resource, were not appropriate.

Indeed, it was hard to believe that a mental health professional who makes such a statement could possibly be involved in any type or form of crisis intervention. He was essentially saying that using NO crisis intervention techniques was the proper thing to do and that shooting Bryan instead was the appropriate method of resolving the crisis. Mohandie was clearly acting as an advocate for the deputies and attempting to facilitate their defense. His finding ran from the absurd to the dishonest in my mind. First of all, how did Bryan demonstrate an unwillingness to talk when the total face-to-face time the deputies had with him was exactly five seconds? How was he to make any demands in that amount of time? I was at a loss to understand how Dr. Mohandie got from Bryan arming himself with the knife, which he never raised against the deputies, to "drug-induced violent impulses." I wondered if he even considered that perhaps Bryan was preparing to protect himself from the attack of a police

K9. And finally, his statement that Bryan "attacked" the deputies with the knife led me to believe that he never bothered to even watch the video. There clearly was no attack by Bryan prior to stepping one foot off the steps and getting shot twenty times.

It was obvious that the defense in this case brought in Dr. Mohandie to make the case that Bryan committed "suicide by cop." Many behavioral science professionals deplore the term because it has the effect of removing responsibility for certain types of police shootings from the officers involved and placing it squarely on the victim. No one truly "commits" suicide by cop. They place themselves in

a situation where the officers involved choose to commit the lethal act, an act they are trained to avoid, and in many cases do. It is an unscientific term that is often used as a "get-out-of-jail-free" card by the law enforcement community to address problematic shootings. Dr. Mohandie's report appeared to me to be intended to facilitate the officers' defense. He even made the rather unbelievable statement that no crisis intervention techniques or protocols were appropriate. Such techniques and protocols are ALWAYS appropriate when responding to a crisis, even if their effectiveness may be limited by various factors.

I eventually flew out to Santa Barbara for my deposition. Bill Schmidt, a pilot, flew in from Fresno and met me there. We expected a tough line of questioning from the defense attorney, who is also an attorney for Santa Barbara County. It was especially tough during the five hours of questioning. I stood my ground however, especially when it came to Dr. Mohandie's report. I knew suicide by cop was their defense strategy, so I focused as much as I could on refuting that assertion. I expected that they would file a Daubert motion basically arguing that I was not qualified to question one of the nation's leading authorities on the issue. In the end, no motion was offered. A short time following my deposition, Santa Barbara County agreed to settle the case for $850,000.

Every day in America the police offer the phenomenon of suicide by cop to justify a questionable shooting. More often than not it works, typically because they hire an expert who makes the case for them using an unscientific mix of anecdotes, urban legend, and purported personal experience. Very few pro-police experts are even qualified to discuss the issue. It is a powerful argument because it has the effect of causing a jury or even a judge to look no further for a justification for the officer's decision to shoot. The only reason we were able to prevail in Bryan Carreño's case was because it was captured on video, a video that refuted both Dr. Mohandie's conclusions, as well as the statements of the officers involved. Sadly, there have been hundreds of such cases over the years that were not captured on videotape. We will never know how many of those shootings were truly justified and how many slipped through the cracks.

Bryan Carreño was a young man who needed help. A nonlethal shot from a Taser or a burst of OC pepper spray was all that separated him from a mandatory psychiatric evaluation. Perhaps it would have been life-changing for him. Perhaps he would have received the right mix of medication, counseling, and the support of his family to have a lasting effect. Instead, he was killed instantly in such a fusillade of gunfire that it lit up the night sky, and then blamed for his own death through a coordinated use of the script by five different deputies. In this case, the script came face-to-face with an unflinching attorney in Bill Schmidt and the most powerful weapon that can be employed to neutralize its calculated impact—a truthful and open-minded analysis of the evidence and a willingness to listen to the story it has to tell, regardless of where that story leads.

By the time the Carreño case settled, I had become a target of the police unions from one coast to the other. In almost every case there was a concerted effort to get me disqualified from testifying. Attorneys from different cases, sometimes in completely different parts of the country, were coordinating their efforts. Numerous times during depositions a question would be asked that I recognized from some other deposition in a completely different case. I knew the game. The two attorneys had discussed my testimony, and now one was trying to get me to answer differently from the previous deposition. Of course, if I did, then that inconsistency would be part of a Daubert motion to get me disqualified. It never worked. In nearly 200 cases, I was disqualified only twice. In one of the cases, I had already terminated my involvement in the matter for reasons related to the competency of the attorney who hired me. I frankly felt that he was purposely trying to lose his own case and I did not want to be part of it. Consequently, when the Daubert motion was filed, I was not able to defend my qualifications with an affidavit as I normally did. And in the second case, all four of the experts involved were disqualified just a few weeks before the trial. I recognized that the judge was attempting to pressure the lawyers to settle the case rather than go to trial. If that was his intent, and disqualifying all the experts was a good way to do it, then it worked. The case settled a few days later for over $2 million.

I think what upset the deadly force industry the most was that I never hesitated to play the same games they did, only better. Unlike the other retired cops I knew who were providing expert witness testimony on behalf of plaintiffs, and there were only a few, I never tried to finesse my way through a case without offending the police establishment. When they brought out a shooting victim's criminal history in an effort to publicly crucify them, I highlighted in my report the officer's lies and inconsistencies to publicly crucify them right back. When a pro-police expert used junk science to make their case, I used an abundance of sophisticated and peer-reviewed legitimate science to make them look foolish. And when an attorney or expert representing a large department like the LAPD or Chicago Police Department tried to minimize my experience by pointing out with a snicker that I worked for a rural sheriff's department with less than a dozen deputies, I never hesitated to point out that an officer from one of those departments would have no clue how to patrol 325 square miles by themselves and with no back-up anywhere near. The key was to fight back and not be bullied, which is one of the tactics used very effectively by the deadly force industry.

CHAPTER 16

The Case of John Cruz Jr.

Edgewater, Colorado

The Cost of Being Expendable

If there is one case that causes me to lay awake at night, it is the case of John Cruz Jr. He represents a class of people the criminal justice system traditionally sweeps under the rug with little deliberation. He was, and remains, one of society's expendables. On July 12, 2019, John was 40 years old, unemployed and never married, and still living with his aging parents. He had an undiagnosed mental illness, paranoid schizophrenia no doubt, and was a drug user on top of that. He had all the characteristics that force people like him to struggle through life with few advocates and little hope of living even a small part of the American dream. When they find themselves on the wrong end of a police response, especially one involving SWAT, there is seldom a positive outcome.

On the day he was arrested, John had committed no proven crime, at least not before the police arrived, and the only crime he was even accused of committing was shooting at a neighbor's house with a BB gun, a neighbor he was convinced worked for the CIA. When he finally walked out of his house hours later to surrender to SWAT, he was charged with attempted murder after purportedly shooting at the officers. None were hurt, but John found himself facing a nearly 40-year prison term. The district attorney agreed not to argue against a sentence of twenty-one years, the minimum for the crimes he was eventually charged with, if John would agree to plead guilty, which he eventually did.

My involvement in this case was somewhat unique. I seldom worked criminal cases, and I had never worked one that was already finished except for the sentencing hearing. I was contacted by John's lawyer, Denver civil rights attorney Luke McConnell. Luke explained that he was looking for an expert who could offer an opinion on the police response, given John's mental illness. Was their response carried out appropriately, or did it make things worse by provoking John to respond the way he did, something they should have anticipated and tried to avoid? Luke also explained that he had been caught in somewhat of a trick bag regarding John's decision to plead guilty. It is something prosecutors will often do, especially with expendables like John. They give the defendant a choice. They can plead guilty and receive a lengthy sentence, or they can exercise their constitutional right to a trial and risk going to prison for twice as long if they lose. It is one of the most cynical and offensive aspects of the criminal justice process because it penalizes a defendant for exercising their constitutional rights. I totally understood the corner Luke was in when he recommended that John enter a guilty plea. Colorado is a law-and-order state. The downside is that prosecutors and judges in such jurisdictions tend to give little weight to a defendant's cognitive or emotional shortcomings when meting out justice. They will find much in aggravation to support a longer prison sentence, but little in mitigation to support a shorter sentence. Knowing the likely futility of advocating for a shorter sentence, I agreed to take the case.

The initial complaint in this matter came from a neighbor of John's directly across the street. Two Edgewater police officers, Robert Brink and Tristan Robenalt, responded, with Officer Brink acting as the lead officer. The neighbors reported that they were in their yard when they heard four to five "pops" and then something hitting their house. They neither saw where the shots came from, nor did they see John outside. This was not the first time Officer Brink had dealt with this situation. In October 2018, the same neighbor had reported that she found either a pellet or bullet hole in her front door. Officer Brink was the responding officer, and after concluding that the hole was caused by a pellet, he surmised that someone passing by in a vehicle had likely fired it. Then, in July 2019, the same neighbor reported finding a bullet or pellet hole in her front window. In neither case did Brink take the time to question John, and in neither case was any evidence found that would connect the shots to any weapons owned by John, which included a number of pellet and BB guns, two handguns, a shotgun, and at least two assault rifles.

There was no indication in the investigative documents I reviewed that Officer Brink retrieved any of the pellets or inspected the points of impact, or even confirmed that there were points of impact before moving forward with his actions that morning. It must be assumed that he believed the shots were from a pellet gun rather than a firearm, given the neighbor's description. The neighbor knew where the projectiles had hit the house. Had they come from a firearm, there would have been obvious bullet defects. None were mentioned in the report. In fact, no evidence at all was later found by the crime scene technician at the neighbor's residence except evidence from the prior incidents.

Given that the only report from the neighbor was that she and others had heard "pops," and given that Officer Brinks failed to locate any pellets or even impact points, the question that arises is why the officers did not simply knock on John's door and attempt to speak to him. Instead, they took positions of cover while Brink ordered him out of his house over a loudspeaker. Little did they know that John was in bed asleep. This is not to discount the possibility that a pellet gun can be a dangerous weapon, but there did not seem to be a compelling reason to attempt to communicate with John from a distance and over the loudspeaker. Speaking to him face-to-face could have accomplished a number of important goals. First, it could have provided probable cause for an arrest or search warrant, or both. And second, short of an arrest, it may have helped to de-escalate the situation and prevent further problems. Because they failed to properly investigate the initial report, the officers lacked probable cause to arrest John. And without that, they lacked the authority to force him from his own residence.

As more officers began to arrive, a call was made to John's father. Both of his parents were inside the house. They agreed to come outside and meet with officers. Once outside, they were not allowed to return. John would later state during an interview with detectives that when he awoke and found his parents gone, he initially believed they had left for the gym. Moments later, responding to the sound of the loudspeaker, he opened his front door to the sight of numerous police officers taking positions of cover with their guns drawn. Not surprisingly, John responded by slamming the door shut. One can only imagine what he was thinking at that point, given his obvious paranoia.

As discussed throughout this book, all police officers in the United States now complete de-escalation training. They complete an abbreviated course during their initial academy training, and then most complete an advanced 40-hour training later in their careers. This training, commonly called CIT training, provides officers the knowledge to recognize various types of mental illness and teaches them the techniques to de-escalate individuals suffering from mental illness, as well as ways to avoid escalating them unnecessarily. There was enough information known to the responding officers, especially after talking to John's parents, that he was suffering from some type of mental illness. They should have recognized that paranoia was part of that illness. During the initial response, their training should have informed them of the ease with which John's behavior could be unnecessarily escalated if they did not handle the situation with that in mind. Unfortunately, rather than talking to him in a manner designed to avoid escalation, they chose to have his parents leave the house, and then took defensive positions with their weapons drawn and commanding him over a loudspeaker to exit. There is little doubt that in John's mind the police were preparing to use force to extricate him from his own home. Escalating his behavior at that point was likely unavoidable. And again, with no probable cause to make an arrest, John was under no obligation to leave his own home simply to be questioned by the police about having possibly fired a pellet or BB gun at his neighbor's house.

A little over an hour after Officer Brink's arrival, and after John refused to come outside, there was a dispatch by Brink that John was possibly "barricading" himself inside the house. The use of this label was not an accident. A barricaded suspect is typically the necessary criteria for a SWAT callout. By this point, John had done nothing but refuse to come outside. He had not yet been observed with a weapon, and if there was no probable cause for an arrest, then he was under no obligation to comply. Also, by this time, no effort had been made to secure a search warrant or an arrest warrant, nor was there probable cause to do so. The officers had already escalated John with their numbers and show of force, and now they were about to make things even worse by calling out SWAT. John's parents provided no information to corroborate the neighbors' claims. They were cooperative; however, there appears to have been no effort made to use them as an investigative resource to determine exactly what had happened earlier that morning.

At 9:18 a.m., a page was sent activating SWAT. It appears from the record that Officer Mark Donohue from the Golden Police Department was commanding the regional team. They deployed to three different locations. An arrest team was positioned in the driveway behind the cover of a Bearcat armored vehicle. A second team was positioned at the rear of the house. A third team (snipers) was positioned to the northeast of the house to cover a blind spot at the rear corner. At the time of the callout, John still had not fired a weapon, nor had he been seen displaying one.

While Donohue may have been commanding SWAT, there is no indication in the record that the operation had a unified and single commander directing the various entities. In fact, the record indicates that there was no single commander. This is an absolute necessity, especially when the operation involves regional and multijurisdictional units. Unbelievably, when Donohue was later interviewed by detectives, he stated that at some point John may have been connected to a negotiator or dispatcher, but he was not sure. It is hard to imagine that a SWAT commander could possibly carry out an operation without even knowing whether a negotiation was taking place. In fact, there was a negotiator talking to John, and obviously Donohue was not even listening. Done properly, an operation such as this is under the command of a single senior officer. That commander at various times assigns control of the operation to others. For example, when a negotiator is communicating with a subject, that negotiator is given full control unless the commander intervenes. The decision to begin an escalation of force by SWAT does not rest with the SWAT commander until the negotiator relinquishes control back to the scene commander, who in turn gives control over to the SWAT commander to move forward with their tactical plan. This only confirms that no one appears to have been in charge. Even Officer Brink can be heard in the dispatch recordings continuing to direct officers after SWAT was deployed. This lack of coordination only caused John to become even more escalated as time passed.

The goal of SWAT is not de-escalation, but rather to achieve their objective through a gradual escalation of force until the suspect complies with their commands. When SWAT is deployed, there is a high probability that some level of force will be used. It is thus imperative that the SWAT commander have timely and accurate intelligence from the officers at the scene. It is obvious this was not the case with Officer Donohue. In his interview he admitted that he did not recall specifically all that he was told when he arrived on-scene. This interview occurred just three days after the incident. He stated that he did recall being told that John's family believed he had the potential to fire upon the police. There is no indication in the statements and affidavits of the uniformed officers, especially Officer Brink, that this statement was ever made by John's family members. Donahue also stated that the police were not sure if a pellet gun or .22 firearm had been fired at the neighbor's residence. The statements and reports of the uniformed officers indicate that there was never a suspicion that anything other than a pellet gun had been fired at the house and, further, that no one at the house across the street had actually witnessed John fire it.

After pulling the Bearcat in front of the house, Donohue announced over the loudspeaker that John was under arrest and commanded him to leave the residence. At this point there was no arrest warrant or search warrant secured or even applied for. It remains unclear what probable cause Donahue was relying on to make such a demand. At approximately 10:38 a.m., SWAT officers began breaking out windows. They do this to provide an avenue for introducing weapons and technology (e.g., gas cannisters, drones). At the time the windows were broken, John still had not fired a weapon, nor had he been seen holding one. Instead, he called 911 to report that the police were breaking out his windows. The call was patched through to Deputy Denise Denuzzie, a trained negotiator. A second deputy was assigned to serve as a back-up negotiator.

Denuzzie had significant information about John prior to her contact with him. She knew he suffered from hallucinations, delusional thinking, and extreme paranoia, and was a drug user on top of that. A trained negotiator knows that such a person is easily escalated and will not process the happenings around them in a rational way. They also know to be extremely careful in what they say to avoid elevating the person's level of paranoia. As soon as Denuzzie made contact with John, all SWAT activity should have ceased. Furthermore, Denuzzie should have shared the information she had about John with Officer Donohue, and the two of them should have coordinated their activities, with Denuzzie having temporary control of the scene. The Bearcat should have been pulled back out of sight, and SWAT officers should have done the same while maintaining a containment perimeter. This was not done, even when John showed a willingness to talk to Denuzzie. It was a missed opportunity to begin de-escalating the situation by minimizing their force profile.

The most important task of the negotiator early on is to build trust and rapport with the individual. In this case, Denuzzie immediately focused the conversation on whether John had any guns in the house and repeatedly asked him to come outside. She already knew from the family members that he had a number of guns, and it was too early in the dialogue to expect him to simply walk outside. John was willing to talk, but rather than allowing him to do so, and then acknowledging his concerns, Denuzzie unwittingly projected the message that her only goal was to convince him to exit the house. For a person suffering from paranoia, her efforts were almost immediately counterproductive.

Early on, John requested that he be allowed to speak to a federal law enforcement officer. This request was based on the delusional belief that he was an employee of the U.S. Treasury Department. Nonetheless, it was a reasonable option to pursue. The goal should have been de-escalation, and to pursue this option meant nothing more than exchanging a local negotiator with a federal negotiator. Every FBI field office has trained negotiators. There was no reason not to pursue this option. At that point there was no arrest warrant. Again, it is questionable whether they even had probable cause at that point. Whenever a barricaded suspect makes a request or demand that can potentially bring the situation to a peaceful conclusion, it is an opportunity that must be pursued. This was not a hostage negotiation. There was no need for a "this-for-that" strategy. Denuzzie advised John that she would try to get in touch with someone at Treasury, but that he would have to come out first. The message she was giving to John was that she was not taking his request seriously. This message was reinforced numerous times when she switched back and forth between telling him she was working on getting a federal agent there and telling him he would have to come out first. At one point she even told John, "you know as well as I do, John, that getting a hold of the feds for anything is pretty difficult." She later told him that the feds would not come to the house. In reality, no federal agency was even contacted.

Approximately five minutes into the conversation, John asked, "Why are they even here?" This was a rational question that should have been answered honestly. Instead, Denuzzie responded that she was unsure why and then asked John what had happened earlier in the morning that upset him and made him angry. There was no indication that he was upset or angry about anything. Again, when the police arrived, John was asleep in bed. Furthermore, a negotiator's goal is to get the suspect to tell them how they are feeling and to acknowledge those feelings with empathy. It is not for the negotiator to tell the suspect how the suspect is feeling and why. It was a mistake to say she was not sure why the police were there. After all, she was the police. Again, her response was counterproductive to building trust and rapport. When John again demanded to know why they were there, Denuzzie answered that there was "possibly" a warrant for his arrest and then asked John if that was true. Obviously, he would not have known. At that point, a warrant had not even been applied for. She then admitted that there was no warrant. Already, just over five minutes into the negotiation, she was losing credibility and establishing no effective rapport.

At eleven minutes into the conversation, John again stated that he would come outside for a federal law enforcement officer. Unbelievably, at the same time Denuzzie is responding to this statement, SWAT can be heard in the background yelling commands over a loudspeaker. I was able to discern "DO IT NOW!" in the background of the recording. It was obvious to me that there was no centralized and coordinated command. It was also obvious that John was becoming more emotionally escalated. Never should there be a situation where multiple SWAT officers are yelling commands at a suspect while a negotiator is on the phone trying to negotiate a peaceful resolution. At that point, at least in my mind, the police response had devolved into a disorganized mess, and it was about to get worse.

At approximately fifteen minutes into the conversation, as John continued to ask for a federal agent, the sound of SWAT breaking the windows can be heard. I knew what this meant. They were about to introduce gas into the house. At that point, Denuzzie tells John, "John, take a deep breath for me . . . don't listen to them, just talk to me." It was an absurd thing for a negotiator to say. At that point, the negotiation was of no value. Denuzzie had no credibility, she had demonstrated no real intention of having a federal agent respond to the scene, and SWAT, continuing their response during the negotiation, only sent the message to John that he was being tricked into coming out of the house or exposing himself. At that point, Denuzzie should have been replaced by the back-up negotiator, and SWAT should have been directed to back off. Unfortunately, neither happened.

The negotiation in this case accomplished little and in fact likely escalated John's level of paranoia. It is a basic principle of crisis negotiation that you do not lie to the person you are negotiating with. It was obvious that John figured out quickly that a federal agency was not being called. Denuzzie also was unprepared. She did not know for certain if there was a warrant and really did not seem to have a clear understanding of the allegations regarding the pellet shots earlier in the morning. The most striking aspect of the negotiation was that John himself made it clear how the situation could be resolved. He wanted only for a federal agent to respond to the scene to confirm for him that the officers were truly police officers. He stated multiple times that he would then come out. Why that call was never made is a mystery. It would have been a simple resolution to the crisis, and it could have been done in a manner that safeguarded the federal agent's safety.

Immediately after SWAT began breaking the windows, officers heard gunshots coming from inside the house. These shots were later found to have been fired by John into a bedroom floor with one of his handguns. In response to the sound of the shots, the SWAT officers began a significant escalation of force, including the introduction of both OC and CS (chlorobenzalmalonitrile) "hot" gas into the house. The latter is extremely flammable and dangerous. They also deployed Stinger balls, robots, drones, 40 mm baton rounds, and flash grenades. John did not come out, and in fact, it was not even clear where in the house he was hiding. A small drone was deployed through a broken window, but the operator was unable to find him. It was obvious that SWAT had lost sight of the fact that there still was no probable cause even to arrest John. It is not a violation of law for someone to shoot a gun into the floor of their own house.

At approximately 11:45 a.m., after delivering a fresh round of gas into the house, Sergeant Donahue again ordered John to come out of the house over the loudspeaker of the Bearcat, which was now parked in the driveway at an angle. Donahue was sitting in the passenger seat. There were multiple SWAT officers standing behind the Bearcat with their assault rifles at the ready. Then all hell broke loose. Multiple officers stated they observed John fire an AR-15 style rifle toward the Bearcat from a window on the side of the house under the carport. A drone overhead and at least one media camera positioned down the street were recording at that moment and captured the passenger side window of the Bearcat being struck by a bullet. The bulletproof window, next to where Donahue was sitting, shattered but remained intact. In the moments that followed, multiple officers returned fire at the window where John was spotted. Wood and glass flew in all directions as the high-velocity bullets penetrated the side of the house. Miraculously, John was not shot as he retreated away from the window.

For the next twelve hours John refused all further attempts by the police to communicate with him and remained silent. At around midnight the decision was made to breach the house. By now, new SWAT members had relieved the original team. When SWAT decides to breach a structure, it means they are done waiting and intend to enter by any means possible, typically with explosives or some other type of destructive force. It is a dangerous point in any SWAT encounter. Anyone who watched events unfold during the 1993 standoff in Waco, Texas, with the Branch Davidians, watched as the FBI breached the side of the structure with a battering ram attached to a tank. The results were deadly. In this case, SWAT made the decision to take a similar action with a battering ram attached to a Bearcat. With little effort they destroyed the south wall of the house. As they prepared to make a tactical entry, John exited the house with his hands in the air and surrendered.

The case against John seemed strong at first glance. There was no doubt in my mind that the police had provoked his actions unnecessarily. But it is nearly impossible to successfully argue self-defense against the police, even when the individual defending himself suffers from some type of mental illness. The evidence favored the police, or so I initially thought. Like every case I worked, I set out to reinvestigate this one, first by analyzing the evidence provided by the police and the district attorney. When I finally did, I had more questions than answers, and began to consider that John never fired at all. Of course, if he did not fire the gun, then he did not commit the felony offenses he was preparing to plead guilty to in return for a 21-year prison sentence.

The first thing I found were significant inconsistencies in the officers' descriptions of John firing at the Bearcat, his most serious offense. Deputy Chad Bingham, who was sitting inside the Bearcat, stated that he observed John stretch his arms out the window while wearing a motorcycle helmet and fire an AR-style rifle several times at the Bearcat. Sergeant Donahue stated that John was actually climbing out of the window when he fired. He observed John hanging out of the window with his entire torso exposed. Deputy Anthony Brown reported that he could see John's head silhouetted in the window immediately after he fired. He said nothing about John wearing a motorcycle helmet. Another officer stated that John was holding a rifle with an orange tip, indicating a BB or pellet gun. And another described John holding a handgun rather than a rifle. Additionally, there was little agreement on how many shots John had fired. The statements ranged from a single shot to as many as five.

I immediately began to question the officers' accounts. For starters, the drone video was clear that the officers returned fire immediately after the bullet struck the Bearcat's window. If John really were hanging out of the window when he fired, I wondered how he could possibly have returned inside quick enough to avoid being shot. Also, the only motorcycle helmet recovered from the residence following the incident was found on the front porch right where John was seen dropping it earlier in the morning by multiple officers. But for me, the most important evidence would have been the location where John's empty casings were found. If he really was leaning or climbing out of the window when he fired, then his casings would surely have ejected close by onto the driveway. Even if the gun was mostly inside the window when he fired, the empty casings should have been easily found inside the house. To my surprise, no casings were found, neither inside nor outside the house. This seemed impossible to me if John truly had fired his weapon.

There were three known shots that were fired in the direction of the Bearcat. One hit the Bearcat's window. Another was found embedded in the window trim in a small in-law residence across the street. And the third entered a house across the street and to the north of the in-law residence. I expected that the bullet that struck the Bearcat was likely destroyed and beyond analysis. And I knew from the reports that the bullet that entered the house was not found. But the bullet that was found embedded in the in-law residence was found and recovered. Furthermore, I found a report from the detective who recovered it and confirmed that he had delivered it to the crime lab. This would be conclusive evidence since the rifle found in the house was a .223 caliber. The SWAT officers were carrying 5.56 caliber weapons. So, if the bullet was determined to be a .223, then there would be no question that John did in fact fire his weapon.

I was unable to find any crime lab reports in the materials that were provided by the police department. I advised Luke McConnell of this, and he agreed to request them. During the wait, I decided to again review the video footage, especially the drone video, to see if a SWAT officer could be spotted to the rear of the residence with a shot trajectory that matched the three shots. I had worked other cases where it was later determined that the police in the chaos of the moment had actually fired a shot originally believed to have been fired by a suspect. When I watched the video, this time keeping a close eye on the alley behind John's house, I could not believe what I saw. Not only was there a SWAT officer in the alley, but in the seconds just before the Bearcat window can be seen shattering, the officer is seen leveling his rifle in a shooting position and bracing it atop a garbage can. The rifle was pointed in the direction of the Bearcat! Unfortunately, just before the Bearcat was struck, the drone abruptly changed positions and lost sight of the officer in its field of view. I advised Luke of what I found, and that the lab report was now critical. If the bullet retrieved from the in-law residence was a 5.56, it would be conclusive evidence that John did not fire at the Bearcat. Adding to this possibility, when John's .223 rifle was finally recovered from inside the house, it was unloaded, and a BB was found in the barrel. It seemed a bit impossible that a BB could survive inside the barrel after three bullets roughly the same diameter as the barrel had passed through.

I would not say I was surprised when Luke called to tell me the bullet had never been analyzed and that all testing had stopped once John agreed to plead guilty. The police and the prosecutor were willing to send a man to prison for twenty-one years without even knowing for certain if he had committed the crime. It was such a basic investigative step, and for reasons that were never shared, was simply ignored. I knew the ugly reality of the criminal justice system, especially for someone like John. If Luke now asked that the sentencing hearing be postponed, allowing time to have the bullet tested, the prosecutor would likely withdraw their agreement to a twenty-oneyear sentence. If the bullet was identified as a .223, John would again be facing the maximum thirty-eight years, even with a guilty plea. If it was found to be a 5.56, Luke would have to go to trial to argue his case. Even then, there was no guarantee that a law-and-order jury in a law-and-order state would agree. It was the impossible corner criminal suspects find themselves in every day in the United States. It is a corner even the best lawyers are unable to get their clients out of. I considered Luke one of the more able lawyers I had worked with, but I could hear the hopelessness in his voice.

On August 7, 2020, John was sentenced. There is another dirty little secret in the criminal justice system that played out that day. Prosecutors have the ability to execute a formal plea agreement that includes an agreed to sentence the judge will impose. But they also at times will simply agree not to argue against a particular sentence recommended by the defense attorney without a formal agreement. The prosecutor in this case agreed not to argue against twenty-one years rather than the maximum thirty-eight the judge could impose under the law. Often, this course by a prosecutor amounts to little more than a wink and a nod to a presiding judge that the prosecutor will stand to the side if the judge chooses to impose a harsher sentence. After all, if a prosecutor honestly believes a lighter sentence is appropriate for whatever reason, then there will likely be a formal plea agreement. Also, it is a great way for a prosecutor to wash the blood from their hands, so to speak, and to blame an extremely harsh sentence on a judge who does not have to campaign against a primary challenger every four years.

Before the judge imposed his sentence on John, Luke attempted to offer evidence that the police had provoked John's actions, that they had failed to properly investigate the matter, and that John suffered from mental illness. It had little effect. After Luke asked for twenty-one years, followed by the prosecutor agreeing not to argue against the recommendation, the judge sentenced John to thirty-eight years in the Colorado Department of Corrections. For John, who by then was 42 years old, it amounted to what could potentially end up being a life sentence.

There is no doubt that John could have avoided all of this by simply walking outside to meet with the officers. But it is also true that he enjoyed the constitutional right, as do all citizens, to remain inside the privacy of his own home and refuse to talk to the police when there is neither a warrant for his arrest nor to search his house. John was acting in self-defense. The shots he allegedly fired were reactive and defensive in nature. He fired five shots into the floor of his house with a .22 caliber revolver when SWAT began breaching his windows, and then allegedly fired at the Bearcat after they introduced gas into the house. Was it reasonable for John to take such action? Reasonableness is a relative term, and for someone suffering from mental illness with schizophrenic-like symptoms, made worse by illicit drug use, it probably seemed completely reasonable at the time and, in fact, necessary.

It is easy to dismiss John Cruz Jr. as someone who got what he deserved for firing upon police officers. But when you strip away the layers, you find that SWAT responded to John's house and began breaking his windows and shooting highly flammable "hot gas" into the residence for nothing more than a couple of BBs that were never found; that struck a residence in an area that was never located; and that were fired by an individual who was never identified. Did John fire the BBs? Probably. But the police have no authority to make arrests and use force based on "probably." Those activities are based on the legal standard of "probable cause," and "probably" does not rise to that level. Neither the prosecutor nor the judge even considered that the actions of the officers in this case were unlawful. Once John reportedly climbed out a window wearing a motorcycle helmet to confront a police tactical team—is there a better description of mental illness?—then the question of lawfulness became a moot point.

Somewhere in the evidence room of the Edgewater police department is a box with John's name on it that contains, among other items, a single bullet that was never analyzed. If that bullet is a .223 caliber, then we can conclude that John did in fact fire upon the officers. But if it is a 5.56 caliber, then an innocent man is now spending the better part of his remaining life in prison. Either way, at the end of the day, John Cruz Jr. was guilty most of all of the crime of mental illness. He is one of the expendables to whom the criminal justice system assigns little to no inherent value, and who now sits in a prison cell to be quickly forgotten by a society that has never been quite capable of facing its own darkness. And so it is that life goes on, the conveyor belt of justice keeps creeping forward along its pitted path, and if you listen closely, you can hear in the distance the faint sound of the band continuing to play on, uninterrupted by an inconvenient distraction like John Cruz Jr.

- CHAPTER 17-

The Case of George Floyd

Minneapolis, Minnesota

Lessons Learned and the Path Forward

The truth is always somewhere in the middle. It is a lesson I learned long ago, and nowhere is that truer than in a questionable deadly force case. In almost every such case, both sides—the police and those who advocate on behalf of the victim—will circle the wagons and interpret the incident from their own worldview and be influenced by their own implicit bias. Every deadly force incident is a complex psychological exchange between two or more people with elements critical to the outcome occurring sometimes in a fraction of a second. A case is never as simple as the press reports it or as the attorneys tend to describe it when they get in front of a microphone. What sometimes appears obvious to the untrained eye on a dash or body cam is anything but obvious to an expert who must set aside any preconceived ideas, check their bias at the door, and reach conclusions based on science rather than public opinion.

I began my expert witness career during the social unrest in Ferguson, Missouri, in 2014. I decided to end it with the nationwide unrest following the George Floyd incident in Minneapolis in 2020. I set out to level the playing field for the families of police violence, and eventually found myself defending police officers who were being wrongly accused by prosecutors kowtowing to radical organizations dead set on defunding law enforcement in the United States. It seemed that America had completely lost sight of the middle ground, that place where truth resides, and that any hope of leveling the playing field was lost. After nearly 200 cases in six short years, I decided it was time to retire.

The George Floyd case would be my final foray into the world of civil rights litigation. I was hired by Chicago attorney Antonio Romanucci, one of Chicago's top civil rights lawyers, and his associate, Bhavani Raveendran. I must admit that I had second thoughts about working the case. There were multiple attorneys involved on the plaintiff's side. I was brought in specifically to address the Monell issue, or whether the Minneapolis Police Department held any liability for the officers' actions. My efforts would involve primarily a review of the department's policies and training to determine if there were deficiencies in either that may have contributed to the outcome. I had reservations about working the case because of the highly publicized ways in which the public, the media, and the political establishment were all behaving in the incident's aftermath. It was a level of mass hysteria that not even the Michael Brown or Rodney King cases had caused. I knew the objective truth of what had happened was lost somewhere in the middle, and in this case the middle itself was lost.

One of the first public responses to the death of George Floyd was a nationwide call to ban choke holds by the police. I found this peculiar since choke holds have always been banned in law enforcement except in cases where deadly force is justified, in which case the officer can gouge out a suspect's eyes if necessary to prevent death or serious injury to themselves or others. The public and political establishments were both confusing a choke hold with a carotid neck restraint, a classic "sleeper hold" that is applied by a properly trained officer without obstructing the suspect's breathing. It is used to briefly incapacitate a suspect who cannot otherwise be restrained to give the officer time to apply handcuffs. Done properly, the suspect will become momentarily unconscious from the reduced flow of blood to the brain.

What happened to George Floyd was neither a choke hold nor a carotid neck restraint. The officers should have recognized that Floyd was demonstrating the symptoms of excited delirium by the time they had him in handcuffs and pinned to the ground next to the police vehicle. This was evident on the body cam videos that were released. The police are trained to recognize this condition, and they are well aware of the potential deadly outcome if the individual's movement is restricted while pinned to the ground in a prone position. The risk of sudden death is greatly increased. Although the individual may be able to breathe, their respiration can be restricted enough to prevent adequate oxygenation of the blood (hypoxia), causing the heart to become distressed and eventually fail. The risk of this outcome is increased if the individual has a history of heart disease and substance abuse.

When the autopsy report was finally released by the Hennepin County Medical Examiner's Office, the cause of death was listed as "cardiopulmonary arrest complicating law enforcement subdual, restraint, and neck compression." Prosecutors were quick to point out, at least initially, that the autopsy revealed no physical findings that supported a diagnosis of traumatic asphyxia or strangulation. George Floyd had died of heart failure, likely caused by a near lethal amount of Fentanyl in his system, a powerful opioid that can cause respiratory distress and death when taken in high doses. The medical examiner also found evidence of "atherosclerotic and hypertensive heart disease." Medically speaking, Floyd was a walking time bomb, something the officers could not have known.

A second independent autopsy was conducted by Dr. Michael Baden and an associate on behalf of Floyd's family. Baden, a former chief medical examiner of New York City, left no room for doubt. He found the cause of death to be "mechanical asphyxiation" resulting from compression on the neck and back, which restricted Floyd's blood flow and breathing. Baden also found no underlying conditions that would have contributed to Floyd's sudden death, neither his history of heart disease nor the toxic level of Fentanyl in his system. In fact, Baden concluded that Floyd was in good health.

So here we were. The rioting had begun. Parts of Minneapolis and other cities were being burned to the ground. The officers were all charged with serious crimes, including murder. And the truth of what had happened was lost somewhere in the no-man's land of the political extremes. Had George Floyd died of heart failure because of body compression or in spite of it? With two opposing autopsy reports, it would be up to a jury of citizens who likely possessed no medical experience or knowledge whatsoever to decide which was right. And while I did provide my opinions to Tony Romanucci regarding the Monell issue, I decided early on that I would refuse to serve as the prosecution's expert witness in the criminal case. As a civil matter, the case was a good one. The officers, three of them at least, clearly violated their training by applying their weight to Floyd's back and neck while he was handcuffed and in a prone position on the ground. The burden of proof in a civil case is met when the plaintiff convinces a jury that there is a greater than 50% chance that the allegations are true. This lower burden of proof leaves room for doubt on issues such as whether body compression caused or hastened Floyd's heart failure. If it is more likely than not that it did (51%), then the burden is met.

The burden of proof in a criminal matter is much more stringent, however. To convict someone of a crime in the United States, the prosecution must prove the allegation beyond a reasonable doubt. In other words, even with opposing autopsies, to convict the officers of the crimes they were charged with, the prosecution would have to prove that Floyd died of heart failure because of the body compression rather than in spite of it. In cases like young Nicholas Dyksma in Georgia, there were no preexisting conditions to cast doubt on the cause of death. In the case of Floyd, however, with a history of heart disease and a near lethal level of Fentanyl in his system, there were all kinds of doubt. Had they not been on top of him, and had he struggled while the officers attempted to get him in handcuffs without compressing his body, would his heart have failed anyway? Floyd's preexisting conditions greatly complicated the case, and when even the pathologists could not agree, in my mind it seemed impossible to prove beyond a reasonable doubt that the body compression caused his heart to fail.

The officers in this case were not charged with intentionally killing Floyd, or aiding and abetting in an intentional killing, but rather with knowingly committing a felony assault that unintentionally caused the death. Not only would the prosecution now have to prove that the body compression caused Floyd's heart to fail, but they would also have to prove that the officers' restraint of Floyd, especially Officer Chauvin's, was an intentional felony assault. This muddied the waters even further because now they would have to prove that the officers intended to assault Floyd rather than simply restrain and control him until they could get him to jail.

Regarding the Monell issue, and the potential liability of the Minneapolis Police Department for the officers' actions, I did uncover a gaping hole in the MPD policies. I discovered that while the MPD use-of-force policy provides guidelines for using either a conscious or unconscious neck restraint (MPD policy no. 5-311), that policy refers to legitimate restraint techniques MPD officers are trained to properly apply in appropriate circumstances. Officer Chauvin did not apply a legitimate neck restraint. He also did not choke Floyd. On the date of the incident then, there was in fact a deficiency in the MPD policies that has been corrected by most departments. The policy provided for the following:

1. A choke hold is defined as applying direct pressure to the front of the neck to block or obstruct the airway and can only be used when deadly force is justified (policy 5-311, section I).
2. A neck restraint technique is defined as compressing one or both sides of the neck without blocking or obstructing the airway and can be used in an appropriate situation if the officer has been properly trained (policy 5-311, section I).

What was absent from the policy, and perhaps still is, was a prohibition on compressing one or both sides of the neck without using a legitimate technique, as was the case here. What Chauvin did fits neither of the definitions provided. While it may be that at some point George Floyd did have his airway blocked (a choke hold), given the amount of time that passed before he became unresponsive, it must be assumed that the larger problem was compressional asphyxia related to hypoxia. While many departments now have specific policies related to compressional/positional asphyxiation, it does not appear that the MPD did at that time. Some departments include these guidelines and prohibitions in their "Arrest and Control" policies. A review of the MPD policies, specifically "Handcuffing Arrestees/Detainees" (policy 9-109) and "Prisoner Control, Safety, and Transportation" (policy no. 9-110), confirmed that the MPD had no policy specifically addressing compressional/positional asphyxia. In short, it could be argued that Chauvin did not violate MPD policy, notwithstanding the fact that he clearly violated his training. The argument could perhaps be made that he violated the MPD's deadly force policy, but again, what Chauvin did was not spelled out in the MPD policies as constituting deadly force.

In March of 2021, the city of Minneapolis agreed to settle the case for $27 million. There was never any doubt that the case would settle, but I wanted to believe that at least part of the reason the amount was so high was because of my conclusion that a deficient MPD policy had contributed to Floyd's death. I had to laugh when people who knew about my involvement in the case, mostly family and close friends, asked me what my percentage of the settlement amount was. The fact is, independent experts are precluded from working for a percentage, nor can they charge only if the side that hires them wins. Either circumstance creates a bias in the expert and allows the opposing side to argue that the expert is motivated to win at all costs for financial gain. Their independence is thus lost. My fee for uncovering a policy deficiency that may have contributed to the multimillion-dollar settlement amount was $1,000.

When the criminal trial finally began, I chose not to watch. I knew it would be anything but a search for the truthful middle. Rather, it would be a display of two diametrically opposed arguments that both pulled to the fringes. I viewed it as impossible to determine if Chauvin's knee caused or even contributed to Floyd's death. In a strangulation case there are physiological signs that can point to the crime—petechiae of the eyes (burst blood vessels), swollen tongue, neck injuries and bruising. But those manifestations were not found in Floyd. In fact, the autopsy report specifically stated that no petechiae or neck injuries were identified. And while the postmortem condition of the heart can sometimes point to asphyxiation, Floyd already had a severely damaged heart from excessive drug use. It seemed to me that to prove beyond a reasonable doubt that Chauvin's knee caused or contributed to Floyd's death, absent the physical manifestations of strangulation or asphyxiation (hypoxia), then someone would have to testify to the amount of pressure Chauvin applied to Floyd's neck and then compare that to some legitimate science indicating how much pressure would be fatal. I knew that the former would be impossible.

In the end, the science, even an absence of supporting science, did not matter. There was probably never any doubt that Chauvin would be convicted of the most serious offense. And perhaps he should have been. But true justice is not a guessing game. It is based on evidence. And when the evidence is lacking, justice is found somewhere in the middle. There was no doubt that Chauvin had violated his training, and with the deficiency in the MPD policies making the department itself culpable, a sizeable civil judgment was appropriate and just. As for the criminal charges, the most serious offense required the prosecution to prove that Chauvin knowingly committed a felony offense and that that action contributed to Floyd's death. I did not believe a felony could be proven without having some ability to quantify the amount of pressure applied to Floyd's neck, especially with no physical signs of strangulation or asphyxiation. I considered the two lesser charges the most just outcome.

In the end, the jury convicted Chauvin on all three charges. The ghosts of little Eddie Garner, Rodney King, and Michael Brown had finally come to haunt, and Officer Derek Chauvin would now take his place in infamy, as well as in the Minnesota Department of Corrections, as a metaphor for the accumulated sins of the police establishment. Perhaps it was the most just outcome after all. Perhaps, because it was the most needed outcome at this juncture in our nation's history. Time will tell. When the inevitable appeals finally run their course, and when the image of Chauvin's knee on George Floyd's neck begins to fade from the collective memory of most Americans, only then will we know if lasting change has finally taken root, or if it remains as elusive as ever. Only time will tell.

When I look back on the last six years, having worked nearly

200 cases involving police violence in thirty-two states, cases that have resulted in nearly $100 million in civil judgments, there are a number of lessons I have either learned or have had reinforced. One of the most important is something I already knew, that the vast majority of police officers in the United States are among the best and brightest men and women this nation has to offer to public service. They truly represent the thin blue line, but it is not a line of silence as many have argued. Rather, it is the line that separates freedom from tyranny, social order from anarchy, and hope from hopelessness when help is needed fast. It is an honorable profession with honorable people who are willing to sacrifice, sometimes with their lives, for even the lowest among us in society.

But we must also recognize the profession's shortcomings. In working excessive force cases all over the country, those shortcomings have been laid bare at my feet on numerous occasions. One of the most critical is the continued inability of law enforcement to effectively respond to the mentally ill. Sadly, the majority of cases I have worked have involved mentally ill individuals who had either committed a minor offense or no offense at all. In spite of the widespread de-escalation training that occurs, police officers still have a difficult time using those techniques when they are needed most. They have a difficult time adapting their response to a medical emergency rather than a traditional offender-arrest scenario. And if there is a weapon involved, which is almost always a knife or other type of contact weapon, in many cases all efforts to de-escalate are abandoned while the officers yell commands to drop the weapon. It is more likely than not that the officers will actually escalate rather than de-escalate the person, and the more escalated they become, the greater the likelihood that ultimately, they will be shot and killed. De-escalation efforts must occur in spite of the presence of a weapon—not to include a firearm—and never made contingent on the person dropping the weapon.

Another major shortcoming, and one that has deadly implications almost daily in the United States, is what I refer to as "linear thinking" by the police. Traditional thinking among police officers, just like the force continuum, is that the intensity of their response and level of force used to achieve compliance is steadily escalated until compliance is achieved. The police are trained, and socialized by their own culture, never to back down. This is why vehicle pursuits are so dangerous, not only during the pursuit, but immediately after. Even with most jurisdictions now restricting vehicle pursuits, it is difficult for a police officer to simply slow down and allow the vehicle being pursued to drive away. Their linear thinking causes them to approach the situation with only one possible outcome on their mind, the person's arrest. This thinking is only intensified once the vehicle is stopped or boxed in. Suddenly, the person who was being stopped, perhaps only for a minor traffic offense, ends up shot a dozen times after attempting to leave again.

It is also linear thinking that causes so many suspects to be asphyxiated by the police, an outcome I have dealt with many times as an expert. Once an arrest begins, a police officer typically has no other thought but to complete the arrest by getting the individual restrained. Many times, a deadly cycle begins if the person resists arrest. More officers pile on and apply pressure to the person's back. This may cause the person to struggle even more violently in an effort to breathe, which in turn causes the officers to apply even more pressure. Not once in my expert career have I ever heard an officer on a body cam tell a group of other officers to get off a resisting suspect and allow him or her to roll over, sit up, or stand. Instead, their linear thinking causes them to escalate their efforts as much as needed until the handcuffs are applied.

Linear thinking impacts just about every aspect of a police officer's job. It results from a mix of police training, the police culture, and Hollywood and television depictions of how police officers do their jobs. Each of these things combines to create what the law enforcement profession as a whole views as the ideal police persona—the individual who never backs down and who always gets their man (or woman). Police officers receive a great deal of training on when to act with varying levels of force. But they receive very little training on how to recognize when it might be the best option to instead swallow their pride and not act. There are too many "Pavlov's bells" in law enforcement—a vehicle speeding away from a traffic stop; a teenager running from a stolen vehicle; a suicidal person waving a knife; a suspect pulling away when an officer grabs their wrist; even a belligerent citizen exercising their constitutional right to free speech and being verbally abusive toward an officer. Linear thinking seldom causes the little voice in the officer's head to ask, "What would Andy Griffith do?" Rather, it is "Dirty Harry" who typically guides their behavior. They consider what began the incident (e.g., speeding away from a traffic stop) and how it will end (arrest). In between there will be little thought given to anything other than a gradual escalation of force until the end is achieved.

Another shortcoming of modern law enforcement is how police officers are trained to use their firearms. There is a desperate need for retooling deadly force training. Any police officer who comments on the subject will say things like "We don't shoot to injure"; "If we are justified in shooting at all, then we are justified in shooting to kill"; and "We never shoot to kill, only to stop the threat." All are word games designed to lessen an officer's sense of responsibility for making the subjective decision to kill another human being. Such words tend to make deadly force a black and white issue with few nuances and no middle ground. But that is not reality. The messages that should be instilled in new police officers should include, "When we shoot, we shoot to kill, and when we kill, we leave behind children, spouses, and parents"; and "If we are justified in shooting, perhaps there are still ways to avoid doing so." Police officers receive a great deal of training on how to kill. They receive very little training on how not to kill, even when killing might be legally justified. Deadly force is not a clinical exercise, but that is what it has become.

Police officers are trained to "stand their ground." And in fact, the law supports them when they do. And while many, if not most, instances of deadly force demand that they do stand their ground, there are still times when deadly force could have been avoided had an officer simply backed down from the precipice. When I was a young police cadet attending the academy, I recall an especially good and "old school"-type instructor providing the class a scenario where the officer gets out of his vehicle on a minor loud music complaint, and as he does, a large man holding a large knife comes out of the house saying, "I'm going to kill you, pig!" Without exception, those in the class, including me, raised our hands when the instructor asked how many would draw their weapons and fire if he got close. He then offered an alternative. How about just getting back in your squad, locking the doors, and letting him stab the vehicle while you wait for back-up? That lesson stuck with me because it made perfect sense.

Today's police training leaves little room for improvising in this manner. And in the case of the mentally ill there is actually a conflict in the training that has never been resolved. Police use-of-force training instructs officers to never back down, yet CIT training instructs those same officers to do whatever they can, including backing down, to de-escalate the situation. Unfortunately, in most cases, by the time the officer receives the latter training, they have already assimilated into their profession with the former.

One final area that police use-of-force training must address more intensively involves the number of shots that are fired at a suspect, including the phenomenon of contagious shooting when multiple officers fire. The police like to always point out a few anecdotes where an individual was still able to attack an officer even after being shot in center mass (chest and abdomen). But frankly, those examples are few and far in-between. I personally have never worked such a case. The police use ammunition that has a devastating effect on the body as the bullet passes through. There really is a small chance that after being shot once in center mass the person will not collapse. Just in some of the cases discussed in this book, consider the number of times each was shot. In each case, most of the shots occurred while they were already on the ground or falling:

- Kajieme Powell—Shot 12 times by two St. Louis, Missouri, officers
- Dontre Hamilton—Shot 14 times by a Milwaukee, Wisconsin, officer
- Michael Brown—Shot 7 times by a Ferguson, Missouri, officer
- Anthony Soderberg—Shot 17 times by multiple LAPD SWAT officers
- Jorge Ramirez—Shot 10 times by multiple Bakersfield,
- California, officers

The number of shots typically fired by the police, especially by multiple officers, is out of control. It is indeed part of the deadly force script that when an officer involved in contagious fire has no plausible way to argue that the suspect was a danger to them personally—in many cases the suspect does not even see some of the officers who fire—they will invariably state that they feared for the safety of the other officers when they fired. Without exception, the deadly force policies of police departments state that deadly force is justified to protect themselves and others from a lethal threat. None of them, however, addresses the issue of when "others" includes or is limited to well-trained and heavily armed police officers who are quite capable of protecting themselves. And at this point the courts have mostly found this to be an acceptable practice. Police officers must never be restricted in their efforts to protect the innocent from a lethal threat, but there must be reforms in police training and policy to prevent this circumstance when only police officers are in harm's way, as well as to reduce the likelihood of contagious fire when multiple officers have responded to a lethal threat.

And that of course brings us to the deadly force script itself. The courts must recognize its existence and widespread use. There is no available database that reports on the various defenses police officers use across the country in questionable deadly force cases. If there were, I am certain judges and prosecutors would be quite shocked at how often and consistently the deadly force script's various components are used. Police officers arguing that a suspect reached for his waistband; that they had superhuman strength or a thousand-yard stare; that the officer was sure they were going to die; or that they were under so much stress that they were sure they saw a gun in the suspect's empty hand, occur daily in the United States. If the officer fails to invoke the script immediately following the incident, by the time they give their account to detectives with their union representative and lawyer seated next to them, the script will be offered up with the skill of a Shakespearean actor. The beauty of the script, at least for the officers involved, is that its various components cannot easily be disproven, yet they can so easily be used to bolster an officer's defense. Ultimately, it will require that judges and prosecutors recognize the script when they see it and either demand corroborating evidence or limit its use.

So, other than retooling many aspects of police training, how do we reduce the amount of unjustified police violence in the United States? I believe the first answer to that question is the establishment of a national certification and oversight agency. Each state in the nation has such an agency, but if you look at who makes up the principals of those agencies, they are typically retired and former chiefs and sheriffs who maintain close ties to their state's law enforcement community. Many of these agencies have either limited or no authority at all to investigate and decertify officers who have engaged in questionable uses of force. Those that do seldom use it to the fullest extent possible.

A national certification for police officers, along with insurance companies cooperating by requiring this certification before providing a department liability coverage, would place responsibility for recruitment and training standards, as well as the continued employment of problem officers, square in the lap of a truly independent agency with no political or professional ties to the law enforcement community. It would serve two important functions. First, they would review all disciplinary actions, which would be reported by the departments via an online portal. All cases involving the use of deadly force, regardless of whether disciplinary action was taken by the department, would receive a mandatory review. The agency would then have the option, based on established criteria, to decertify an officer and prevent their continued employment.

The second function of the agency would be to review all investigations of deadly force across the United States. One of the biggest problems that has existed for decades is that law enforcement simply cannot investigate itself, at least not without oversight. Local prosecutors cannot be trusted to provide that oversight. Many approaches have been tried, and all have failed. In some jurisdictions, multiagency task forces have been established. Other jurisdictions carry out their own investigations. Some have tried supposed independent and impartial examiners, most of whom turn out to be anything but independent and impartial. And still others have tried the idea of a citizen's advisory committee, perhaps the least effective option of all. You simply cannot select a group of citizens with no law enforcement experience and expect them to be able to understand the complexities of a deadly force case. They tend to be advised and fed evidence by the very apparatus that has little interest in bringing to light the truth of what happened.

I have always said that the important thing is not who investigates a police shooting, but rather, who investigates the investigation of the police shooting. There is nothing about a police shooting that requires specially trained investigators. The investigation is completed like any other homicide. And while it is best to have such a case investigated by other than the involved department, what is more important is that an independent and truly impartial entity have complete access to the investigative materials to complete a full review. The agency I propose would be that entity. Such a review would include a written report that prosecutors, civil attorneys, and the public would have unrestricted access to. Additionally, when the report is submitted, it would include the agency's own decision about the continued certification of the officer(s) involved independent of any criminal or civil litigation.

Not only is this proposed solution doable, but there is a perfect model already in place in the securities industry. It is called the Financial Industry Regulatory Authority (FINRA). Regardless of the state, when an individual wishes to sell investments or provide investment advice for a fee, they must be registered by FINRA. This is a national registration, and it can be denied for past conduct, not just in the securities industry, but in the applicant's private life. Once they are registered, all disciplinary actions and client complaints against the individual are submitted by the employer and kept in a national registry. At any time, FINRA has the capability of opening a case and pursuing administrative charges against the individual that can lead to their registration being terminated. If they conduct an investigation, the individual's employer must provide all requested documentation and give FINRA complete access to their files.

The FINRA model would work perfectly for the law enforcement community. FINRA even provides public access to certain data to allow a consumer to check if their broker has had past consumer complaints and disciplinary actions. Such a portal could also be made available to municipalities to allow for better background investigations of job applicants, and possibly even allow for public access on a limited basis to allow citizens to see how many officers are employed by their department with questionable backgrounds.

One additional function that could be carried out by such an agency, or perhaps by some other existing agency, is a national certification, based on established and stringent criteria, for expert witnesses who testify in use-of-force and police practices cases. In six years, I was never seriously challenged by an opposing pro-police expert. It is not that I was so much better than them, but I had the one credential essentially none of them had—an academic background in the behavioral sciences. You cannot truly analyze and opine on cases of excessive force without understanding the underlying behavioral dynamics of the exchange. You must understand phenomena such as perception, human reaction time, and the effects of stress to understand why the officer did what they did when they did it. Many pro-police experts I have faced have attempted to employ psychological concepts and research, but in almost every case they either misunderstood, misapplied, or mischaracterized those concepts. Many were ultimately disqualified or limited in their testimony following a challenge by the plaintiff's attorney with an affidavit I wrote.

Unfortunately, the world of expert testimony, at least in civil rights cases involving the police, is a relatively unregulated free-for-all. At the end of the day, there are no real criteria for establishing whether an individual is truly an expert. The decision boils down to the subjective determination of a judge who may have a bias in favor of or against the police. Not once have I been involved in a case where a judge actually verified an expert's credentials, including my own. The majority of pro-police experts I have come up against are little more than firearms instructors who will justify an officer's actions no matter how egregiously wrong they were. They tend to come from a preferred expert list provided by the police unions, and they will reverse-engineer their conclusions and use pseudoscientific research, itself mostly reverse-engineered, to give the appearance of credible science. At least in the realm of civil litigation, there is not an area of reform more desperately needed than the court certification of expert witnesses. Physicians who testify as experts enter the courtroom with a medical degree; engineers with an engineering degree; and legal experts with a law degree. Yet in a case where a police officer kills a 15-year-old kid because he purportedly reached for his waistband, and many other cases like it, I have seen supposed experts enter the courtroom with nothing more than a high school diploma and some unverified one-day police training to argue that the officer had no choice but to shoot.

Politicians too must take responsibility for correcting the problem of police violence with legislation. First on the chopping block must be the qualified immunity defense. I have found the law to be sufficiently imprecise to allow a judge to rule however they wish to rule on this issue. I have seen well-reasoned thirty-page decisions from judges on this issue, but I have also seen two-page decisions that were nearly incoherent and based on a misunderstanding of the evidence. I have always found it interesting how we trust lay juries to rule on whether an officer's use of force was appropriate or excessive, but we do not trust them to rule on the lesser issue of whether the officer should be immune from litigation. Victims of police violence, including the families who are left behind, are never guaranteed a day in court to face the individual who killed their loved one, which seems a constitutionally sound precept. Instead, they are guaranteed only that a single judge, one appointed by a politician from one party or the other, will decide for them whether that day will ever come. And while there is certainly an appeals process, the deck of cards is always stacked in favor of defense attorneys who typically enjoy the security of an insurance company bankrolling their efforts, while the plaintiff's attorney must continue to work for free in hopes of an eventual judgment in their favor. It is a risk versus no-risk proposition, and it is never a fair fight.

Additional legislation that could be pursued would include a law that when an officer lies during a compelled Internal Affairs interview, there is a mandatory administrative hearing to rule on the officer's certification to continue working as a police officer. Additionally, I have always wondered why police departments will demand a polygraph exam of their job candidates, but one is never demanded of an officer who uses deadly force. I believe it should be law that every officer involved in a deadly force incident must submit to a polygraph exam if requested. There would be limits placed on using the results of the exam in a criminal proceeding, but those limits would not apply to an administrative hearing focused on certification. The exam would be standardized with questions that focus on administrative rather than criminal issues. For example, rather than a targeted question like, "Did you believe (name) had a gun in his waistband when you fired your weapon?," the questions would instead be something similar to, "In your IA interview on (date), were you completely truthful with detectives?"; or, "Are there details about the incident you have failed to disclose to detectives?" Such questions, if structured correctly, do not provide specific information that could be used to bring criminal charges against the officers, but they would be sufficient for use in an administrative hearing with a lower burden of proof. Across the United States, polygraph exams are used with convicted sex offenders to measure their level of risk to the community and are used in conjunction with other methods and techniques to reach decisions about whether an offender will remain in or be returned to a secure treatment facility. They are administrative or civil decisions made under a state's "sexually violent persons" law. These laws provide due process to the offender in the form of an appeal process. The same would be afforded to a police officer who is decertified in-part because of a failed polygraph exam.

And that brings me to the end of this book, which hopefully will assist in educating a public that is woefully lacking in its understanding of the phenomenon of deadly force. As I write these final pages, even as people in Minneapolis are still celebrating the outcome of the Derek Chauvin trial, several other U.S. cities are again experiencing turmoil. Within minutes of the Chauvin verdict, a White police officer in Columbus, Ohio, shot and killed a 16-year-old Black girl who was preparing to plunge a knife into another young girl, likely saving her life. Not surprisingly, the wagons began to circle almost immediately. Politicians, all the way up to the president, took to the microphones to bemoan the problem of systemic racism. The civil rights leaders for hire, those who are paid large sums of money to make an appearance at such happenings, boarded their airplanes for

Columbus. Celebrities took to Twitter to condemn the officer. NBA star Lebron James even posted his picture online with the caption, YOU'RE NEXT. And almost immediately, representatives from the various police unions around the country began appearing on radio and television to explain why the shooting was justified even before a proper investigation of the matter was complete.

As I sat in front of my television watching the truthful middle once again get lost in the preemptive rhetoric and political agendas, wondering if we had learned anything at all these past few years, all I could do was shake my head and end this journey the way I began, with a cynical chuckle that seemed to spontaneously escape my lips:

Every society gets the kind of criminal it deserves. What is equally true is that every community gets the kind of law enforcement it insists on.

—Bobby Kennedy, 1964

INDEX

A

action *v.* reaction argument, 11, 32
actively *v.* passively resisting, 88–89, 158
Alercon, Alex, 167, 179

B

Bakersfield Police Department, 166, 179
barricaded subject, 99, 100, 101, 214–215
Beagley, Jess, 168, 169, 170–171, 74, 177, 179. *See also* Ramirez, George
Blood Is at the Doorstep, The (Hamilton Case Documentary), 63
body cam recording, 87, 90, 91-93, 113, 119, 120, 123–124, 125, 153
Brewer, Daniel, 167–169, 174, 175–176, 179. *See also* Ramirez, Jorge
Brink, Robert, 212–213, 214–216. *See also* Cruz, John, Jr.
Brown, Michael, 11, 15, 65–83
    case settlement, 83
    crime detailed, 68–70
    deadly force script testimony, 75–77
    evidence *v.* reported version of

    events, 72–75, 79–80
    expert testimony, 67–68
    grand jury proceedings, 66
    just-in-case defense, 77
    overview of, 65
    refuted statements of accused, 80–81
    report conclusions, 81–82
    shots fired at, 237
    testimony inconsistencies, 66–67, 68, 70–73, 77–80
burden of proof, 230

C

Campiche, Jeffrey, 43, 181, 183, 187, 191
canines, police, 88, 197–198
carotid neck restraint, 228
Carreño, Bryan, 195–210
    case file review, 197–198
    case settlement, 208
    deputies' interviews following shooting, 199–201
    information responding officers had concerning, 198–199
    medical examiner report, 198
    Mohandie's suicide by cop report and, 204–208
    OC pepper spray question, 203

overview of, 195–197
Taser *v.* gun question, 201–202
21-foot rule and, 202–203
Casillas, Casimero, 40–41
casings. *See* empty casings
Chandler, Stuart, 43, 140, 149
Chatman, Cedrick, 25–34, 52, 97
  evidence/case facts review, 27–28
  expert witness report, 27–28
  flaws in studies used against,
    28–33
  overview of, 25
  perceptual distortion argument
    and, 28–29
  Rule 26 reports, 25–26
  studies used by prosecution
    against, 28–31
Chauvin, Derek, 231–233
chief or sheriff in deadly force
  theater, 37–42
Chisholm, John, 52, 58
choke holds, 228
CIT (Crisis Intervention Team)
  training, 54–55, 88, 214, 236
Cockrell, Joshua, 198, 201, 202–
  203. *See also* Carreño, Bryan
Coffman, Brian, 25, 33, 34, 43, 52
compressional asphyxiation, 96, 135,
  138, 161. *See also*
  Dyksma, Nicholas;
  Edwards, Drew
concentric muscle contractions, 132
confounding variable, 30
contagious fire, 166
coup-de-grace shot, 167, 179
Crump, Ben, 67, 82
Cruz, John, Jr., 211–225
  barricading dispatch, 214–215
  Denuzzie negotiations with,
    216–219
  inconsistencies in officers'

descriptions, 221–222
  initial response details, 212–214
  negotiator de-escalation error
    made, 217–219
  overview of, 211–212
  police response expert, 212
  sentencing of, 223–224
  shell casing/recovered bullet
    evidence, 213, 222–223, 225
  SWAT dispatch, 215–216
  SWAT escalation of force, 219–221

D

Daubert motion, 62, 208, 209
Dawson, Heath, 130, 132, 133–135.
  See also Dyksma, Nicholas
deadly force acronym
  (Mark V. Bart), 3–4
  "B" (burglary) example, 4–5
deadly force industry, 7, 10
  Lewinski and, 23
  perceptual distortion academic
    studies used by, 28–29
  pro-police expert witnesses for,
    46–47
  speed/efficiency of response by,
    18–19
deadly force script, 5–6, 10–11, 45,
  238
Brown case and, 75
Carreño case and, 200
Dial case and, 120–123
Hamilton case and, 51–52, 58
  Powell case and, 21–22
  thousand-yard stare and, 75–76
  21-foot rule and, 19–21
deadly force theater, 35–49
  Casillas example, 40–41
  defense lawyers, 43–46
  department chief or sheriff, 37–42
  detectives/evidence technicians, 36

Dotson example, 38–39
Dyer example, 39–40
expert witnesses, 46–47
FBI and, 41–42
judge, 47–49
local prosecutors, 42–43
officer interviews, 36–37
police union representative, 35–36
private attorneys, 43
public safety walk-through, 36
union lawyer, 37
DeBarge, Robert, 198, 199, 201.
  See also Carreño, Bryan
de-escalation, 54, 55, 85, 88, 214,
  216. *See also* Cruz, John, Jr.;
  Deming, John, Jr.
defense lawyers in deadly force
  theater, 43–46
Deming, John, Jr., 85–96
  case review, 86
  case settlement, 95
  de-escalation principles and, 88
  evidence v. reported version of
    events, 86–91
  overview of, 85–86
  physical evidence review, 92–93
  report conclusions, 95–96
  sequence of events
    determination, 94–95
timeline analysis of events, 91–92
Denuzzie, Denise, 216–219. *See also*
  Cruz, John, Jr.
Department of Justice (DOJ),
  158, 159
Dial, Michael, 113–126
  case settlement, 126
  deadly force script, 120–123
  evidence v. reported version of
    events, 116–120
  officers cleared in shooting of,
    114–115

overview of, 113–114
recorded police radio traffic,
  119–120
report conclusions, 123–125
use of force narrative used, 116
vehicle pursuit of, 114, 115–116
Donohue, Mark, 215, 216. *See also*
  Cruz, John, Jr.
Dotson, Sam, 16, 38–39, 41
Dunaway, Bryant, 114, 116, 124
Dyer, Jerry, 39–41, 141, 145, 148, 150
Dyksma, Nicholas, 127–138, 230
  autopsy report, 129, 131
  case settlement, 136
  dash cam video, 128–129, 130
  deputies involved reports, 131
  evidence v. reported version of
    events, 131–135
  obstacles faced in justice for,
    136–138
  overview of, 127–128
  police officer first aid for, 135–136
  report conclusions, 136

E

eccentric muscle contractions, 132
Edwards, Drew, 151–163
  arrest decision process, 161–162
  arrest report review, 155–156
  autopsy report review, 154–155
  case settlement, 163
  excited delirium and,
    153–154, 161
  overview of, 151–153
  Taser use by Owen, 152–153,
    156–161
electronic control weapons (ECWs).
  See Tasers
empty casings
  in Brown case, 73–74
  in Cruz Jr. case, 222

in Deming Jr. case, 92–93
in Hamilton case, 60–61, 63
in Le case, 183
in Myers Jr. case, 39
in Ramirez case, 167, 168, 172
in Soderberg case, 105, 107
Esparza, Lerry, 166–167, 177–178.
    See also Ramirez, Jorge
evidence contamination, 200
excited delirium, 152, 153–154.
    See also Edwards, Drew
expert witnesses, 25–26, 27–28
    in deadly force theater, 46–47
    national certification for, 240–241

F
FBI investigations, 41–42
5150, 87, 96
Financial Industry Regulatory
    Authority (FINRA), 240
firearm use training, 235–236
Fitchett, Robert, 53–54, 55, 58
Flannery, Jason, 38–39
Flores, Juan, 108–109. See also
    Soderberg, Anthony
Floyd, George, 227–233
    autopsy reports, 229
    burden of proof in case of, 230–
       231
    case settlement, 232
    Chauvin criminal trial, 232–233
    Monell issue and, 231
    MPD policies and, 231–232
    overview of, 227–228
    public responses to death of,
       228–230
Foothill Patrol Division, LAPD,
    98, 103
foot pursuits, weapons fired during,
    141–143
Force Science Institute, 23, 26, 32,
    62, 192
forensic psychology, 14–15
Fournier, Lisa, 32–33
Fraternal Order of Police (FOP), 10,
    18–19, 35–36
Fresno, California, Police
    Department, 39–40, 140
frisking. See pat-down search
    procedures
Fritz, Jerry, 108. *See also* Soderberg,
    Anthony
Fry, Kevin, 27, 28, 34
Fuerte, Andrew, 53–54, 55, 58

G
Galipo, Dale, 41, 43
Garner, Eddie, 4–5
Garrett, Chad, 168, 169, 170, 174.
    See also Ramirez, Jorge
Geragos & Geragos, 86, 167
Gora, Eric, 87–89. See also Deming,
    John, Jr.
Graham v. Connor, 6–7
deadly force script and, 10–11
    first public test of, 8–9
Gray, Anthony, 65, 67–68, 82
Gulbrandson, Erik, 55–56
Gurvitch, Ellin, 86, 95

H
Hamilton, Dontre, 51–63, 75
autopsy report, 53
CIT training and, 54–55
crime scene story of, 62–63
empty shell casing evidence,
    60–61
eyewitness accounts, 59–60
Manney account of, shooting,
    51–52, 58–59
media accounts of, 52–53
    Milwaukee settlement in

case of, 62
pat-down search of, 55–58
shots fired at, 237
Harger, Justin, 166, 167, 169, 170,
    172–176, 178. *See also*
    Ramirez, Jorge
Harmon, Joe, 128, 130, 131–133.
    See also Dyksma, Nicholas
Harris County Sheriff's Department,
    136–137
hired guns, 27–28
hot gas, 105, 106, 107, 110, 220, 224
hot prowl burglary, 98, 99
Hymon, Elton, 4–5

J

Johanknecht, Mitzi, 192–193
Johnson, Dorian, 68–70. *See also*
    Brown, Michael
Jones, Craig, 43, 128, 131, 136, 138
Joyce, Jennifer, 22, 39
judge in deadly force theater, 47–49
justified *v.* excessive police
    shootings, 13–14
    Powell example of, 17–18
just-in-case rationale, 57, 77, 148

K

King, Rodney, 7–10, 11
King County Sheriff's Department,
    182, 184, 186, 191
Kirakosian, Greg, 98, 100–101
Koon, Stacey, 8–9
Kunkel, Daniel, 87, 89–95. *See also*
    Deming, John, Jr.

L

Land, Clay, 137–138
Lantz, Eric, 167, 169, 177
law enforcement leader types, 37–38
Le, Tommy, 181–193

autopsy report, 183–184
case settlement, 192
evidence *v.* reported version of
    events, 187–192
investigative file, 184–186
overview of, 181–183
physical evidence analysis,
    183–184
wood chip evidence, 186–187
legislation, police violence, 241–243
Lewinski, Bill, 23, 32
linear thinking, police, 234–235
local prosecutors in deadly force
    theater, 42–43

M

Manney, Chris, 51–63. *See also*
    Hamilton, Dontre
McConnell, Luke, 212, 222–225
McCulloch, Bob, 66–67, 73
mechanical asphyxiation, 229
memory contamination, 200
memory distortion, 30
mentally ill individuals, law
    enforcement response to, 234
Milwaukee Police Department, 51–63.
    See also Hamilton, Dontre
Minneapolis Police Department
    (MPD), 228, 231
    Arrest and Control policies,
        231–232
Mohandie, Kris, 196, 204–208
Molina, Cesar, 182, 184, 186,
    187–191. *See also* Le, Tommy
Monell issue, 228, 230, 231
Moore, Ken, 197, 200–201. *See also*
    Carreño, Bryan
Moreno, Isaac, 108. See also
    Soderberg, Anthony
Mudd, William, 72, 77
Murrietta, Isaiah, 139–150

case settlement, 150
investigative stop of, 143–145
overview of, 139–140
report conclusions, 148–149
research of unarmed person
    findings, 142–143
video evidence of, 145–146
Villalvazo interview, 146–148
waistband defense and, 141–
    142,147–148
Murrietta, Israel, 140, 150
Myers, VonDerrit, Jr., 38–39

N
negotiators, 215–217
neuromuscular incapacitation (NMI),
    157–158
9/11 attacks. See September 11, 2001
    terrorist attacks
Nixon, Jay, 15–16, 66
number of shots fired at suspects, 237

O
O'Brien, Dave, 153, 154, 157, 162
OC (oleoresin capsicum) pepper
    spray, 18, 203
Otterness, John, 169–170, 177.
    See also Ramirez, Jorge
Owen, Mike, 151–153, 161–162.
    See also Edwards, Drew
Taser use by, 156–161
Owens, Tanner, 182, 184, 188,
    190–191. *See also* Le, Tommy

P
passively v. actively resisting, 88–89,
    158
pat-down search procedures, 55–57
PCP defense, 7–10
perceptual distortion argument, 11, 28,

97–98. *See also* Soderberg,
    Anthony
SWAT team and, 98
Pierson, Tommy, 128, 129, 130,
    137–138. *See also* Dyksma,
    Nicholas
PIT (pursuit intervention technique)
    maneuver, 117, 118, 123
Pleasanton Police Department, 87, 96
Police Executive Research Forum
    (PERF), 158, 159
police officer certification,
    independent agency for,
    238–240
police profession's shortcomings,
    234–238
    deadly force script, 238
    firearm use training, 235–236
    linear thinking, 234–235
    mentally ill response, 234
    stand their ground training, 236
    use-of-force training, 236–238
police violence legislation, 241–243
positional asphyxia, 161
Powell, Kajieme, 13–23, 29, 34
    deadly force industry and, 18–19
    deadly force script and, 21–22
    Dotson description of incident,
        16–17
    shots fired at, 237
    21-foot rule and, 19–21
    YouTube video of incident, 17–18
Powell, Laurence, 8, 9
private attorneys in deadly force
    theater, 43
probable cause arrest, 155–156
psychological contagion, 166
public safety walk-through, 36

Q
qualified immunity, 47–48

R

Ramirez, Jorge, 165–180
  case settlement, 179
  contagious fire phenomenon and,
    166, 178
  evidence v. reported version of
    events, 171–178
  officer statements, 168–171
  overview of, 165–167
    shots fired at, 237
    shots fired review, 167–170
    waistband defense, 171
    wounds to, 175
reasonableness in police shooting,
  29–30
reasonable officer state of mind,
  6, 11
  King trial and, 8–9
Romanucci, Antonio, 228, 230
Rule 26 reports, 25–26
Rushing, Ken, 197, 199, 200.
  See also Carreño, Bryan

S

Schmidt, Bill, 41, 43, 140, 197,
  203–204, 209
Schroeder, Steve, 151–152,
  161–162. *See also* Edwards,
  Drew
September 11, 2001 terrorist attacks,
  10, 11
shell shock, 76
Shipman, Trevor, 40–41
shortcomings. *See* police profession's
  shortcomings
Shoupe, Oddie, 113–114, 119–120,
  124–126. *See also* Dial,
  Michael
Simms, Charlie, 114, 117–118, 124.
  See also Dial, Michael
social blindness, 8

Soderberg, Anthony, 97–111
  case settlement, 111
  chronology of events, 100,
    101–103
  definitions/response to threat in
    case of, 99–100
  evidence *v.* reported version of
    events, 101–109
  incident details, 98–99
  misperceptions presented in case,
    107–109
  overview of, 97–98
  perceptual distortion argument
    and, 97–98
  shots fired at, 237
special officer's badge, 45
spent casings. *See* empty casings
state of mind, 1–4
  of reasonable officer, 6
St. Louis County Police
  Department, 66, 78
St. Louis Metropolitan Police
  Department, 16, 38–39
studies used by prosecution, 28–30
  confounding variable rendering,
    invalid, 30–31
Sturdevant, William, 128, 130. *See
  also* Dyksma, Nicholas
Suicidal Mind, The (Shneidman), 205
suicide by cop, 17, 195. *See also*
  Carreño, Bryan
  as challenging *v.* begging police,
    196
  Mohandie on, 196–197, 204–208
superhuman strength defense, 8, 9,
  11, 52, 75, 185
SWAT (special weapons and tactics)
  team, 98
  aerial platform sniper (APS) team,
    102, 103–104
  Cruz case and, 215–216, 219–221

synchronous fire, 166
systemic racism, 243

T
target lock, 146, 149
Tasers, 18, 45, 88–89, 132–133,
    184–185. See *also* Edwards,
    Drew; Le, Tommy
  Carreño case and non-use of,
    201–202
  threat level to deploy, 158
Tennessee Bureau of Investigation
    (TBI), 115, 124
Tennessee v. Garner, 4–6
Terry v. Ohio (1968), 55
thousand-yard stare, 11
  Brown case and, 75–76
  Carreño case and, 200–201
  Hamilton case and, 51–52
  Ramirez case and, 178
threat, defining, 99
time drift, 91
timeline analysis of events, 91–92
21-foot rule, 10, 19–20
  Carreño case and, 202–203
  origins of, 20
  Powell case and, 19–21

U
union representative. *See* Fraternal
    Order of Police (FOP)
use-of-force cases, Rule 26 reports
    and, 25–26
use-of-force training, 236–238

V
Vaughn, Ryan, 168, 169, 170, 174.
    See also Ramirez, Jorge
vehicle pursuits, 113–126. *See also*
    Dial, Michael
video cameras, 9, 10

Villalvazo, Ray, 140–141, 144–148,
    150. *See also* Murrietta, Isaiah

W
waistband defense, 1, 11, 45, 241
  in Brown case, 77, 78–79
  in Hamilton case, 52
  in Murrietta case, 139, 141–143,
    146–149
  in Ramirez case, 170, 171, 178,
    179
  in Soderberg case, 106
Wallach, Ian, 52, 62
wannabe attorneys, 45–46
Washington University, 14–15, 19,
    29, 65
weapons fired during foot pursuits
    research, 141–143
West, Adam, 114, 119, 120, 121–122,
    123–124, 126. *See also* Dial,
    Michael
Wheeler, Lanny, 117–118, 121, 125.
    See also Dial, Michael
Wilson, Darren, 65–83. *See also*
    Brown, Michael
Wimbish, Rick, 167–169, 175, 176,
    179. *See also* Ramirez, Jorge
Winebrenner, Dustin, 198, 201, 202.
    See also Carreño, Bryan

Y
Young, Brandon, 115, 118, 122–123,
    125. *See also* Dial, Michael

Z
Zeimet, Brendan, 152, 153, 160.
    See also Edwards, Drew